Africa

An Encyclopedia
for Students

GEOPOLITICAL

MOROCCO
TUNISIA
ALGERIA
LIBYA
EGYPT
WESTERN SAHARA
MAURITANIA
MALI
NIGER
CHAD
SUDAN
ERITREA
SENEGAL
GAMBIA
GUINEA BISSAU
GUINEA
SIERRA LEONE
LIBERIA
BURKINA FASO
BENÍN
NIGERIA
DJIBOUTI
SOMALIA
CÔTE D'IVOIRE
GHANA
TOGO
CAMEROON
CENTRAL AFRICAN REPUBLIC
ETHIOPIA
EQUITORIAL GUINEA
SÃO TOMÉ AND PRINCIPE
GABON
UGANDA
KENYA
RWANDA
CONGO (Kinshasa)
19,341 ft.
CONGO (Brazzaville)
BURUNDI
COMOROS
TANZANIA
ANGOLA
ZAMBIA
MALAWI
MOZAMBIQUE
ZIMBABWE
MADAGASCAR
NAMIBIA
BOTSWANA
SWAZILAND
LESOTHO
SOUTH AFRICA

ELEVATIONS OVER 1,640 FEET

Africa

An Encyclopedia for Students

John Middleton, Editor

Volume 3
Leakey–Rwanda

CHARLES SCRIBNER'S SONS

GALE GROUP

THOMSON LEARNING

New York • Detroit • San Diego • San Francisco
Boston • New Haven, Conn. • Waterville, Maine
London • Munich

Developed for Charles Scribner's Sons by Visual Education Corporation, Princeton, N.J.

For Scribners
PUBLISHER: Karen Day
EDITORS: John Fitzpatrick, Brad Morgan
COVER AND INTERIOR DESIGN: Jennifer Wahi
PHOTO RESEARCH: Kelly Quin
PRODUCTION SUPERVISOR: Mary Beth Trimper

For Visual Education
PROJECT DIRECTOR: Darryl Kestler
WRITERS: John Haley, Charles Roebuck, Rebecca Stefoff, Joseph Ziegler
EDITORS: Noëlle Y. Child, Cindy George, Guy Austrian, Charles Roebuck
ASSOCIATE EDITOR: Cheryl MacKenzie
COPYEDITING SUPERVISOR: Helen A. Castro
ELECTRONIC PREPARATION: Fiona Torphy

Contributors
Nancy E. Gratton, Kevin van Bladel, Frank Griffel, Jeremy Raphael Berndt

Library of Congress Cataloging in-Publication Data

Africa: an encyclopedia for students / John Middleton, editor.
    p. cm
  Includes bibliographical references and index.
    ISBN 0-684-80650-9 (set : alk. paper) —ISBN 0-684-80651-7 (v. 1) —
ISBN 0-684-80652-5 (v. 2) —ISBN 0-684-80653-3 (v. 3) —
ISBN 0-684-80654-1 (v. 4)
    1. Africa–Encyclopedias, Juvenile. [1. Africa—Encyclopedias.] I. Middleton, John, 1921–

DT3 .A249 2001
960'03—dc21

                    2001049348

Table of Contents

VOLUME 1
Abidjan—Economic History

VOLUME 2
Ecosystems—Laws and Legal Systems

VOLUME 3
Leakey Family—Rwanda

VOLUME 4
Sadat, Anwar—Zulu

List of Maps

Table of Contents

Color Plates

Volume 1
Peoples and Cultures

Volume 2
The Land and Its History

Volume 3
Art and Architecture

Volume 4
Daily Life

A Time Line of Africa

4 m.y.a.*	Australopithecines *(early hominids) live in northern Rift Valley (Ethiopia, Kenya).*
2.5 m.y.a.*	*Early Stone Age;* Homo habilis *appears (Olduvai Gorge, Tanzania).*
1.5 m.y.a.*–150,000 B.C.	Homo erectus *appears.*
240,000–40,000 B.C.	*Middle Stone Age.*
80,000–20,000 B.C.	*Late Stone Age.*
20,000–10,000 B.C.	*Farming introduced in lower Nile Valley.*
10,000–6000 B.C.	*Cattle domesticated in northern Africa.*
	Millet and sorghum grown in western Africa.
6000–5000 B.C.	*Khoisan hunters of southern Africa create rock paintings.*
3000 B.C.	*King Menes unifies Lower Egypt and Upper Egypt.*
	Agriculture develops in Ethiopian highlands.
2000–1000 B.C.	*Horses introduced in Sahara region.*
	Bananas grown in central Africa.
332 B.C.	*Greeks occupy Egypt.*
200 B.C.	*Romans gain control of Carthage.*
32 B.C.	*Royal city of Meroë flourishes in what is now Sudan.*
A.D. 300s	*Aksum invades Meroë; Aksum king adopts Coptic Christianity.*
530s	*Byzantine empire takes Mediterranean ports.*
600s	*Muslim Arabs invade North Africa.*
ca. 1000	*Shona begin building Great Zimbabwe.*
1200s	*Portuguese voyage to northwest coast of Africa.*
	Sundjata Keïta founds Mali kingdom.

*m.y.a. million years ago

1312–1337	*Mansa Musa rules Mali and makes pilgrimage to Mecca.*
1400s	*Benin kingdom flourishes.*
1498	*Vasco da Gama sails around the southern and eastern coasts of Africa on the way to India.*
1505–1510	*Portuguese seize Swahili towns in eastern Africa and fortify Mozambique.*
	Kongo king Afonso I converts to Christianity.
1517	*Ottoman Turks conquer Egypt and port towns along the Mediterranean.*
1578	*Moroccans defeat Portuguese, remaining free of colonial control.*
1591	*Al-Mansur invades Songhai.*
1600s	*French, English, and Dutch establish trading posts along western coasts to export gold, ivory, and slaves.*
	Akan state emerges.
1650s	*Dutch settle at Cape of Good Hope in southern Africa.*
	Arab traders settle on East African coast.
1700s	*French and British establish network for slave trade in Central Africa.*
	Zanzibar prospers as Arab trading center.
1721	*French colonize Mauritius.*
1787	*British missionaries found Sierra Leone.*
1795	*British seize Cape Colony from Dutch.*
1798	*Napoleon leads French invasion of Egypt.*
1805	*Muhammad Ali takes power in Egypt, breaking free of Ottoman control.*
1807	*Britain and the United States abolish slave trade.*
1817	*Shaka emerges at head of Zulu kingdom in southern Africa.*
1821	*Freed slaves from the United States settle in what is now Liberia.*
1828	*Queen Ranavalona takes throne in Madagascar.*
1830s	*French rule proclaimed in Algeria.*
	Slave trade continues in western Africa.
1835	*Dutch settlers in southern Africa head north in "Great Trek."*
1840s–1880s	*Slave trade flourishes in East Africa.*
1847	*Republic of Liberia is established.*
1852–1873	*David Livingstone explores Central and East Africa.*
1858	*Portuguese abolish slavery in Central Africa.*

1855–1868	*Emperor Téwodros rules Ethiopia.*
1859–1869	*Suez Canal is built.*
1869	*Diamonds are discovered at Kimberley in northern Cape Colony.*
1880–1881	*Afrikaners rebel against Britain in the First Anglo-Boer War, and British withdraw from Transvaal in southern Africa.*
1885	*Mahdist forces capture Khartoum.*
1880s–early 1900s	*European powers colonize most of Africa (present-day names of countries listed):*
	Belgians in Congo (Kinshasa);
	British in Nigeria, Ghana, Sierra Leone, the Gambia, Uganda, Kenya, Somalia, Mauritius, Seychelles, Zambia, Zimbabwe, Malawi, Botswana, Lesotho, and Swaziland;
	French in Mauritania, Niger, Burkina Faso, Mali, Algeria, Tunisia, Morocco, Senegal, Guinea, Ivory Coast, Bénin, Central African Republic, Gabon, Congo (Brazzaville), Chad, Djibouti, Madagascar, Réunion, and the Comoro Islands;
	Germans in Togo, Cameroon, Namibia, Tanzania, Rwanda, and Burundi;
	Portuguese in Guinea-Bissau, São Tomé and Príncipe, Cape Verde, Angola, and Mozambique;
	Spanish in Western Sahara and Equatorial Guinea.
1893–1895	*Africans in King Leopold's Congo revolt.*
1895	*France forms federation of colonies that becomes French West Africa.*
1896	*Ethiopian emperor Menilek defeats Italians, maintaining country's independence.*
1899–1902	*Afrikaners defeated by British in Second Anglo-Boer war.*
1910	*Union of South Africa formed.*
1914–1918	*World War I: French and British capture German Togo; Africans fight on the side of various colonial powers in Africa.*
1922	*Egypt gains its independence.*
1930	*Haile Selassie I crowned emperor of Ethiopia.*
1935	*Italians invade Ethiopia.*
1936	*Union party in South Africa revokes voting rights of blacks.*
1939–1945	*World War II: many major battles fought in North Africa; Africans in French and British colonies drafted to fight in Europe and Asia.*
1940s	*First nationalist political parties are formed in western Africa.*

1944	William Tubman becomes president of Liberia.
1945	Arab League, an organization of Arab states, is founded in Cairo.
	Ethiopia regains its independence.
1948	Policy of apartheid introduced in South Africa.
1950s	Several independence movements against colonial rule develop.
1951	Libya declared an independent monarchy under King Idris I.
1952	Gamal Abdel Nasser seizes power in Egypt.
1953	Northern Rhodesia (Zambia), Southern Rhodesia (Zimbabwe), and Nyasaland (Malawi) join to form the Central African Federation.
1954	War breaks out in Algeria.
1956	Sudan, Morocco, and Tunisia become independent.
1957	Ghana achieves independence, with Kwame Nkrumah as president.
1958	Guinea, under Sékou Touré, becomes independent.
1960	Independence achieved in Cameroon (French Cameroun), Chad, Congo (Brazzaville), Congo (Kinshasa), Dahomey (Bénin), Gabon, Ivory Coast, Madagascar, Mali, Mauritania, Niger, Nigeria, Senegal, Somalia, Togo, and Upper Volta (Burkina Faso).
1961	Rwanda, Sierra Leone, and Tanganyika become independent.
1962	Independence achieved in Algeria, Burundi, and Uganda.
1963	Kenya (under Jomo Kenyatta) and Zanzibar become independent.
	Central African Federation ends.
	Organization of African Unity is founded.
	FRELIMO begins armed struggle for liberation of Mozambique.
1964	In South Africa, Nelson Mandela stands trial and is jailed.
	Tanganyika and Zanzibar join to form Tanzania.
	Malawi and Zambia become independent.
	Hutu overthrow Tutsi rule in Burundi.
1965	Rhodesia declares independence under Ian Smith.
	Mobutu Sese Seko takes power in Congo (Kinshasa) and renames it Zaire.
	King Hassan restores monarchy in Morocco.
	The Gambia gains independence.
1966	Independence achieved in Lesotho and Botswana.

1967–1970	*Biafra attempts to secede from Nigeria.*
1968	*Swaziland becomes independent.*
1969	*Muammar al-Qaddafi seizes power in Libya.*
1970	*Egypt/Sudan: Aswan Dam is completed.*
1974	*Guinea attains independence.*
1975	*Cape Verde and Angola become independent.*
	FRELIMO government gains independence in Mozambique.
1976	*Spain withdraws from Western Sahara; Morocco and Mauritania fight over territory.*
	Residents of Soweto and other South African townships begin violent protests.
1970s–1990s	*War erupts across the continent within the countries of Angola, Chad, Congo (Brazzaville), Congo (Kinshasa), Ethiopia, Guinea-Bissau, Liberia, Rwanda, Sierra Leone, Somalia, Sudan, and Western Sahara, and between the nations of Ethiopia and Eritrea, Ethiopia and Somalia, and Sudan and Uganda.*
1980	*Zimbabwe becomes independent.*
1990	*Nelson Mandela released from prison.*
	Namibia becomes independent.
1993	*Apartheid ends in South Africa.*
	Eritrea gains independence from Ethiopia.
1994	*Rwandan and Burundi presidents assassinated; ethnic violence between Hutu and Tutsi continues.*
	Nelson Mandela becomes first black president of South Africa.
1995	*Outbreak of deadly Ebola virus in Congo (Kinshasa).*
1997	*Laurent Kabila takes power in Zaire and renames it Democratic Republic of the Congo (Kinshasa).*
1999	*Libya hands over two suspects in 1986 airplane bombing over Lockerbie, Scotland.*
2000	*Ghana chooses president John Kufuor in free elections.*
	Paul Kagame is the first Tutsi to become president in Rwanda.
2001	*Congo (Kinshasa) leader, Kabila, is assassinated; Kabila's son, Joseph, succeeds him as president.*

Leakey Family

For two generations, the Leakey family of KENYA has contributed significantly to paleoanthropology—the study of early humans and their ancestors—in Africa. Fossils discovered by the Leakeys helped establish the continent as the site of human origins. Members of the family who participated in this research include Louis S.B. Leakey (1903–1972); his second wife, Mary Douglas Leakey (1913–1996); their son, Richard E.F. Leakey (born 1944); and Richard's wife, Meave Gillian Leakey (born 1942).

The son of British missionaries stationed in Kenya, Louis Leakey was trained as an archaeologist and anthropologist*. In 1936 he married Mary Douglas Nicol, an archaeologist. They began investigating the history of early humans in Africa, focusing their research on a place called Olduvai Gorge in TANZANIA. At Olduvai, Mary Leakey unearthed the oldest group of stone tools ever found.

In 1959 Mary Leakey discovered the skull of an early hominid, a member of the *Hominidae* family that includes modern humans and their ancestors. Known as *Australopithecus boisei,* it was 1.75 million years old. This find helped to expand scientists' understanding of human evolution*. A few years later Louis Leakey found the first fossils of another hominid, *Homo habilis.* By writing and lecturing on these and similar discoveries, Louis Leakey aroused wide interest in paleoanthropology and inspired a generation of younger researchers. After Louis's death, Mary Leakey continued her work. At Laetoli, Tanzania, she discovered fossils of hominid footprints that were about 3.5 million years old.

Richard Leakey's major contribution to paleoanthropology was his discovery of a site called Koobi Fora in Kenya. It proved to be the world's richest known source of hominid remains. Together with Meave Leakey, he conducted a series of expeditions there from the late 1960s onward. In 1999 Meave Leakey and a team of researchers discovered the skull of a hominid called *Kenyanthropus platyops* in Kenya. About 3.5 million years old, it provided new information about the history of human ancestry. (*See also* **Archaeology and Prehistory, Humans, Early.**)

Lebanese Communities

West Africa is home to many Lebanese immigrants and their descendants, most of whom are shopkeepers and small business owners. The first Lebanese arrived in the region in the late 1800s, and many of those who came later were following relatives. Lebanese immigration increased sharply between World Wars I and II. Many of the immigrants settled in SENEGAL and other French territories because France ruled Lebanon at the time. For the most part, the early arrivals were Maronite or Greek Orthodox Christians, but after 1920 the majority were Muslims from southern Lebanon. Today IVORY COAST boasts the largest Lebanese community, consisting of perhaps 100,000 people.

Many Lebanese became entrepreneurs* in Africa, buying crops from farmers and selling them to European merchants. After World War II, they expanded into other areas of activity, such as trading in gold and diamonds and importing foreign goods. Wealthier Lebanese invested in firms making building materials, plastics, and cosmetics. Others owned hotels, pharmacies, restaurants, gas stations, and insurance companies. However, most Lebanese businesses are small and family-owned.

1

The Lebanese have a complex relationship with African peoples. They often learn the local languages and contribute to local schools and hospitals. Yet many go back to Lebanon, Europe, or the Americas when they retire instead of remaining in Africa. Some Africans resent the Lebanese immigrants' financial success and political influence and their reluctance to integrate or intermarry with local populations. (*See also* **European Communities, Indian Communities**.)

Lenshina, Alice

1920–1978
Zambian religious leader and prophet

Alice Lenshina was the founder of a PROPHETIC MOVEMENT that gathered tens of thousands of followers. In the 1960s she led an uprising against the colonial government in ZAMBIA.

Lenshina was born in northern Zambia among the Bemba people. As a young woman, she was preparing to join the Presbyterian Church at the mission center of Lubwa. She failed to complete her religious studies, but she became familiar with the Bible.

Alice married Petros Chintankwa Mulenga and had five children. In 1953, after experiencing several bouts of serious illness, she met with the Reverend Fergus Macpherson at the Lubwa mission. She told him that she had died four times, met with Jesus Christ, and risen from the dead. She said that Jesus had taught her hymns, shown her special religious texts called the Book of Life, and given her certain spiritual powers.

After meeting with Reverend Macpherson, Alice resumed her religious studies. However, she soon left the Presbyterian Church and founded the Lumpa Church, an independent Christian group. She became known as Alice Lenshina, from the Bemba pronuciation of the Latin *regina* (queen). Her fame as a healer and prophet spread rapidly. By 1959 the Lumpa Church had between 50,000 and 100,000 members and nearly 150 congregations, mostly in northern and eastern Zambia.

* **secular** nonreligious; connected with everyday life

As Zambia moved toward independence, Lenshina told her followers to withdraw from all secular* activities, a move that angered colonial officials and local chiefs. In 1964 fierce battles raged between Lumpa followers and other Zambians. Over 700 people died before army troops stopped the fighting. Many Lumpa were placed in prison camps and others fled the country. Arrested by the authorities, Lenshina was released in 1975 and kept under house arrest in the city of LUSAKA until her death. (*See also* **Christianity in Africa**.)

Leo Africanus

ca. 1485–ca. 1554
Arab geographer

Leo Africanus was an Arab geographer who make numerous journeys in the northern and western regions Africa and wrote a book about the places he visited. Born in Spain and educated in MOROCCO, he traveled extensively throughout North Africa and made three trips to EGYPT. South of the Sahara, he visited Gao and TIMBUKTU in the Songhai Empire of western Africa.

Alice Lenshina, shown here holding an unknown child, was the founder of the Lumpa Church, which had more than 50,000 members. In the 1960s, she led an uprising against the colonial government in Zaire that ended with her arrest.

Around 1520 pirates captured him off the coast of TUNISIA and presented him to Pope Leo X as a slave. The pope freed him and baptized him as a Christian. At the pope's request, Leo Africanus wrote *Description of Africa*, which became an important source of information about this period in African history. The book, which appeared in 1526 (five years after the pope died), has been published in many editions and has been translated into several languages. He remained in Rome most of his life but returned to Tunis before his death. Some people say that Leo Africanus returned to Islam before his death, but that remains uncertain. (*See also* **Sudanic Empires of Western Africa, Travel and Exploration.**)

Lesotho

Lesotho

* **protectorate** weak state under the control and protection of a strong state

A small, mountainous country in southern Africa, the Kingdom of Lesotho is completely surrounded by SOUTH AFRICA. Before gaining independence in 1966, Lesotho was a British protectorate* known as Basutoland. Today it is dependent on South Africa economically and for access to the outside world.

Lesotho is located in the Drakensberg Mountains at the edge of the southern African plateau. The western part of the country contains a narrow strip of lowlands ranging in elevation from 5,000 to 6,000 feet. The eastern highlands, crossed by a number of rivers, contain peaks of more than 11,000 feet. The climate is generally moderate, with average temperatures between 45°F and 70°F and a rainy season from October to April. Severe droughts occur occasionally.

History and Government. In prehistoric times Lesotho was inhabited by KHOISAN hunter-gatherers. From about the 1500s BANTU PEOPLES began migrating into the area and settled among the Khoisan groups. In the early 1800s, a leader named MOSHOESHOE I united some 22 separate clans* under his authority. When the area was invaded by other groups, including the ZULU, Moshoeshoe successfully repelled them. His followers became known as the Basotho, and their homeland was called Basutoland.

* **clan** group of people descended from a common ancestor

In 1834 a new threat emerged. White settlers of Dutch ancestry, called Afrikaners, began migrating northward from Cape Colony in South Africa and seized land belonging to the Basotho. The Basotho fought the Afrikaners for decades. The conflict intensified in 1854 when the Afrikaners established a new colony, the Orange Free State, west of Basutoland. The Basotho sought protection from the British, who annexed* Basutoland as part of Cape Colony in 1871. Twelve years later Basutoland became a protectorate under British colonial authority. The Basotho chiefs were allowed to continue enforcing traditional laws.

* **annex** to take over or add a territory to an existing area

Between the late 1800s and mid-1900s, Basutoland moved slowly toward self-government, which it achieved in 1965. The following year the country gained full independence as the Kingdom of Lesotho. A constitutional monarchy, Lesotho has a king who serves as head of state, an elected assembly, and a prime minister who leads the government.

Since independence, rivalries within Lesotho have caused political instability. In 1966 the king, Moshoeshoe II, demanded greater power and Prime Minister Leabua Jonathan placed him under temporary house arrest. Four years later, when Jonathan faced defeat in the national elections, he declared a state of emergency, suspended the constitution, arrested opposition leaders, and sent the king into exile. Jonathan held power as a dictator until 1986, when he was overthrown by the military under General Justin Lekhanya.

Lekhanya installed a military dictatorship in Lesotho, but by 1990 he faced political unrest. In an effort to win support for his government, he put Moshoeshoe II back on the throne—with limited powers. However, when Moshoeshoe opposed some of Lekhanya's policies, the king was replaced by his son, Letsie III. The following year, Lekhanya was overthrown.

Moshoeshoe I (1786–1870) united the Basotho people and established the kingdom that later became Lesotho.

* **Insurrection** violent uprising against authority; rebellion

The new head of government, General Elias Ramaema, agreed to hold elections in 1993. This resulted in the restoration of democracy under Prime Minister Ntsu Mokhehle. However many junior army officers opposed the new government, and fighting soon broke out within the army. During one of the struggles, the deputy prime minister was killed. King Letsie III stepped down in 1995 to allow his father to return as king, but Moshoeshoe II died the following year in an automobile accident. Letsie once again took the throne.

Following the election of Pakalitha Mosisili as prime minister in 1998, a wave of protests swept through Lesotho. Fearing an insurrection*, the government asked South Africa and BOTSWANA for assistance. Many businesses and government offices were looted and destroyed in rioting before troops of soldiers were able to restore order.

Lesotho

The Kingdom of Lesotho

POPULATION:
2,143,141 (2000 estimated population)

AREA:
11,720 sq. mi. (30,555 sq. km)

LANGUAGES:
English, Sesotho (both official)

NATIONAL CURRENCY:
Maloti

PRINCIPAL RELIGIONS:
Christian 80%, Traditional 20%

CITIES:
Maseru (capital), 400,200 (1995 est.); Leribe, Mafeteng

ANNUAL RAINFALL:
25 in. (635 mm)

ECONOMY:
GDP per capita: $2,240 (1999 est.)

PRINCIPAL PRODUCTS AND EXPORTS:
Agricultural: livestock, mohair, corn, wheat, sorghum, peas, beans, potatoes, asparagus
Manufacturing: food and beverages, textiles, vehicles, handcrafts
Mining: diamonds

GOVERNMENT:
Independence from Great Britain, 1966. Parliamentary constitutional monarchy. Prime minister elected by universal suffrage. Governing bodies: two-house parliament.

HEADS OF STATE SINCE INDEPENDENCE:
Kings:
1966–1990, 1995–1996 King Moshoeshoe II
1990–1995, 1996– King Letsie III (formally Prince Mohato)
Heads of government:
1966–1986 Prime Minister Leabua Jonathan
1986–1991 Military Council chief Major-General Justin Lekhanya
1991–1993 Colonel Elias P. Ramaema
1993–1998 Prime Minister Ntsu Mokhehle
1998– Prime Minister Pakalitha Mosisili

ARMED FORCES:
2,000

EDUCATION:
Compulsory for ages 6–13; literacy rate 71%

Economy. Lesotho is a poor country with few natural resources. Although the economy is based primarily on farming and raising livestock, only about 10 percent of the land is suitable for agriculture. The main crops are corn, sorghum*, wheat, and beans. Unable to produce enough to support the population, Lesotho imports about 25 percent of its food.

Lesotho's few industries export items such as clothing, pottery, and leather goods. Tourism, especially from South Africa, has been increasing in recent years because of the country's scenic beauty.

Poverty, unemployment, and the lack of natural resources have made Lesotho economically dependent on South Africa. For decades, tens of thousands of workers have migrated from Lesotho to South Africa to work in industries such as mining. However, in the late 1980s South Africa began to restrict the number of foreign workers in the country, which has left many people in Lesotho unemployed.

Peoples and Cultures. Almost all the people in Lesotho are Basotho. Most are Christian, though about 20 percent practice traditional religions. Despite the country's great poverty, about 70 percent of the population is literate*. Both English and Sesotho, the Basotho language, are spoken.

Lesotho is still primarily a rural society, and nearly 80 percent of the people live in small villages. Apart from Maseru, the capital, there are no other large towns or cities. Many Basotho continue to follow traditional ways of life, living in thatched houses and accepting the authority of

* **sorghum** family of tropical grasses used for food

* **literate** able to read and write

6

the chiefs. Clan and family loyalties play an important role in Basotho society, creating a strong sense of cultural unity. (*See also* **Afrikaner Republics, Colonialism in Africa, Ethnic Groups and Identity, Kings and Kingship, Southern Africa, History.**)

Liberia

ocated on the Guinea Coast of West Africa, Liberia is the oldest black republic in Africa. It was founded by free blacks from America in 1847 and maintained its independence throughout the years of European rule in Africa. At one time the country had one of the world's fastest growing economies. However, since 1980 Liberia has been wracked by civil war and violence that have devastated the social and economic fabric of the country.

GEOGRAPHY AND ECONOMY

The geography of Liberia has played a significant role in the country's development. Its swampy coastline and heavily forested interior not only discouraged European settlement but also determined the farming methods used by colonists.

Geography. Liberia's location just north of the equator gives it a tropical climate marked by warm temperatures and high humidity. The country experiences distinct dry and rainy seasons each year, and annual precipitation averages 190 inches.

Tropical rain forest covers nearly 60 percent of the country's interior. At one time these forests probably extended to the Atlantic coast. However, several hundred years of human settlement have produced a savanna*-like environment along the coast. The coastline itself features many narrow barrier beaches and coastal lagoons but no natural harbors. The lack of harbors is undoubtedly one reason Europeans established few trading posts in the area and later made no real effort to colonize it.

Moving inland from the broad coastal plain, the elevation increases, with rolling hills, tropical forest, and eventually high plateaus and mountain ranges in the north and west. The Nimba Mountains, the highest part of Liberia, are rich in iron ore and also contain deposits of diamonds, gold, and other minerals.

The nation's current boundaries are the result of territory the American founders purchased from indigenous* people. Liberia was under constant threat from surrounding French and British colonies until well into the 1900s. It now shares borders with SIERRA LEONE on the west, GUINEA on the north, and IVORY COAST on the east and northeast.

ECONOMY

Liberia's economy has traditionally been based on agriculture, primarily subsistence farming*. Dry upland rice, the most important staple* crop, is planted in fields created by clearing forests. In dry rice farming the fields are left fallow* for 7 to 12 years between crops to allow the soil to become fertile again. The system makes it difficult for the country to pro-

* **savanna** tropical or subtropical grassland with scattered trees and drought-resistant undergrowth

* **indigenous** native to a certain place

* **subsistence farming** raising only enough food to live on

* **staple** major product of a region; basic food

* **fallow** plowed but not planted during the growing season

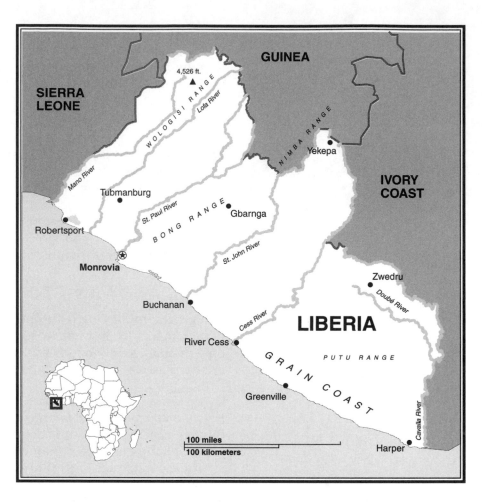

* **cassava** starchy root plant; source of tapioca

* **exploit** to take advantage of; to make productive use of

* **infrastructure** basic framework of a society and its economy, which includes roads, bridges, port facilities, airports, and other public works

duce enough food for its population, and Liberia depends heavily on imported food. Cassava*, eggplant, corn, okra, and peppers are often planted along with the rice. Many Liberian farmers also grow crops such as citrus fruits, bananas, and sugarcane.

The economy of the country has also depended heavily on exports of raw materials, particular rubber and iron ore. In many cases the Liberian government sold the rights to exploit* these products to foreign companies. Liberians received little benefit from their country's leading exports because foreign firms controlled them. In any event, after civil war broke out in Liberia, rubber and iron exports plummeted.

Development of other areas of the economy, such as manufacturing and commerce, has been held back by the country's poor infrastructure*. In addition, the civil war destroyed many of the country's roads, railroads, and industrial facilities. Future economic development will require massive amounts of foreign aid and a climate of stability that will attract foreign investment.

HISTORY AND GOVERNMENT

Many historical accounts claim that Liberia was founded by freed American slaves. However, like many statements about Liberian history, this is an oversimplification of some complicated events.

8

From Prison to Promised Land

Liberia's name came from the fact that its freed black settlers saw it as a land of liberty. However, the country grew out of an idea that was far from liberating. Haunted by the fear of a violent slave revolt, legislators in Virginia proposed establishing a separate colony for rebellious blacks. They asked President James Monroe to acquire land in Africa for that purpose. The idea was never pursued, but it led in 1816 to the organization of the American Society for Colonizing the Free People of Color. The efforts of this group, later known as the American Colonization Society, eventually resulted in the founding of Liberia.

Early History. The original inhabitants of Liberia were Mel-speaking peoples who were joined by Mande speakers from the northern forests and savannas in the 1400s. Long before the arrival of Europeans on the Atlantic coast, these groups were involved in trade across the SAHARA DESERT in pepper, gold, ivory, and other products. When European traders appeared in the 1500s, trading activity moved toward the coast. Mande and Mel chiefdoms provided slaves for the Atlantic trade, while Kru-speaking peoples of southeastern Liberia served as dockworkers, deck hands, and laborers.

U.S. involvement in Liberia grew out of the efforts of the American Colonization Society (ACS), a group of wealthy white Americans who worked to resettle free blacks in Africa. This group sought to remove free blacks from America because their presence served as a challenge to the moral and legal basis of SLAVERY. Formed in 1816, the ACS brought the first black American immigrants to Liberia in 1822. Many of them were educated business and professional people who felt a sense of superiority to both the local population and to the freed American field slaves who came to Liberia later.

In 1847 the educated black immigrants declared independence from the ACS and founded Liberia as a republic modeled after the United States. These settlers were determined to end the SLAVE TRADE and take over the dominant position in the coastal economy. Using a combination of military force, treaties, trade agreements, and political marriages into prominent local families, they managed to extend their control over the region. These Americo-Liberians controlled power in Liberia and discriminated against indigenous peoples in education, business, and civil service. However, because the local population was not racially distinct from the newcomers, some indigenous peoples were able to gain access to positions of influence. This contrasted sharply with European colonies in which skin color presented a steep barrier between the rulers and the ruled.

The Tubman Era. Perhaps the most important political figure in Liberian history, William TUBMAN served as the nation's president from 1944 to 1971. His election ushered in a new era in Liberian politics because he did not belong to one of the prominent families that dominated the capital city of Monrovia.

Although a loyal member of the True Whig Party, which had controlled Liberian politics since 1877, Tubman tried to reach out to indigenous peoples. He launched what he called the Open Door Policy to provide economic opportunities for all Liberians by making the country more attractive to foreign investors. He also gave indigenous people the right to vote and lowered property qualifications for voting. At the same time, though, Tubman introduced programs designed to continue minority rule while creating the illusion of sharing power with the African majority.

Under Tubman, Liberia continued to be a one-party state, but Western leaders found his policies attractive. Liberia was the first nation in Africa to earn a seat in the United Nations Security Council. President John F. Kennedy made Liberia a focus of the Peace Corps, whose members helped build many schools and hospitals in the country. Tubman want-

President of Liberia from 1944 to 1971, William Tubman extended full rights of citizenship to all Liberians. Here Liberians line the streets of Monrovia to greet their president.

* **coup** sudden, often violent, overthrow of a ruler or government

ed to be a leader of the newly independent African states, and his politics had a great deal of influence on the ORGANIZATION OF AFRICAN UNITY.

When Tubman died in 1971, his vice president, William Tolbert, succeeded him. The new president claimed to be interested in listening to and meeting the needs of the indigenous population, but he continued most of the policies established under Tubman. By the mid-1970s, Liberia's government faced a number of political and economic challenges. Tensions came to a head in April 1979, when police and army forces fired into a crowd of unarmed protesters, killing an unknown number of people. A year later, Tolbert was overthrown in a military coup* and assassinated.

Military Government and Civil War. The leader of the coup, Samuel Doe, formed a military government and promised to hold elections in five years. During that time he appointed members of his own ethnic group, the Krahn, to many government and army posts. This marked the first time that ethnic identity was introduced as a factor in Liberian politics.

When elections were held in 1985, Doe claimed victory even though he actually lost by a wide margin. An army general attempted a coup a month after the election, but Doe survived and retaliated brutally against members of the Dan, the general's ethnic group. In December

Liberia

POPULATION:
3,164,156 (2000 estimated population)

AREA:
43,000 sq. mi. (111,370 sq. km)

LANGUAGES:
English (official); Mande, Kru, Bassa, Vai, Kpelle, others

NATIONAL CURRENCY:
Liberian dollar

PRINCIPAL RELIGIONS:
Traditional 70%, Muslim 20%, Christian 10%

CITIES:
Monrovia (capital), 962,000 (1999 est.); Greenville, Buchanan, Robertsport, Harper

ANNUAL RAINFALL:
Ranges from 203 in. (5,210 mm) on northwestern coast, to 100 in. (2,540 mm) at southeastern tip of country, to 70 in. (1,780 mm) on central plateau

ECONOMY:
GDP per capita: $1,000 (1999 est.)

PRINCIPAL PRODUCTS AND EXPORTS:
Agricultural: rubber, rice, palm oil, cassava, coffee, cocoa beans, sugarcane, timber, bananas, eggplant, corn, okra, peppers, livestock
Manufacturing: rubber processing, palm oil processing, construction materials, food processing
Mining: diamonds, iron ore, gold

GOVERNMENT:
Independence from the American Colonization Society, 1847. Republic with president elected by universal suffrage. Governing body: National Assembly (legislative house).

HEADS OF STATE:
1943–1971 President William Tubman
1971–1980 President William R. Tolbert
1980–1990 General Samuel K. Doe
1990–1994 Interim President Amos Sawyer
1994–1997 Several chairmen of Council of State
1997– President Charles G. Taylor

ARMED FORCES:
14,000 (2001 est.)

EDUCATION:
Compulsory for ages 7–16; literacy rate 38% (2001 est.)

1989, Charles Taylor, a former member of Doe's government, led a small force into Liberia from Ivory Coast. The local people supported the invaders and civil war erupted.

In 1990 an international military force led by NIGERIA intervened in Liberia and prevented Taylor from taking Monrovia. In the meantime a rival group had captured and killed Doe. A regional alliance, the Economic Community of West African States, then set up a civilian government led by Amos Sawyer, another former Doe supporter. Sawyer and his forces controlled the towns, but Taylor held the countryside.

The civil war ended with a cease-fire in 1997, and later that year Taylor was elected president. He has run Liberia like a warlord, with his security forces arresting and executing opponents of his regime*. Taylor has also plundered Liberia's resources for his personal gain and helped destabilize the area by supporting rebels fighting the government of neighboring Sierra Leone. By the year 2001, the Liberian economy continued to deteriorate, and a return to peace, democracy, and stability appeared a dim hope.

* **regime**   current political system or rule

PEOPLES AND CULTURES

Liberia's people are divided into three major language groups: the Mande, Mel, and Kruan. The largest of these is the Mande, who mainly inhabit the north and west along with the Mel. The Kru-speakers live mainly in the southeast. Many Liberians share ethnic identity with people living in the neighboring countries of Guinea, Sierra Leone, and Ivory Coast.

Liberia

* **hierarchical**   referring to a society or institution divided into groups with higher and lower levels

* **Islam**   religion based on the teachings of the prophet Muhammad; religious faith of Muslims

The Mande and Mel have hierarchical* societies in which individuals trace ancestry through the male line. Both societies are also characterized by the existence of SECRET SOCIETIES. The Kruan peoples are less hierarchical, and secret societies do not exist among them.

Traditional religions feature ancestor worship and have been influenced by Western religions. Many Liberians are members of Christian churches as well. Islam* has also become an important force in the country. In the past, religious and ethnic group affiliations were not terribly important in Liberia. This provides some hope that the people can overcome the divisive effects of civil war and build a unified national identity. (*See also* **Ethnic Groups and Identity**, **History of Africa**, **Tribalism**, **United Nations in Africa**.)

Libya

Bordering the Mediterranean Sea, Libya has played a significant role in North Africa and the Middle East since ancient times. For centuries the country's three distinct regions—Tripolitania, Cyrenaica, and Fezzan—were ruled by foreign powers such as the Romans, the

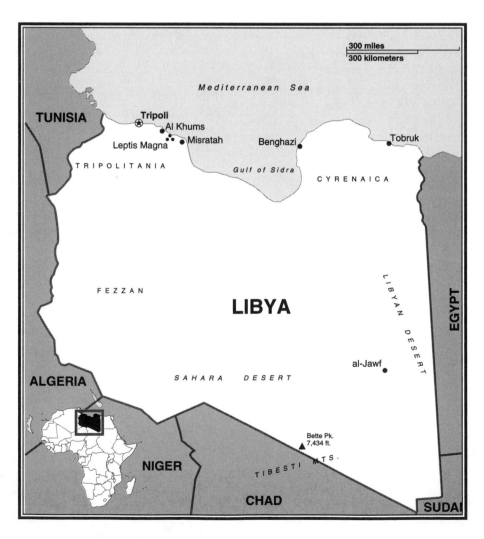

Tobruk

A port city in northeastern Libya, Tobruk changed hands many times over the centuries. The Greeks established a farming colony, called Antipyrgos, there. Later the Romans built a fortress on the site to defend the borderland between Cyrenaica and Egypt. In 1911 the Italians used the harbor as a naval base. During World War II, the city was the scene of combat between the British and the Germans. When Libya became a kingdom in 1951, King Idris I lived in Tobruk. Today the city is the endpoint of the oil pipeline that runs from the Sarir oil field to the coast.

* **exploit** to take advantage of; to make productive use of

* **socialism** economic or political system based on the idea that the government or groups of workers should own and run the means of production and distribution of goods

* **indigenous** native to a certain place

See map in Archaeology and Prehistory (vol. 1).

* **maritime** related to the sea or shipping

Muslim Arabs, and the Ottoman Turks. During the period of European colonial rule, Italy united these regions and created the borders of the modern state of Libya.

Since gaining independence in the 1950s, Libya has exploited* its rich oil reserves and experienced a period of unprecedented prosperity. Beginning in 1969 the revolutionary government headed by Colonel Muammar al-QADDAFI introduced reforms based on socialism* and ideals of Arab and African unity. However, Qaddafi's policies have alienated Libya from Western nations and many of its potential allies.

THE LAND AND ITS PEOPLE

The fourth largest country in Africa, Libya has a total area of nearly 680,000 square miles. It is surrounded by ALGERIA and TUNISIA on the west, CHAD and NIGER on the south, and EGYPT and SUDAN on the east. Most of the population lives in the northern region along the coast. The remainder of the country lies in the SAHARA DESERT.

A series of ridges known as the Jebel run along the southern edge of the region of Tripolitania. South of the Jebel is Fezzan, mostly barren desert broken up by oases. In eastern Libya, Cyrenaica rises in a series of ridges along the coast and extends into the desert in the south.

The vast majority of Libyans are Muslim Arabs and about 5 percent are BERBERS, an indigenous* people of the region. A large number of immigrant workers employed by Libyan businesses live in the country. To increase the size of the workforce, the government has encouraged Libyans to have large families. As a result much of the population is very young. The two largest cities, Tripoli and Benghazi, are on the Mediterranean. Most of the people in rural areas live near oases where they can obtain water to irrigate their farms.

HISTORY

Each of the foreign powers that conquered Libya contributed to the country's cities and towns as well as its culture. Since independence, the revolutionary government has tried to limit Western influences on Libyan society. It has also become deeply involved in Middle Eastern politics.

Ancient Times. Libya had extensive contact with the various civilizations that grew up around the Mediterranean Sea. The Egyptians used the name *Libya* to refer to a Berber people who lived west of the NILE RIVER. The Greeks and Romans used the term to refer to Cyrenaica, the North African coast, or sometimes even the entire continent.

The two coastal regions of Tripolitania and Cyrenaica had distinct cultures made up of Berbers and immigrants from other areas. In the late 600s B.C., the Greeks colonized Cyrenaica. The local people adopted Greek culture, and the region produced a number of important writers and philosophers. By the 400s B.C., Phoenicians from Lebanon had settled in Tripolitania and built a powerful maritime* empire in the region.

During the 200s and 100s, the Romans conquered the western Mediterranean, including Tripolitania. Shortly after, they gained control

13

Libya

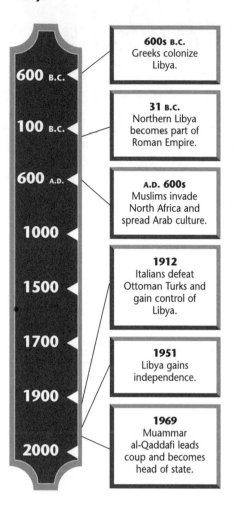

600s B.C.
Greeks colonize Libya.

31 B.C.
Northern Libya becomes part of Roman Empire.

A.D. 600s
Muslims invade North Africa and spread Arab culture.

1912
Italians defeat Ottoman Turks and gain control of Libya.

1951
Libya gains independence.

1969
Muammar al-Qaddafi leads coup and becomes head of state.

600 B.C.
100 B.C.
600 A.D.
1000
1500
1700
1900
2000

* **Islam** religion based on the teachings of the Prophet Muhammad; religious faith of the Muslims

* **nomadic** referring to people who travel from place to place to find food and pasture

* **dynasty** succession of rulers from the same family or group

* **Sufi** member of a Muslim movement characterized by mysticism and dedication to poverty and prayer

of Cyrenaica as well. North Africa remained part of the Roman Empire for almost 700 years. Evidence of this long association with Rome can be seen at Leptis Magna in Libya, the site of some of the best-preserved remains of a Roman city.

By the A.D. 400s, Rome's control over its vast empire began to weaken. The Vandals, a Germanic people from northern Europe, migrated south into Africa and took over Tripolitania. The Vandals dominated trade in the Mediterranean until the Byzantines in the eastern half of the Roman Empire reconquered the lost territory in 533.

Muslim Influence. The arrival of Islam in the 600s changed North Africa forever. Muslim Arab forces conquered vast portions of territory around the Mediterranean, including what is now Libya. The Berber groups that inhabited Tripolitania, Cyrenaica, and the surrounding deserts adopted Islam. Although some local people continued to speak Berber, most learned Arabic, which replaced Greek and Latin as the language of literature and law. Meanwhile, several waves of nomadic* Bedouins migrated into the region, bringing with them their own ways of life.

After the Muslim takeover, a series of Islamic dynasties* ruled Libya. The powerful Abbasid dynasty appointed the Aghlabids to govern the region. The Aghlabids restored the Roman irrigation system and made Libya increasingly prosperous. During the 900s the Fatimids brought most of northern Africa under their control.

By the 1500s the coast of northern Africa was famous for its pirate kings, who often came into conflict with the European states across the Mediterranean. In 1551 the Ottoman Turks conquered Libya, which became a Turkish province known as Tripolitania. The Turkish sultan appointed a series of rulers to govern the province.

European Colonization. By the late 1800s, Britain, France, and Italy were looking for opportunities to establish settlements and expand their trading interests in North Africa. To gain control of Libya, Italy declared war on the Ottoman Turks in 1911. The Turks surrendered the region a year later. However, led by members of the Sanusi, a Sufi* religious order, the Libyans resisted Italian rule. Italy succeeded in dominating Libya until the 1940s, and thousands of Italians settled in the colony.

After World War II, France and Britain won control of Libya. In 1951 they decided to grant the territory independence. A council of leaders from Libya's three regions met and declared the new country to be a united kingdom headed by Muhammad Idris. A hero of the Sanusi resistance against the Italians, he became King Idris I.

Modern Libya. At first the new kingdom of Libya was very poor and required large amounts of aid from Western powers to survive. In 1955 the discovery of rich petroleum resources in Libya ushered in an era of prosperity. Yet even with the benefit of its oil wealth, the country faced many challenges in developing a diverse modern economy.

During the 1960s, changes in other Arab countries, particularly a movement for Arab unity, began to affect Libyan society. Conflicts between various Arab states and Israel, as well as uncertainty about the fate of the Palestinian people, helped win support for the movement. In 1969 a group of military officers led by Colonel Muammar al-Qaddafi carried out a coup* that ended the monarchy. Colonel Qaddafi took over as head of the revolutionary government and introduced wide-ranging social, political, and economic reforms. Under his rule all public institutions, including schools, businesses, and the media, were administered by "people's committees." The military and foreign relations remained outside the people's control.

* **coup** sudden, often violent, overthrow of a ruler or government

In an old quarter of Tripoli, the Libyan capital, narrow passageways lead to markets and historic mosques.

Libya

 Libya

POPULATION:
5,115,450 (2000 estimated population)

AREA:
679,400 sq. mi. (1,759,540 sq. km)

LANGUAGES:
Arabic (official); Italian, English, Berber dialects

NATIONAL CURRENCY:
Libyan Dinar

PRINCIPAL RELIGIONS:
Muslim (Sunni) 97%

CITIES:
Tripoli (capital), 1,822,000 (2000 est.); Benghazi, Misurata

ANNUAL RAINFALL:
Varies from about 4 in. (100 mm) in the steppe to less than half an inch (12.5 mm) in parts of the Sahara desert

ECONOMY:
GDP per capita: $7,900 (1999 est.)

PRINCIPAL PRODUCTS AND EXPORTS:
Agricultural: barley, wheat, sorghum, dates, olives, citrus, almonds, figs, grapes, peanuts, tobacco, livestock
Manufacturing: food and beverage processing, textiles, petrochemicals, aluminum, cement, leather goods
Mining: crude oil, natural gas, natron, potash, iron ore, salt, gypsum, manganese, sulfur

GOVERNMENT:
Independence from Italy, 1951. Third International Theory, an Islamic Arabic Socialist state of the masses (called Jamahiriya). In theory, governed by the people through local councils; in fact, a military dictatorship. Governing bodies: General People's Congress (legislative body) and General People's Committee (cabinet).

HEADS OF STATE SINCE INDEPENDENCE:
1951–1969 King Idris I
1969– Colonel Muammar al-Qaddafi

ARMED FORCES:
65,000

EDUCATION:
Compulsory for ages 6–15; literacy rate 76%

In 1973 Qaddafi launched a "cultural revolution" aimed at eliminating foreign influence and creating a society based on Muslim principles and socialism. He also made several unsuccessful attempts to unite Libya with other Arab countries. Relations with Western powers became strained after the Libyan government was suspected of supporting international terrorist activities and the United States placed economic sanctions* on Libya.

In 1986, following charges of terrorist activities by Libya, the United States bombed important Libyan sites. Two years later an American passenger airline exploded over Lockerbie, Scotland, and British and American authorities claimed that Libyan terrorists had caused the explosion, increasing tensions even more. Libya was punished by the United Nations and various other organizations until 1999, when the Libyan government turned over two suspects in the explosion. The trial in Lockerbie, Scotland, resulted in a split verdict. One suspect received a life sentence, and the other was found not guilty.

* **sanction** measure adopted by one or more nations to force another nation to change its policies or conduct

ECONOMY

Libya's economy is more like that of the oil-rich states of the Persian Gulf than that of its neighbors in Africa. The main source of the country's income, oil has made Libya one of the wealthiest states in Africa. Nevertheless, the government continues to put great emphasis on agriculture. Farmers raise livestock and plant crops such as barley, wheat, sorghum*, almonds, citrus fruit, apricots, and figs. To increase agricultural production, the country has built extensive irrigation works in the last several decades. The largest program, the Great Man-Made River

* **sorghum** family of tropical grasses used for food

See map in Minerals and Mining (vol. 3).

project, consists of a huge pipeline to carry water from wells in the southern Sahara to the coastal region. Libya has also launched programs to prevent desertification—the spread of desert conditions to usable stretches of land. (*See also* **Arabs in Africa, Colonialism in Africa, Deserts and Drought, Energy and Energy Resources, Islam in Africa, North Africa: Geography and Population, North Africa: History and Cultures, Roman Africa.**)

One of the greatest challenges facing modern Africa is increasing the rate of literacy—the ability to read and write—among its population. Studies have shown that literacy leads to improvements in many areas of life. These include better health and nutrition for mothers and their children, a lower infant death rate, higher productivity in agriculture, and increased political participation. However, in recent years the economic and political troubles of many African nations have led to a decline in the availability and quality of educational programs.

Literacy has benefits on many levels. It helps people to improve their thinking skills and absorb information more readily. It also changes the way that they view themselves and relate to others. On a practical level, literacy enables individuals to read printed materials such as the instructions that come with medicines and agricultural chemicals. Literate adults are more likely to understand the information and to prepare and use the products correctly. In this way, the benefit of literacy can extend beyond individuals to their families and society as a whole.

Measuring Literacy. Literacy is often difficult to measure. It does not always relate to the number of years of schooling a person completes. The quality of the educational program can make a difference in how well students learn to read and write. In some African societies the most common form of reading material is sacred texts, used for religious ceremonies. Individuals might be skillful in reading these texts but inexperienced with other types of writing, such as technical instruction manuals.

In many African countries, more than one language is spoken. Children may be taught to read in an indigenous* language or in another language such as English or French. Estimating the level of literacy across the population may be complicated by the variety of languages and schools found in the culture.

Literacy in Africa. In 1961 African ministers of education met in ADDIS ABABA, ETHIOPIA, and pledged to eliminate illiteracy in 30 years. They planned to achieve this goal by making primary education universal by 1980 and by sponsoring adult education programs. The early results were impressive: by 1980 nearly 80 percent of African children were enrolled in elementary schools. In addition, some countries such as Ethiopia and TANZANIA launched large-scale adult literacy campaigns during the 1970s and early 1980s. Between 1970 and 1990, the illiteracy rate among African adults dropped from 77 to 53 percent.

* indigenous   native to a certain place

In recent years, social, economic, and political problems have hindered efforts to increase literacy in Africa. Many countries have experienced high population growth and economic decline. Others have been devastated by political unrest and even civil war. By 1997 only about half of African children were attending school. Those who do attend are often taught by untrained teachers.

All of these factors have widened the gaps in literacy among African countries. By 2000 Botswana had achieved a literacy rate of 70 percent, while Burundi had a rate of only 35 percent. One promising trend noted by researchers is that parents involved in literacy programs are more likely to send their children to school and to keep them there. For this reason, various countries, including Ghana and Senegal, have recently launched national literacy campaigns. (*See also* **Education, Languages, Literature, Publishing, Writing Systems.**)

Literature

African literature has developed from sources and influences that originated both within and outside of the continent. One major source, Africa's rich tradition of oral stories and histories, is much older than the continent's written literature. Written scripts arose in Africa in Egyptian hieroglyphs, a complex system of picture-writing used by the ancient Egyptians. However, written scripts using alphabets and words did not appear in Africa until traders, missionaries, colonists, and armies from foreign lands brought them.

This process occurred in three waves, separated by time and location. In the first, which took place during the first thousand years B.C., scripts from the Semitic peoples of the Middle East and Arabia arrived in eastern Africa. In the second wave, which began in the A.D. 600s, the Arabic language and Islamic* religion swept across North Africa. The third wave, which started with European trading posts on the western coast of Africa in the late 1400s and engulfed the whole continent by about 1900, brought European languages and the Roman alphabet.

* **Islamic** relating to Islam, the religion based on the teachings of the prophet Muhammad

The Arab and European invasions had far-reaching consequences for every aspect of African life, including its literature. Africans adopted and adapted the languages and scripts used by the invaders. Some Africans began writing in these foreign languages, while others used the alphabets to create written forms for indigenous* languages. Africans wrote in these new forms to express their feelings about the profound social and psychological changes caused by conquest and colonization. Women writers in particular have turned to literature to consider their position in society and to struggle for their own liberation.

* **indigenous** native to a certain place

AFRICAN LITERATURE IN ARABIC

In A.D. 632, Muslim Arabs invaded EGYPT, and by 1000 they had conquered all of North Africa. Parts of East Africa and West Africa also came under Islamic influence, and several cities became centers of Islamic learning.

The Spread of Islam and Arabic. From the 1400s to the 1600s, the city of TIMBUKTU in MALI produced a rich body of literature in the form of historical chronicles and works of Muslim science, law, medicine, and theology*. Over time, indigenous languages were written in Arabic script as well. This development made it easier to spread Islam among the African peoples and led to the beginnings of written literature in African languages such as FULANI, HAUSA, and WOLOF.

* **theology** study of religious faith

A second source of Arabic influence came by way of Arabia and Persia to East African coasts along the Indian Ocean. After A.D. 700, immigrants and merchants from those areas arrived in the region that is now KENYA and TANZANIA. There they interacted with local BANTU-speaking peoples and forged a common culture and tongue known as SWAHILI. At some point Swahili also began to be transcribed into Arabic script. The earliest known Swahili manuscripts date from the early 1700s and feature mainly religious and secular* poetry.

* **secular** nonreligious; connected with everyday life

Islam and the Written Word. Islamic culture holds the written word in high esteem, and where Islam appeared in Africa, African versions of Arabic script often followed. Many written works from East and West Africa are known as Afro-Islamic, based on indigenous tongues that have absorbed much Islamic expression and content. However, some cultures with Afro-Islamic literature, such as Somali and Mandingo, still favor oral over written literature.

Islamic literature made its greatest contribution in the area of poetry. A wide range of themes—from the life of the prophet Muhammad to works about society, religion, and politics—can be found in Islamic poetry. The period from about 500 to 1500 was a golden age of poetry among the educated aristocracy* of North Africa and the Middle East.

* **aristocracy** privileged upper classes of society; nobles or the nobility

Colonial North Africa. During the 1800s and 1900s, the role of Islamic prose expanded considerably in North Africa. Some authors revived forms and themes from classical Arabic literature while dealing with the people and politics of their own times. Novels and novellas appeared chapter by chapter in popular newspapers and magazines, often written by the publishers themselves. Authors began to use common forms of Arabic instead of the classical Arabic of high culture, and readers and writers from the lower classes began to take part in literature.

During the mid-1900s, literature played a crucial role in North Africans' struggles against French and British rule. Islamic associations and schools encouraged people to speak and write in Arabic rather than French or English, and writers responded with powerful portrayals of colonial society.

After independence, many writers turned their criticism on the new governments' corruption and incompetence. Both male and female authors have campaigned to free women from strict Islamic religion and culture. Modern Arabic literature has developed a wide range of fantasy and realism, tradition and innovation, culture and politics. Yet many writers continue to explore the relationship between Islam and modern Western culture, and fierce debates rage over the choice of language. Meanwhile, international fame has come to some, such as Egypt's Naguib MAHFOUZ, who won the Nobel Prize in 1988.

Literature

Keepers of the Lost Ark

The biblical tale of the Queen of Sheba is familiar to many Western readers. However, the Ethiopian version, the Kibre negest, adds some interesting details. In this version, the Queen of Sheba travels from Ethiopia to Israel, where she converts to Judaism and bears a son by King Solomon named Menilek. When he reaches adulthood, Menilek returns to Israel for a visit with his father. Solomon sends Menilek back home with priests to teach the law and set up a Jewish state in Ethiopia. But Menilek also takes with him the Ark of the Covenant, the chest containing the tablets of the Ten Commandments. Ethiopian religious leaders say that the ark is still in their country.

* **dynasty**   succession of rulers from the same family or group

LITERATURE IN AFRICAN LANGUAGES

Many African cultures had oral traditions that formed the basis for indigenous literature after written scripts were created. For example, the arrival of Arabic script in East Africa in the A.D. 900s led to writing in the Swahili language and in time to Swahili literature. Other languages such as Somali, however, did not have a written form until quite recently.

Ethiopian Literature.   The earliest evidence of written African literature comes from the ancient kingdom of AKSUM, in what is now ETHIOPIA. Inscriptions there are written in a Semitic script native to southern Arabia. Around the 300s B.C., Egyptian monks converted Aksum to Christianity and eventually translated the Bible from Greek into the local Ge'ez language. Although Ge'ez died out as a spoken language and was replaced by Amharic, it has remained the language of Ethiopian Christianity, and the 1300s and 1400s marked the golden age of Ge'ez literature.

Ethiopian literature was largely religious in nature, and much of it came from the traditions of Egypt's Coptic Christian Church. But by writing in Ge'ez, the Ethiopians preserved their own independent culture. The first works in Ge'ez were the Gospels, followed by other religious books. Ethiopian literature went into a decline in the 900s, but it revived with the Solomonic dynasty* of kings that took power in 1270. This period produced a work of national history and myth called the *Kibre negest* (*Glory of the Kings*), a version of the biblical tale of the Queen of Sheba's visit to King Solomon of Israel. The story originally appeared in Arabic, which may mean that Ethiopian writers once used Arabic as well as Ge'ez.

The most productive author of traditional Ethiopian literature was the emperor ZARA YA'IQOB, who ruled from 1434 to 1468. He wrote many stories about miracles involving the Virgin Mary, as well as religious essays, prayer books, and hymn books. But by the end of the 1500s, civil wars and a Muslim invasion brought literary activity to an almost complete halt.

In response to these pressures, Ethiopian rulers moved their capital to the city of Gondar, where literature enjoyed another revival. This period produced many hymns, such as the *ginie,* individual poems composed for each particular day and sung only once. Though an old form, the *ginie* became newly popular at that time.

The end of the Gondarite period in 1755 also brought a decline in Ge'ez literature. Amharic rose to challenge Ge'ez as a literary language, helped along by Catholic missionaries who used it to communicate with local populations. Early Amharic authors focused on theology and Christian ethics, and they criticized tradition as an obstacle to progress.

Modern Amharic literature deals mostly with universal themes such as love, death, and social problems. Meanwhile, civil unrest has driven many Ethiopians to live abroad, where they have produced a body of non-African Amharic literature. It includes not only creative writing but also several types of Amharic computer software created by Ethiopian engineers.

Swahili Literature. Swahili culture arose from interactions between Bantu-speaking East Africans and Arabs from Persia and Arabia. The main form of Swahili literature has been poetry, which reached a peak with warrior-hero Fumo Liyongo. The style of Liyongo, who may have lived as early as the 900s, shows so much polish and skill that scholars believe Swahili poetry was already highly developed by his time. Later Swahili poets based their work mainly on forms he used. Poems were generally passed on orally, although some religious poetry was written down.

In the 1800s and 1900s, colonial rule had a major impact on Swahili literature. The translation into Swahili of English novels such as *Treasure Island* and *Gulliver's Travels* led to the rise of Swahili novels. The best-known early Swahili novelist was SHAABAN ROBERT, who drew heavily on traditional stories for inspiration. Later Swahili novels turned more to realistic portrayals of modern life. Modern Swahili literature deals mainly with the colonial experience and its effects on Africa. Novelists have also grappled with the conflict between rural and urban life.

Somali Literature. The East African nation of SOMALIA has produced some of the most experimental fiction on the continent. After the government adopted the Roman alphabet for the Somali language in 1972, works by a new group of writers appeared that combined traditional oral poetry and written forms. A more political group of novelists, including Nuruddin Farah, had novels published in installments in newspapers and journals until stopped by government censorship. During the Somali civil war of the 1980s and 1990s, many novels were written and published thanks to new desktop computers and the absence of a strong government to censor the works.

Hausa Literature. The written literature of the Hausa, an ethnic group in northern NIGERIA, blossomed shortly after 1800. Prior to that time, the Hausa oral tradition consisted mainly of praise songs. Among the aristocracy the songs praised traditional leaders and patrons, while common people sang of farmers, hunters, boxers, and wrestlers. This tradition continues today with popular singers who chant alongside music and choruses both to praise patrons and to address social issues such as poverty and drug abuse.

In 1804 an Islamic holy war produced much Hausa religious poetry written in both Arabic and the local Fulani language. After conquering the Hausa, the military leader Shehu UTHMAN DAN FODIO used poetry to win his new subjects over to Islam. He and his daughter Nana ASMA'U wrote poetry in Hausa that explained the principles of Islam and attacked non-Islamic ideas. Modern Hausa poets still use these forms to debate politics, economics, and culture.

Prose writing in Hausa began with a colonial competition in 1933 and has recently developed into a full social and political force. Novelists such as S. I. Katsina have focused on Nigeria's ruling class and the corruption of the oil industry and national elections.

Yoruba Literature. The Yoruba of southwestern Nigeria, neighbors of the Hausa, also have a rich oral tradition. Their chant poetry, called *ewi,*

Wole Soyinka, Nigerian author and political activist, wrote a play in honor of his country's independence in 1960. The play celebrated the end of colonial rule but warned Nigerians of other forms of tyranny. In 1986 Soyinka won the Nobel Prize for literature.

plays an important part in Yoruba life. Important public ceremonies almost always include a local poet performing *ewi*. Poets also chant *ewi* to make comments on modern society.

Written Yoruba literature did not appear until English missionaries collected and published a vocabulary of Yoruba words in 1828. The first collection of Yoruba poetry appeared 20 years later, and the first Yoruba newspapers began in 1859. The papers printed long stories in serial form. Daniel O. Fagunwa, the first major Yoruba novelist, wrote fantasy novels inspired by oral traditions. However, a call for more realistic works produced a generation of writers who have concentrated on modern life.

The Yoruba novel is growing, but traditional Yoruba THEATER is on the decline.

South African Literature. Southern Africa, and the nation of SOUTH AFRICA in particular, includes ethnic groups speaking languages such as ZULU, XHOSA, Nguni, Sotho, and Tswana. Several South African languages have strong oral traditions that include praise poetry, stories, proverbs, and riddles. A professional praiser was present at the ceremony that installed Nelson MANDELA as president of South Africa in 1994. Many of the oral traditions include human encounters with a trickster* god, who often remains in disguise until the end of the story. Other common themes are meetings with monsters who seem half human and half ogre; the hero of the story must know the ogre's weakness in order to escape.

In the 1800s Protestant missionaries compiled written versions of many languages of southern Africa. Their main goal was to produce Bibles and other religious materials in local languages. However, their works determined which forms and dialects of each language eventually became standard. Later, English novels translated into Zulu, Xhosa, and Sotho inspired indigenous writers to create novels on Christian themes. But since 1960, novels have tended to focus on themes of isolation, self-destruction, and the tension between tradition and modernity.

The apartheid* policies of South Africa had a major impact on Zulu, Xhosa, and Sotho literature. The government controlled many of the publishing houses and censored writing in African languages, aiming to prevent protest literature from reaching its audiences. Many indigenous authors had to use English or Afrikaans (a version of Dutch) to publish their message abroad. The end of apartheid in the 1990s has led to an explosion of South African literature in indigenous languages.

AFRICAN LITERATURE IN ENGLISH

Literature in English—known as anglophone literature—has several sources in Africa. Some is the work of Christian missionaries and European colonists; other material is by indigenous writers. Some African authors wrote in English after they left the continent. A typical example is the autobiography of Olaudah EQUIANO, who was seized in what is now Nigeria and taken to England as a slave. Other African writers began using English while living in Africa. African anglophone liter-

* **trickster** mischievous figure appearing in various forms in the folktales and mythology of many different peoples

* **apartheid** policy of racial segregation enforced by the white government of South Africa to maintain political, economic, and social control over the country's blacks, Asians, and people of mixed ancestry

ature only became established after 1900, as indigenous writers began to record their impressions and feelings about the colonial experience.

Western Africa. The first African work of anglophone fiction was Joseph Casely-Hayford's *Ethiopia Unbound* (1911), which dealt with the European belief in the superiority of Western over African cultures. No significant works of anglophone fiction appeared for the next 30 years. In 1952 Amos TUTUOLA caused a sensation with his novel, *The Palm-Wine Drinkard and His Dead Palm-Wine Tapster in the Deads' Town*. It was a hit with Western readers, who mistook its unconventional style for a bold experiment in language. In fact, the writing reflected Tutuola's lack of familiarity with English.

African critics had harsh words for Tutuola's work, believing that his poor English reflected badly on Africa as a whole. However, his success inspired new authors such as Chinua ACHEBE, a Nigerian who became one of Africa's most celebrated novelists. In *Things Fall Apart* (1958) and other works, Achebe examines both the triumphs and failures of Nigerian history. Other authors have focused on personal lives, including Flora NWAPA in her novels about Nigerian women.

Anglophone poetry in West Africa closely followed Western traditions until the 1950s. At that time poets began to concern themselves with the kind of African experiences that motivated Achebe. In the 1960s, poets such as Lenrie Peters of GAMBIA and Kofi Awoonor of GHANA focused on the tensions between traditional and modern life in Africa.

Drama in West Africa achieved maturity in the late 1950s and early 1960s with playwrights such as Joe de Graft and Ama Ata Aidoo. Their plays deal with themes such as conflict and intermarriage between social groups and the influence of women on history and society. Wole SOYINKA of Nigeria gained fame as Africa's most successful dramatist and won the Nobel Prize for Literature in 1986. In *A Dance of the Forests,* written on the occasion of Nigeria's independence, Soyinka destroyed the myths of a glorious Nigerian past and predicted a bleak future for the new state. Since that time, many of Soyinka's plays have bitterly criticized Nigeria's leaders.

Eastern Africa. From the early 1900s, poetry, prose, and song were key weapons in the struggles against British colonialism in eastern Africa. Some political writing was published in code to avoid censorship. For example, one crucial work, Jomo KENYATTA's *Facing Mount Kenya* (1938), portrayed the GIKUYU culture of Kenya in opposition to the British, and the author later served as the first president of independent Kenya.

Poets, including Julius NYERERE, helped found the political party known as TANU that fought for Tanganyikan independence. Nyerere became the first president of Tanganyika (now Tanzania). Since independence, East African writers such as Abdilatif Abdalla and NGUGI WA THIONG'O have continued to explore colonial history and its impact on Africa.

In their works East African authors have expressed their disappointment with the corruption and violence of their own governments. Both

Afrikaans and Apartheid

The Dutch colonists who settled Cape Colony in the late 1600s developed a distinct dialect of Dutch that the local African population attempted to master. The language, called Afrikaans, fell out of favor among educated South Africans after the British took over the colony in 1806. However, in 1875 a group of white settlers championed the use of written Afrikaans to promote a national identity of white supremacy. Early writers in Afrikaans rarely addressed moral issues such as apartheid. But in the 1960s and 1970s, Afrikaans literature turned critical of South Africa's social policies. Thus, a literature that once promoted racial division eventually helped to end it.

Literature

Abdilatif and Ngugi have worked with human rights organizations to document abuses in Kenya, and Ngugi was imprisoned for his efforts. In Somalia, the government responded to the novels of Nuruddin Farah by sending him into exile on threat of death. A number of East African writers such as Thiong'o have published novels or diaries set in prison.

Following independence, many students and teachers pushed for more works by Africans in college literature courses. This movement also spurred a call for more work in East African languages. A new generation of Kenyan and Tanzanian authors began to write in the Swahili tongue, KiSwahili. Another important development has been the study of spoken compositions known as *orature.*

Southern Africa. The earliest literary works from southern Africa were written by white settlers such as the poet Thomas Pringle, who described his feelings about the land alongside his unease about being part of a brutal colonial society. In the 1880s, Olive SCHREINER received wide attention for her *The Story of an African Farm,* a complex novel expressing critical views of colonialism. However, adventure stories, such as H. Rider Haggard's *King Solomon's Mines,* were also popular at this time. These stories often told of heroic white men exploring and taming the wilderness and conquering the black people who lived there.

The first recognized black writer from southern Africa was Sol PLAATJE. His 1917 novel *Mhudi* attempted to preserve indigenous versions of the region's history. At about the same time, several black literary journals emerged. After 1948, however, apartheid policies drove a wedge into the developing black literary scene. The state of South Africa persecuted talented black writers and censored their work. Many fled the country and published from exile. Meanwhile, some white writers continued to protest the policies of apartheid in their works. Among this group were Nadine GORDIMER, who won the Nobel Prize for Literature in 1991, and Alan PATON, whose novel *Cry, the Beloved Country* (1948) may be the most widely read work of South African fiction. Other well-known writers, both black and white, include J. M. COETZEE, Bessie HEAD, and Athol FUGARD.

AFRICAN LITERATURE IN FRENCH

African literature in French, known as francophone literature, appeared later than African anglophone literature, even though the French arrived on the continent before the British. One possible explanation is that the French discouraged the expression of indigenous cultures and tried harder than the British to impose French culture on their African subjects. In addition, French Catholic missionaries did not share the interest of English Protestant missionaries in compiling written vocabularies of indigenous languages. As a result, francophone literature in Africa began only in the early 1900s.

Western Africa. Apart from a few early novels, the rise of francophone literature can be traced to the NEGRITUDE movement of the 1930s. Negritude developed into the French colonies in the Caribbean as a revolutionary celebration of black African heritage and a reaction to French colonial policies. The movement spread to Paris, where it was adopted by African students such as Léopold SENGHOR and Alioune DIOP of SENEGAL. The movement's main contribution came in the area of poetry, hailed by some critics as the finest in modern Africa.

During the 1950s novels moved to the forefront of francophone literary activity, while poetry declined. Also inspired by Negritude, the novels of this period portrayed French colonial power as corrupt and violent. The works of Mongo BETI, one of the leading novelists, explored how Africans from traditional cultures felt alienated in the world created by colonization. Beti was sharply critical of Guinean novelist CAMARA LAYE, who offered a more positive view of Africans' lives under the French.

Sembène Ousmane of Senegal remains one of the best-known francophone novelists. He has paid little attention to the damage of colonialism, seeing it as a temporary enemy to be defeated. He has focused instead on elements of society, such as traditional religions and the oppression* of women, that he feels held Senegal back. Influenced by Karl Marx, Sembène believes that the truly universal struggle is between the haves and the have-nots, regardless of color or ethnic identity.

As elsewhere in Africa, francophone authors have incorporated the African tradition of spoken works known as *orature*. They have borrowed techniques from *orature*, such as the use of shifting viewpoints to tell a story from many different angles. The novelist Ahmadou KOUROUMA from Ivory Coast used this method in his early novels *The Suns of Independence* and *Monnew*. More recent writers have worked with other features of *orature* such as proverbs, family histories, and recurring images. The main goal is to use language to create a mood and stir the emotions; the plot is secondary.

North Africa. North African countries such as MOROCCO, Tunisia, and Algeria benefited from religious and political efforts to preserve Islamic culture and the Arabic language. Even so, many North African authors chose to write in French, sometimes as a way of expressing the clash of African and European culture. Some of the best-known include Morocco's Driss Chraibi, Algeria's Moulaoud Mammeri, and Tunisia's Albert Memmi. Memmi wrote from the unusual position of a North African Jew caught between tradition, colonialism, and Nazism.

Of the North African nations, Algeria endured the most violent and traumatic colonization, including a bitter war for independence from 1954 to 1962. Many Algerian writers, such as Mohammed Dib in his Algeria trilogy, turned to documentary styles to express the tragedy of this struggle.

Central Africa. Francophone literature developed later in central Africa, often stimulated by the rise of local literary journals. The most influential, *Liaison* and *La Voix du Congolais,* were actually sponsored by colonial governments. However, they provided a place for black African writers to comment on social and cultural issues. Nevertheless, few francophone authors of the region are well known outside their homelands. The two Congolese republics—one a former colony of France, the other of Belgium—have produced the most prominent writers.

* **oppression** unjust or cruel exercise of authority

Congolese poetry blossomed in the late 1960s and 1970s, stimulated by both the Negritude movement and the increasing contact between black writers across the continent. One of its leading figures, Valentin Mudimbe, founded a publishing house to promote Congolese literature. He has since emerged as a prominent novelist and scholar, who lives in the United States.

Congolese literature may be best represented by the comic novels of Jean Malonga and the poetry of Gérard Félix Tchicaya U Tam'si. Beginning his career as a poet, Tchicaya turned to novels and theater in the 1980s. While his poetry is mysterious and religious, his plays and novels face hard realities such as Africa's past and the abuse of power in modern society. Henri Lopès, another Congolese writer, is known for novels that explore serious topics with humor and satire.

WOMEN WRITERS

The development of African literature during the 1800s and early 1900s was largely restricted to male writers. Sexism made it difficult for women to write and to be recognized, both at home and in Europe. But as the movements for African liberation gained strength after World War II, women writers joined the struggle and made significant contributions to African literature and politics. They wrote from their special experience as victims of both colonialism and sexism, and they did not spare their home countries from criticism. Especially since the appearance of Flora Nwapa's famous novel *Efuru* in 1966, women writers have become leading literary voices on the continent and outspoken voices for change.

Issues in Women's Literature. The late development of female literature in Africa has its roots in the attitude of African cultures toward women. Women in traditional societies are often excluded from decision making and are limited to defined roles as wives and mothers, despite significant contributions in farming, housework, and child rearing. Practices such as polygyny, in which a man has more than one wife, also serve to emphasize the power of males over females in such societies. Motherhood is considered the greatest achievement for a woman, and women are often judged on their ability to produce offspring. These bounds on the world of traditional African women severely limit their ability to express their identities, experiences, and hopes.

The work of many male African authors has focused on the conflict between traditional and colonial society, the destruction of indigenous ways of life, the abuses of colonialism, and the corruption of modern Africa's rulers. Many look back on Africa's precolonial* past as a kind of glorious golden age. Many women writers, however, have taken a less romantic view of traditional society. For them, the fight for independence meant not only freedom from European domination, but also from a male-dominated world that did not allow them to have a voice of their own.

Meanwhile, in criticizing African society after independence, women have typically been less concerned with political change at the high levels of government and more concerned with the individual's role in

* **precolonial** referring to the time before European powers colonized Africa

Many of Nadine Gordimer's short stories and novels involve the tensions of everyday life in South Africa during apartheid, the strict racial segregation enforced by the government. In 1991 Gordimer received the Nobel Prize for literature.

society. Many male authors blame corrupt political leaders for the moral breakdown in African society. Women writers, however, often point out that the average person bears much of the blame—and much of the responsibility for progress.

Attitudes Toward Men and Society. Much writing by African women has focused on male behavior—not only on traditional male practices such as polygamy, but also on the sexist attitudes of modern

African men. Female writers accuse African men of allowing the corrupt social structure to continue because it preserves male advantages. This theme runs through Maraima Bâ's novel *So Long a Letter* (1979). It tells the tale of Ramatoulaye, an African woman whose husband takes a very young second wife after 20 years of marriage. He dies, leaving Ramatoulaye to raise 12 children by herself. The book explores her growth as an independent person.

Female writers examine other aspects of the tension between modern and traditional society. Many do not seek to destroy or abandon African culture; they often emphasize that they are African women. But in trying to change their society for the better, they do not disregard all Western influence. For example, many male authors portray Western-style education as a form of colonial domination, but female authors tend to see it as a liberating force for women. Books such as Bâ's *Scarlet Song* (1981) explore the dilemma of educated women in traditional African society, women who find themselves valued by their husbands mainly as wives and mothers.

African women writers see the modern Africa as neither a paradise nor a land without hope. Instead they see a continent still struggling to throw off the oppressions of colonialism and sexism. They work for social change that will allow all Africans, men and women, to reach their potential. (*See also* **Colonialism in Africa, Literacy, Missions and Missionaries, Oral Tradition, Publishing, Theater, Women in Africa, Writing Systems.**)

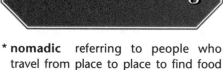

Livestock Grazing

* **nomadic** referring to people who travel from place to place to find food and pasture

* **savanna** tropical or subtropical grassland with scattered trees and drought-resistant undergrowth

Livestock grazing, also known as pastoralism, has been practiced in Africa for many thousands of years. Nomadic* herding cultures existed throughout the continent long before the arrival of Europeans. As colonial governments seized land for agriculture and industry, many pastoral societies were forced to abandon or modify their traditional lifestyles. Nevertheless, some African peoples still depend on herding for their livelihood.

Types of Pastoralism. There are two types of African cultures based on livestock grazing: cattle societies and camel societies. Cattle societies are spread across the savanna* regions of northwestern, eastern, and southern Africa. Camel societies live mostly in the continent's northern and eastern deserts. Herding peoples have historically avoided central Africa, where the tsetse fly is found. Tsetse flies often carry sleeping sickness, which can be deadly to humans and large animals.

Cattle societies place a high value on the ownership of cattle. Individuals who control the largest herds have the most power and prestige. Because cattle do not provide for all of the community's needs, pastoral groups often combine livestock raising with gathering foods that grow wild or farming. They also enter into exchange relationships with agricultural societies, trading meat, milk, and hides for grains, fruits, and vegetables. These economic relations sometimes develop into political ties. In the past the FULANI, a herding people of western and central

Camel caravans, like this one in Niger, transport goods across the Sahara desert. Some herding societies raise camels for use as pack animals.

Africa, had trading relations with farming communities. Fulani leaders later formed states that included the groups in their trading networks.

Camel societies, organized around the use of camels as pack animals, are a relatively recent development. Groups such as the BERBERS of North Africa began using camels to transport goods across the SAHARA DESERT several hundred years ago. Like cattle societies, camel herders rely on exchange with farming peoples to obtain plant foods. They often work as traders, acquiring goods from various groups and distributing them in distant regions.

History of African Pastoralism. Animal bones found in the northern Sahara suggest that people were raising livestock thousands of years before farming took place. The earliest herders kept sheep and goats, but after about 4000 B.C. people began to raise cattle. At that time the Saharan climate was much cooler and moister than it is today, with extensive woods and grasslands.

African rock paintings show scenes of people tending herds of cattle and sheep. Beginning about 2500 B.C., a change in climate caused the Sahara to dry up. Overgrazing—allowing large herds of animals to feed on the land until the surface vegetation is destroyed—may have accelerated the process. The climate change forced pastoralists to move farther south.

In East Africa, cattle raising was firmly established by 2000 B.C. Sheepherding societies flourished in southern Africa during the last centuries B.C. These animals may have come from East Africa or they may have been introduced into the region by BANTU-speaking peoples migrating from west-central Africa.

Colonialism and its aftermath have greatly affected the lives of African pastoralists. The open ranges where they traditionally grazed their herds were fenced in, and their movements were restricted by new political borders. Agriculture and industry damaged some of the grasslands that once supported livestock. In many cases herding peoples whose livelihood was threatened participated in political movements protesting the changes.

Social relations in many livestock-based societies have also altered over the years. People who once measured wealth in animals now measure it in terms of money. Nevertheless, pastoralism is still an important part of the economies of many African countries. (*See also* **Animals, Domestic; Colonialism in Africa; Diseases; Economic History; Ecosystems.**)

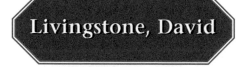

Livingstone, David

1813–1873
British missionary and explorer

David Livingstone went to Africa as a missionary in the mid-1800s and became one of the continent's leading explorers and geographers. He also played a key role in the movement to end the SLAVE TRADE.

Born in Blantyre, Scotland, Livingstone began work in a cotton mill at the age of ten. Determined to become a medical missionary, he studied religion and medicine, and in 1841 the London Missionary Society sent him to SOUTH AFRICA. By the late 1840s, Livingstone was eager to travel into unexplored areas. His long-terms goals in Africa included abolishing the slave trade and achieving a better understanding of the continent and its people. On a journey into present-day BOTSWANA in 1849 he discovered Lake Ngami, for which he received an award from Britain's Royal Geographical Society.

Four years later, leaving his wife and children in Scotland, Livingstone began his greatest journey of exploration. It lasted for more than three years and carried him northeast to Luanda (in present-day Angola) on the Atlantic coast and then across Africa to Quelimane (in present-day Mozambique) on the Pacific coast. In the course of his travels he came upon the ZAMBEZI RIVER and its magnificent waterfall, which he named Victoria Falls after Britain's queen. From 1858 to 1864 Livingstone commanded a British government expedition up the Zambezi. Although he had hoped that the expedition would introduce modern trade to the region, its greatest success was locating Lake Malawi.

Livingstone spent the years from 1865 to his death in what is now TANZANIA and ZAMBIA, investigating the slave trade and exploring. The outside world received no news of the famous explorer. Rumors about his fate prompted Henry Morton STANLEY, an American journalist, to go to central Africa to look for him. In 1871 Stanley met the explorer on the shores of Lake Tanganyika and supposedly remarked, "Dr.

Livingstone, I presume." Despite increasing illness Livingstone refused to accompany Stanley back to the coast. Two years later, at Chitambo in present-day Zambia, Livingstone died. His African servants carried his body to the coast, and he was later buried in Westminster Abbey, London.

Through his journals, letters, and books, as well as speeches in Britain, David Livingstone did much to inform Europeans about Africa. He promoted the view that Africans could become full members of modern civilization, and he aroused strong feelings against the slave trade. (*See also* **Missions and Missionaries, Travel and Exploration.**)

Lobengula

ca. 1836–1894
King of Matabeleland

Lobengula was the last ruler of the NDEBELE kingdom of Matabeleland in present-day ZIMBABWE. After the death of his father, MZILIKAZI, the founder of the kingdom, civil war broke out. Lobengula eventually won the war, and he took the throne in 1870. However, the kingdom remained in chaos.

Lobengula spent much of his reign trying to balance rebellious Ndebele groups and the demands of South African settlers and prospectors for land and mining rights. He agreed to some of their demands under pressure from Europeans, including the adventurer Cecil RHODES. Fearing that his kingdom was threatened, Lobengula also signed an agreement in 1888 with British authorities, pledging that he would have territorial negotiations only with Britain.

In response to continued threats from white settlers and miners, the Ndebele attacked an outpost of the British South Africa Company in 1893. Despite Lobengula's requests for peace, the company retaliated brutally. An army consisting of the company's police force and off-duty British soldiers attacked the Ndebele settlement of Bulawayo and burned it to the ground. Lobengula died of smallpox while retreating. (*See also* **Southern Africa, History.**)

Lugard, Frederick John Dealtry

1858–1945
British colonial administrator

* **protectorate** weak state under the control and protection of a strong state

Frederick John Dealtry Lugard played an important role in British colonial Africa. Lugard worked to end African slavery and slave trading. He also created the system of "indirect rule," which gave traditional African authorities considerable control over their local affairs.

Born in India of missionary parents, Lugard attended school in England and began a career in the military. In the 1890s he led several expeditions in Africa and helped bring the territory of Buganda under British rule. From 1900 to 1906, Lugard served as high commissioner of the protectorate* of Northern Nigeria, where he introduced the system of indirect rule. As governor-general of Northern and Southern Nigeria from 1912 to 1919, he sought to unify these two colonies. Only partially successful, he failed to create an efficient central administration on which to build a united NIGERIA.

After retiring in 1919, Lugard continued working on matters related to Africa. As British representative to a commission on colonial affairs with the League of Nations*, he dealt with issues related to slavery and African labor. An opponent of the transfer of power to European settlers in KENYA, he also opposed the Italian invasion of Ethiopia in 1935.

Throughout his career Lugard worked on behalf of Africans. He believed that the ultimate aim of colonial rule was to grant independence to African peoples. However, he considered his task to be protecting Africans from exploitation* rather than preparing them for independence. (*See also* **Colonialism in Africa, Government and Political Systems, Slave Trade.**)

Lumumba, Patrice Emery

1925–1961
Congolese political leader

Patrice Emery Lumumba was the first prime minister of Zaire, the country now called CONGO (KINSHASA). Known for his fervent nationalism* and his commitment to freeing Africa from colonial rule, Lumumba played a leading role in gaining independence for his country.

Born in the Kasai province of the Belgian Congo, Lumumba received a basic education at Christian missionary schools and then continued to study and read widely on his own. He went to work as a clerk in a post office and held important positions in several employees' organizations. In the mid-1950s, he became active in politics, founding the Congolese National Movement in 1958. His party differed from other parties in its broad appeal to both nationalism and Pan-Africanism—a movement to unite blacks throughout the continent and oppose racism and colonialism. Lumumba and the party worked toward independence from Belgium.

Lumumba was the most important leader in the independence movement for a number of reasons, the most important of which was his political views. Those views were based both on his own experiences in Africa and on the knowledge he gained attending important conferences in Europe. Additionally, Lumumba had excellent public speaking skills and an ability to work with people from many different political parties. When the first general election was held in 1960, his party was the clear winner, despite Belgian opposition.

When the colony gained its independence as Zaire in 1960, Lumumba served as the first prime minister. He immediately faced a number of crises, including secession* movements by the provinces of Kasai and mineral-rich Katanga. Lumumba did what he could to deal with the situation, but his army was weak and his administration inexperienced. When the United Nations ignored his appeals for help, Lumumba sought assistance from the Soviet Union*, a move that alarmed many Western powers and fueled opposition to him within Zaire.

In September 1960, Zairan president Joseph Kasavubu dismissed Lumumba as prime minister. Then, on February 12, 1961, Lumumba was arrested and murdered in the city of Elisabethville by anti-Lumumba forces loyal to Kasavubu. His death shocked and angered many in Africa, and later even his enemies called him a national hero. (*See also* **Independence Movements.**)

Luo

The Luo, an ethnic group of East Africa, inhabit a region on the eastern side of Lake Victoria. They trace their descent from people who migrated south from the Nile Valley region of southern SUDAN about 500 years ago. The majority of the Luo live in KENYA, but sizable numbers are also found in UGANDA and TANZANIA.

Luo territory consists of flat dry country near Lake Victoria and hilly fertile areas to the north and east. The rural Luo live mainly by farming but also engage in livestock herding and fishing. Cattle play an important role in their society, both as ceremonial sacrifices and as bridewealth—payments from a groom and his kin to the bride's family.

Rural Luo generally live in scattered homesteads surrounded by fields. Most Luo towns, including Kisumu, grew up around important marketplaces. Luo-speaking communities can also be found in NAIROBI, Mombasa, and other East African cities. These urban dwellers, who work mainly as laborers, maintain strong economic, social, and spiritual ties to Luo communities in the Lake Victoria region.

* **clan** group of people descended from a common ancestor

Luo society is organized according to clans* that trace descent through male relatives. Inheritance of land and cattle is also through the male line. When a Luo woman marries, she moves to the home of her husband, creating bonds that link various Luo communities. Since Kenya gained its independence, the Luo have tended to play important roles in opposition parties because GIKUYU-speakers and members of Kalenjin groups have dominated the country's political and economic life.

* **Islam** religion based on the teachings of the prophet Muhammad; religious faith of Muslims

Education is very important to the Luo, who are known for their skill in English. Because of this, Luo-speakers have dominated many departments in East African universities. In religion, most Luo practice Roman Catholicism or Protestant faiths, although some are followers of Islam*. Luo country is also home to large numbers of independent Christian churches. (*See also* **Christianity in Africa, Ethnic Groups and Identity, Mboya, Tom.**)

Lusaka

Lusaka, the capital of ZAMBIA, is a sprawling city of about 1.5 million people located in an agricultural region. A financial and commercial center, the city lies at the junction of major rail lines heading to the Copper Belt, the city of Livingstone, and TANZANIA.

Lusaka became the capital of the British colony of Northern Rhodesia in 1935. The city's architecture and design were meant to demonstrate European dominance and to serve as a symbol of the authority and dignity of the British monarchy.

During the colonial period Lusaka was a hub of opposition to British rule. In 1948 various African leaders met there and established the Northern Rhodesia African Congress, a group that worked for African rights and independence. In 1960 Lusaka was the center of a campaign of civil disobedience* aimed at undermining the Central African Confederation of the colonies of Northern Rhodesia, Southern Rhodesia, and Nyasaland, which the British had established in 1953. This cam-

* **civil disobedience** policy of peaceful, nonviolent actions to demonstrate opposition

A major commercial center, the Zambian capital of Lusaka is home to many large and small industries. The men shown here work in a tailor's stall in the market.

paign led to the breakup of the confederation in 1963 and to Zambia's independence a year later. Lusaka remained the capital of the newly independent nation.

In the 1970s and 1980s Lusaka served as headquarters of the African National Congress and other groups involved in fighting white-dominated governments in SOUTH AFRICA, ZIMBABWE, and MOZAMBIQUE. The city's role as a center of opposition to white rule faded in later years as black Africans took power in those three countries. Among the biggest challenges facing Lusaka today are rapid population growth and economic development.

Lutuli, Albert

1898–1967
South African political leader

Albert Lutuli was president of the African National Congress (ANC), a black-led political party in SOUTH AFRICA that fought for African rights. In 1960 he won the Nobel Peace Prize for his leadership in the nonviolent struggle against racism.

The son of a preacher, Albert John Mavumbi Lutuli was born in Southern Rhodesia (present-day ZIMBABWE) and grew up in Natal, South Africa. After graduating from college, Lutuli became a teacher in Natal. Elected a ZULU chief in 1935, he administered local justice and organized peasant farmers.

In 1945 Lutuli joined the ANC. Forced to resign as Zulu chief in 1952 because of his work with the political group, Lutuli was elected ANC president the same year. In this role, Lutuli helped transform the party from a collection of educated and privileged blacks into a broad-based popular movement.

While serving as ANC president, Lutuli was often confined to his neighborhood by government authorities and banned from attending political gatherings. Despite these restrictions, he had considerable influence and enjoyed widespread loyalty from black Africans.

In his later years, Lutuli was considered an honored elder statesman. By this time, however, the ANC had begun to abandon his nonviolent methods and adopt more radical policies. Still confined to his neighborhood by the authorities, Lutuli died in 1967 after being struck by a train near his home. (*See also* **Apartheid**.)

Maasai

* **clan**   group of people descended from a common ancestor

* **pastoralist**   related to or dependent on livestock herding

The Maasai are made up of about a dozen ethnic groups who live in the Rift Valley of east Africa, primarily in KENYA and TANZANIA. These groups speak a language called Maa and share many cultural characteristics, such as the way they dress. Their social systems are based on clans* and age-sets, groups of people of the same age. The society has no centralized political leadership. In the past, the Maasai had an effective military organization for raiding and warfare, and their warriors were known for great courage and strength.

The Maasai have traditionally been cattle herders with a pastoralist* lifestyle. However, many have also practiced agriculture and engaged in trade. Some have close ties through marriage with various Bantu-speaking groups, including the GIKUYU. Photographers and travel writers often portray the Maasai as a "pure" and "untouched" society of cattle herders and warriors. However, some Maasai now live in towns. Perhaps more than other groups in Africa, the Maasai have shown an unwillingness to accept many aspects of Western culture because of a fierce pride in their traditional ways of life. (*See also* **Ethnic Groups and Identity, Livestock Grazing**.)

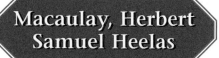

Macaulay, Herbert Samuel Heelas

1864–1946
Nigerian political leader

* **nationalism**   devotion to the interests and culture of one's country

Considered the founder of Nigerian nationalism*, Herbert Samuel Heelas Macaulay promoted self-government in NIGERIA in the early 1900s. Born into an educated, Christian Nigerian family, Macaulay attended school in Lagos. In 1890 he won a scholarship from Nigeria's British colonial government to study abroad. After earning a degree in civil engineering in England, he returned to Nigeria and worked for the colonial administration. In 1899 Macaulay resigned to set up his own business, and he began a career of political protest against colonialism.

Engineering work brought Macaulay in contact with Nigeria's traditional rulers, and he became familiar with the land-ownership customs that had existed before colonial times. He began publishing a newspaper, the *Lagos Daily News,* to champion the land and political rights of

Nigerians. In 1923 he founded the country's first political party, the Nigerian National Democratic Party (NNDP). Twenty-one years later, he was elected the first president of the National Council of Nigeria and the Cameroons (NCNC), one of several parties formed as Britian began to allow its colonies a greater degree of self-government.

Machel, Samora Moises

1933–1986
President of Mozambique

Samora Machel was a leader of the independence struggle in MOZAMBIQUE who became the country's first president in 1975. He became politically active as a young man, joining the movement known as FRELIMO that was dedicated to Mozambique's independence. He volunteered for FRELIMO military training in ALGERIA and was later sent to Mozambique to participate in armed resistance to Portuguese rule.

After FRELIMO's leader Eduardo MONDLANE was assassinated in 1969, Machel took control of the movement. Machel led military campaigns against Portuguese colonial forces in the mid-1970s that resulted in decisive victories for FRELIMO. In 1975 Mozambique gained its independence and Machel was elected president. His presidency was marked by efforts to combat rebels from Rhodesia and SOUTH AFRICA sent to undermine the new nation. In 1986 he died in an airplane crash that many suspect was caused by sabotage. (*See also* **Colonialism in Africa**.)

Madagascar

The island nation of Madagascar lies off the southeastern coast of Africa. A most unusual place, the island contains an amazing diversity of plants, animals, and environments. Perhaps the most intriguing aspect of Madagascar, though, is the origin of its people—trying to determine where they came from and when they arrived.

GEOGRAPHY

Although now an island, Madagascar at one time belonged to a giant continent called Gondwanaland that also included Africa, India, and Australia. This continent broke up some 150 million years ago, and Madagascar drifted to its current location about 240 miles from mainland Africa.

Madagascar consists of low-lying coasts surrounding a central plateau with mountains reaching nearly 9,500 feet. The western half of the island rises gradually from the coast in a series of hills and plateaus to the more mountainous interior. The eastern part contains a narrow coastal strip bordered by steep cliffs and mountainsides that rise abruptly to the central plateau.

At one time rain forests covered much of the island's interior, but over the centuries most of them have been cleared for agriculture. Major forests remain only on the mountains near the eastern coast and in the far northwest. Most of the island's interior hills are covered with thin vegetation. Savannas* dominate the western part of Madagascar, while the south is quite dry and contains large areas of semidesert.

* **savanna** tropical or subtropical grassland with scattered trees and drought-resistant undergrowth

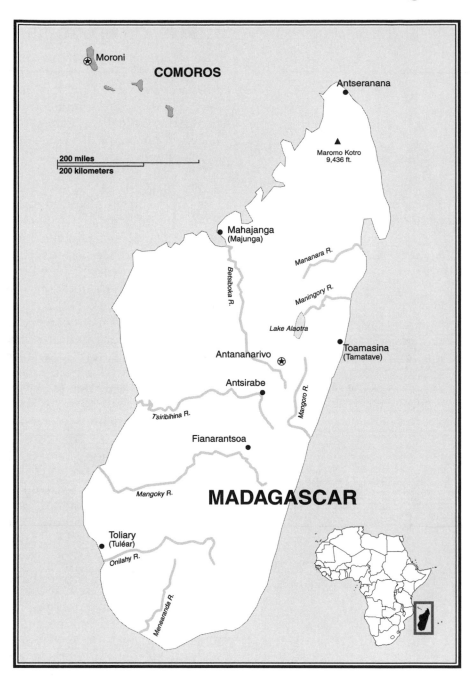

*   **monsoon** seasonal winds, often associated with heavy rainfall

Trade winds from the southeast blow across Madagascar throughout the year. From December to May these winds meet monsoon* winds coming from the northwest. During this period, rain falls almost every day, with the east coast receiving more than the west coast. Between May and October the weather becomes generally cooler and drier, and at higher elevations temperatures can fall to freezing. Madagascar has many local climate variations as well, and changes from one area to the next can be dramatic.

HISTORY AND GOVERNMENT

Although little is known of its early history, it appears that Madagascar was settled by people from lands bordering the Indian Ocean. When they arrived is still a mystery. In a relatively short time these different peoples created a uniform culture, but one with distinctive differences in various parts of the island. This combination of unity and diversity has been an important factor in Madagascar's historical and political development.

Early History. Archaeological evidence indicates that Madagascar was one of the last places on earth to be settled by humans. The earliest traces of humans date back around 1,900 years, but the first continuously occupied site is much more recent—from about the A.D. 700s. Linguistic* evidence suggests that the early settlers probably came from Africa and from what is now Indonesia. Researchers have found a relationship between the local Malagasy language and languages spoken on the Indonesian island of Borneo and have also demonstrated the significant influence of BANTU languages of eastern and southern Africa.

* **linguistic** relating to the study of languages

Genetic evidence indicates that the ancestors of the Malagasy, the people of Madagascar, came from India and lands surrounding the Persian Gulf as well as from Africa and Indonesia. Some scholars believe that Africans were the island's first settlers, joined later by Asians. Others think that the Asian populations came first and the Africans arrived later. Still others suggest that Asian immigrants migrated to Africa where they mixed with local peoples and that the descendants of the mixed population later settled on Madagascar.

In any event, by about 1350 the original inhabitants of Madagascar had spread out across the island and established settlements both along the coasts and in the interior. Most of these early sites were small farming or herding communities, but the northwest coast had an urban trading center called Mahilaka of about 10,000 inhabitants.

Between the early 1500s and mid-1700s, a number of kingdoms arose in Madagascar alongside many scattered groups with no central authority. The largest of these kingdoms, Madagascar, belonged to the Merina. Their king, Ratsimilaho, hoped to unify the island, but he died in 1750 before he could accomplish that task. The failure to unite the various kingdoms marked the beginning of a period of instability that ended with the French conquest of Madagascar in the late 1800s.

Anarchy and Consolidation. After Ratsimilaho died, his kingdom was divided among his four sons and soon fell into disarray. It was not reunited until the reign of King Andrianampoinimerina (1783–1810), who launched a series of military campaigns to conquer neighboring peoples. His successor, Radama I (1810–1828), extended Merina control over about two-thirds of the island.

The British governor of MAURITIUS helped Radama expand, providing military technology and other assistance in hopes of keeping the island out of French hands. Radama was succeeded by Queen Ranavalona I, who came from a nonnoble Merina clan* called the Hova. Under her rule, the Hova increased their power and wealth at the expense of the

* **clan** group of people descended from a common ancestor

The Ways of the Ancestors

The Malagasy have an intense interest in the origins and practices of their ancestors. One way that they express this interest is through an emphasis on proper burial and the creation of large and elaborate tombs. Regardless of how far from home they move, Malagasy try to return to ancestral tombs when a relative is buried. Most such tombs contain several ancestors. Family members assume responsibility for building and maintaining these tombs. Burial itself is an important ritual, and people will often spend most of their resources for a memorable burial as an honored ancestor.

* **exploit** to take advantage of; to make productive use of

* **protectorate** weak state under the control and protection of a strong state

rest of the Malagasy peoples. Ranavalona was more hostile to European influence, even closing the island's ports to outside trade.

Merina rule was far from popular on Madagascar. Most of the conquered peoples had no desire to be governed by the Merina, who exploited* them politically and economically. The situation became worse under King Radama II (1861–1863), who reopened Madagascar to European influence. He rashly adopted many Western ways that were unpopular with most Malagasy. Radama II was assassinated. His brother succeeded him but was overthrown after only one year. In 1864 Rainilaiarivony, the Merina prime minister, took control of the kingdom. Ruling for more than 30 years, he reorganized and modernized the army and adopted more favorable policies toward the non-Merina population.

Rainilaiarivony and his queen, Ranavalona II, converted to Protestantism in 1869. Because only educated Merina followed their lead, the conversion further widened the gulf between the Merina and non-Merina Malagasy. Tensions increased as the Merina became more Westernized. However, internal division was only one problem with which Rainilaiarivony had to deal. His kingdom also faced the threat of France's colonial ambitions.

French Conquest and Colonialism. In the early 1860s, the Merina ruler Radama II signed a treaty with a Frenchman named Lambert. Called the Lambert Charter, it granted the French territorial rights to part of Madagascar. The agreement was later canceled by the Malagasy ruler.

Relations with France grew worse when the Merina kingdom adopted Protestantism (France was a Catholic country). The French responded by claiming the land mentioned in the Lambert Charter. Madagascar appealed without success to both Great Britain and the United States, and in 1883 the French invaded the island.

The Franco-Malagasy War lasted two years and ended in victory for Madagascar, which maintained its independence. In 1890, however, France and Britain signed an agreement that recognized France's right to establish a protectorate* over the island. In return, the French agreed to a British protectorate over ZANZIBAR.

In 1895 the French again invaded Madagascar and quickly defeated Merina forces. The Merina rulers then signed a treaty in which they agreed to the protectorate. The next year Merina nobles led an uprising against French rule. The French crushed the rebellion and exiled the queen, bringing an end to the Kingdom of Madagascar. In the late 1890s and early 1900s, the French put down several other rebellions on the island.

Under French rule, Madagascar's cities were modernized; ports, roads, and railroads were built; and French settlers arrived on the island. These colonists were given various special privileges, such as the right to use forced Malagasy labor. The Malagasy were taxed and compelled to serve in the French army. Those who failed to obey French authority received harsh punishments. The French also outlawed trade unions and restricted freedom of the press. Malagasy discontent with colonial rule rose

Madagascar

after World War I, but in the 1930s a change in the French government led to some improvement in conditions.

Malagasy involvement in World War II helped move the country toward independence. In 1944 Madagascar was allowed to send four elected representatives to the French parliament. Two years later the island's first independent political party was founded. Madagascar became an overseas territory of France, which gave French citizenship to all Malagasy.

Although white settlers and civil servants resisted the changes sweeping Madagascar, nationalist* feelings intensified. In 1947 the Malagasy Revolt erupted. French reaction was swift and brutal, with some 90,000 Malagasy killed in violent reprisals. Although the rebellion was crushed, the island remained in a state of siege for nearly ten years as France tried to maintain control by force.

By this time events were racing beyond French control. In 1956 pressure from abroad led France to allow internal self-rule to its overseas territories. Two years later Madagascar voted to become a self-governing republic within the French community. In 1958 Madagascar adopted a new constitution calling for complete independence, which France granted in June 1960.

The terraced fields carved into the side of a mountain in central Madagascar are planted with rice, a mainstay of the local diet.

After Independence. The first president of the newly independent nation was a former schoolteacher, Philibert Tsiranana. He maintained close ties with France and became one of the founders of the ORGANIZATION OF AFRICAN UNITY (OAU).

Reelected twice as president, Tsiranana hoped to improve the lives of Malagasy peasants. However, he angered the people by trading with South Africa, known for its harsh treatment of blacks and Asians under apartheid*. Moreover, during Tsiranana's rule, Europeans assumed leading positions in Madagascar's economy, which was strongly focused on trade with France. This trade benefited France more than it did Madagascar. The level of corruption in government was also high, and many young Malagasy saw little hope for a better future.

Disappointment with Tsiranana's rule led in 1972 to the rise of a student movement and to a series of strikes and rebellions. The killing of 400 demonstrators by the police caused opposition parties to boycott* elections that year. When the army refused to support Tsiranana, he asked the army commander, General Gabriel Ramanantsoa, to form a new government.

After taking power, Ramanantsoa met with French leaders to arrange the closing of French military bases on Madagascar and the withdrawal of foreign troops. At the same time, he developed closer ties with African nations, released political prisoners, introduced economic reforms, took steps to curb corruption, and replaced French teachers and civil servants with Malagasy.

Despite Ramanantsoa's efforts, opponents attempted a coup* in 1974, and the following year he gave up power. But his successor was assassinated six days later, and the military formed yet another government. The man chosen to lead the country was Lieutenant Didier Ratsiraka, who had served as Ramanantsoa's foreign minister.

Leftist* Ratsiraka nationalized* many businesses and encouraged collective agricultural policies. Moderately successful at first, these policies soon led to economic decline, and Madagascar was forced to adopt tough economic reforms to qualify for international loans. These reforms stabilized some parts of the economy, but also led to higher food prices, food shortages, and greater unemployment as the nationalized companies came under private ownership. Despite these difficulties, Ratsiraka was reelected in 1983.

After his reelection, Ratsiraka tried to turn Madagascar into a one-party state. He restricted freedom of the press as well as the formation of new political parties. Elected again in 1989 with support from the military, Ratsiraka eventually bowed to pressure from church leaders and other groups and restored many of the freedoms he had taken away. However, this did not prevent unrest, and in 1991 a massive demonstration calling for more democracy ended in violence when police fired on the crowd, killing many demonstrators.

During this time a doctor named Albert Zafy emerged as a leading opponent of Ratsiraka's government. In 1992 a new constitution was adopted that limited presidential powers. In elections held later that year, Zafy became president. However, the new government was unstable, with several prime ministers coming and going during the next four years.

* **apartheid** policy of racial segregation enforced by the white government of South Africa to maintain political, economic, and social control over the country's blacks, Asians, and people of mixed ancestry

* **boycott** to refuse to participate or buy goods, as a means of protest

* **coup** sudden, often violent, overthrow of a ruler or government

* **leftist** inclined to support radical reform and change; often associated with the ideas of communism and socialism

* **nationalize** to bring land, industries, or public works under state control or ownership

Madagascar

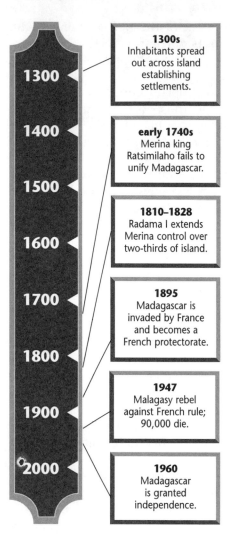

1300s
Inhabitants spread out across island establishing settlements.

early 1740s
Merina king Ratsimilaho fails to unify Madagascar.

1810–1828
Radama I extends Merina control over two-thirds of island.

1895
Madagascar is invaded by France and becomes a French protectorate.

1947
Malagasy rebel against French rule; 90,000 die.

1960
Madagascar is granted independence.

* **staple** major product of a region; basic food

* **literate** able to read and write

In 1996 Zafy was impeached by the parliament after a long-running feud and removed from office. In the elections that followed, the voters returned Ratsiraka to power. Ratsiraka then proposed changes to the constitution that strengthened presidential powers. Voters, not fully understanding the changes and hoping to end some of the instability that plagued Zafy's presidency, approved the measures by a slim margin. Ratsiraka has since made moves to consolidate his power while putting together a government that reflects the diversity of Madagascar's population. His cabinet included members of many different ethnic groups.

ECONOMY

About 75 percent of Madagascar's working population is engaged in agriculture. The staple* crop is rice, which is grown in the lowlands on marshy plains and in the highlands on terraces carved into the sides of mountains. At one time rice was also a major export crop, but the failure of various agricultural policies has forced Madagascar to import rice. The island's main exports now are crops such as coffee, sugar, cloves, vanilla, pepper, and tobacco. The instability of world prices for these products is a major reason for Madagascar's slow economic growth. However, soil erosion caused by the massive clearing of forests and overgrazing of livestock has also led to a decline in agriculture.

Madagascar's industry includes some mining and manufacturing, but these activities play only a minor role in the economy. In the late 1990s, a mining boom in sapphires contributed little to the island's income and caused great environmental damage. As a result of its weak economy and slow economic growth, Madagascar is heavily dependent upon foreign aid, particularly from France.

PEOPLES AND CULTURES

In the colonial era the French divided the Malagasy into 20 different ethnic groups, but ethnicity is not a useful basis for classification. The Malagasy themselves form communities based on KINSHIP, shared location and customs, and common histories and leadership.

The largest Malagasy group, the Merina, make up about 25 percent of the population. They live in the central highlands. Most Merina make their living as rice farmers, but those who live in cities work in government or as traders or teachers. The Merina are highly literate* and largely Christian.

The Betsimisaraka of the central east coast, the second largest group, are also mainly rice farmers. The Betsimisaraka arose from families who banded together to control the SLAVE TRADE. The Merina conquered them during the 1800s, and a shared history of domination by the Merina is part of their group identity. Traditional ancestor worship is still common among the Betsimisaraka, but Christianity has gained converts.

Perhaps the most important distinction among the Malagasy is between the Merina and the *côtier* ("coastal peoples"). The term *côtier* refers to non-Merina groups. These peoples share a history of domination by the Merina that continued under colonial rule. The French relied on the Merina to administer their colonial government, which

Madagascar

POPULATION:
15,506,472 (2000 estimated population)

AREA:
226,658 sq. mi. (587,044 sq. km)

LANGUAGES:
Malagasy and French (both official)

NATIONAL CURRENCY:
Malagasy franc

PRINCIPAL RELIGIONS:
Traditional 52%, Christian 41%, Muslim 7%

CITIES:
Antananarivo (capital), 1,507,000 (2000 est.); Mahajanga, Toamasina, Fianarantsoa, Antseranana

ANNUAL RAINFALL:
Varies from 120–190 in. (3,000–5,000 mm) on the east coast to 20 in. (510 mm) in the southwest

ECONOMY:
GDP per capita: $780 (1999 est.)

PRINCIPAL PRODUCTS AND EXPORTS:
Agricultural: coffee, cloves, vanilla, shellfish, beans, rice, sugar, cassava, peanuts, livestock
Manufacturing: meat processing, textiles, petroleum products
Mining: chromite, graphite, coal, bauxite

GOVERNMENT:
Independence from France, 1960. Republic with president elected by universal suffrage. Governing bodies: Assemblée Nationale, Senate, and prime minister appointed by the president.

HEADS OF STATE SINCE INDEPENDENCE:
1960–1972 President Philibert Tsiranana
1972–1975 Prime Minister Major General Cabriel Ramanantsoa
Feb. 1975 General Gilles Andriamahazo
1975–1993 President Didier Ratsiraka
1993–1996 President Albert Zafy
1996–1997 Interim president Norbet Ratsirahonana
1997– President Didier Ratsiraka

ARMED FORCES:
21,000

EDUCATION:
Compulsory for ages 6–13; literacy rate 46%

gave the group many advantages in education and other areas. The Merina still exercise most economic and political power, though President Ratsiraka is a *côtier*.

While the Merina-*côtier* rivalry pulls the country apart, the common Malagasy language helps to keep it together. Also beneficial is the fact that the national borders are based on geography rather than imposed by colonial powers. Thus, unlike most of Africa, Madagascar has escaped the problem of having competing ethnic groups forced together to form a modern state. (*See also* **Boundaries in Africa, Colonialism in Africa, Ethnic Groups and Identity.**)

Maghreb

Maghreb, or Maghrib, is an Arabic word meaning "west" or "place of sunset." It refers to the area of North Africa west of EGYPT. Known in ancient times as Africa Minor, the Maghreb refers to MOROCCO, ALGERIA, TUNISIA, and sometimes LIBYA. The interior desert regions of these countries are not always considered part of the Maghreb.

The Maghreb contains fertile coastal plains, mountains, and scrubland in the south that merges into the SAHARA DESERT. The area north of the mountains generally receives enough rainfall to support intensive agriculture on the coastal plains, where most of the population lives.

The ancestors of the BERBERS are the original inhabitants of the region. The Arabs conquered the Maghreb between A.D. 643 and 711 and ruled it through semi-independent kingdoms and chiefdoms. From the 800s to the 1300s, the region was the center of an active trading economy

43

* **sub-Saharan** referring to Africa south of the Sahara desert

linked by caravan routes across the desert to sub-Saharan* Africa. Although colonized by European powers in the 1800s and 1900s, the Maghreb has retained much of its Arab heritage, including the Arabic language and Islamic religion. (*See also* **Arabs in Africa, Islam in Africa, North Africa: Geography and Population, North Africa: History and Cultures.**)

See *Witchcraft and Sorcery.*

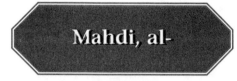

ca. 1840–1885
Sudanese religious leader

See
color plate 8,
vol. 2.

Al-Mahdi, the founder of an Islamic religious movement, seized control of SUDAN and established an empire that lasted for nearly 20 years. Born Muhammed Ahmad ibn Sayyid Abdullah, he began religious studies at an early age and joined a religious order in the capital city of KHARTOUM. He eventually left the order and moved with a number of disciples to an island in the NILE RIVER.

In 1881 he proclaimed that he was al-Mahdi, a religious leader who according to tradition would return to restore and purify Islam. He sent letters to religious leaders in Sudan, urging them to reject the Turkish-Egyptian political rulers who controlled the country. Two months later, against great odds, he and his followers managed to defeat an army sent by the Egyptian government. Over the next two years, three more government armies met the same fate, and many new supporters joined al-Mahdi's cause.

Assembling an army of some 100,000 men, al-Mahdi fought and defeated British troops led by General Charles GORDON and captured Khartoum in 1885. He then established his own capital across the Nile in Omdurman, where he set up an empire based on Islamic law and the teachings of the Muslim holy book, the Qur'an. But less than six months after his victory, he died suddenly, possibly of typhus. The Mahdiya, as his empire was known, controlled all of northern Sudan until 1898, when it was conquered by British troops. Al-Mahdi's successful revolt against foreign domination caused later Sudanese leaders to look up to him as the father of their country's independence. (*See also* **Islam in Africa.**)

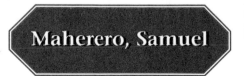

ca. 1854–1923
Chief of the Herero

Samuel Maherero became chief of the HERERO people of NAMIBIA after the death of his father in 1890. Baptized and schooled by German missionaries, Maherero cooperated with German colonists who arrived in Namibia about this time. By selling land to the Germans, he obtained their support in overthrowing and conquering rival Herero chiefs.

In 1904, misunderstandings and tensions led to war between the Herero and white settlers. The Germans defeated Maherero and his followers and drove them into the KALAHARI DESERT. Many died before reaching Bechuanaland (modern BOTSWANA) and receiving sanctuary. Prohibited from returning to Namibia, Maherero led his followers into SOUTH AFRICA. There they worked in the gold mines in exchange for the right to settle in the country. In 1921 he returned to Bechuanaland and died soon afterward. His body was taken back to Namibia where he was buried next to his father and grandfather.

Mahfouz, Naguib

**1911–
Egyptian writer**

Author of 40 novels and short story collections and more than 30 screenplays, Naguib Mahfouz received the Nobel Prize for literature in 1988. He was the first Arabic author to win that honor, which brought attention to his work and to modern Arabic fiction in general. During most of his writing career, Mahfouz also worked in the Egyptian civil service.

Born in Cairo, Mahfouz studied philosophy at Cairo University. In the 1930s he published many articles and short stories. His first novels dealt with ancient Egypt. After World War II, however, Mahfouz became interested in the political and social changes occurring in Egypt and soon began writing about modern life. His masterpiece, a set of three novels called *Al-Thulathiyya* or *The Cairo Trilogy* (1956–1957), tells the story of several Cairo families across three generations. Later works examine issues such as censorship, religion, politics, and the treatment of women.

The opinions Mahfouz expresses have prompted some Muslims to criticize his writing. In 1994 representatives of an Egyptian Islamic movement tried unsuccessfully to kidnap the author. Mahfouz suffered a severe neck injury in the attack, but he continues to write by dictating his work to others. (*See also* **Literature**.)

Maji Maji

* **indigenous**   native to a certain place

Between 1905 and 1907 several small ethnic groups from Tanganyika (present-day TANZANIA) rebelled against German colonial authorities in an uprising known as the Maji Maji Rebellion. Although unsuccessful, the rebellion was one of the most important events in the history of East Africa.

The Maji Maji Rebellion was centered in the southern highlands of German East Africa, a colonial territory that included Tanganyika and present-day RWANDA and BURUNDI. During the uprising, 20 small groups united in opposition to German rule, though they often quarreled among themselves. The groups resented German attempts to force them to grow cotton, pay high taxes, and provide labor for colonists. They also objected to the replacement of indigenous* local leaders with colonial administrators.

The name of the rebellion came from the Swahili word for water, *maji.* In 1902 a healer named Kinjikitile became the guardian of a pool believed to have magical powers. Kinjikitile declared that the people of the region should join together to fight the Germans and that drinking

45

the pool's water would make them immune to German bullets. People also came to believe that drinking the water would cause them to form spiritual bonds with the other groups involved in the struggle.

During a drought in 1904, people came from throughout the area to the magical pool to ask for rain, and Kinjikitile's message spread widely. The first attacks against the Germans came in July 1905. The next month Kinjikitile and one of his assistants were seized and hanged by the Germans. After their deaths, the uprising spread and became more serious. The Germans finally defeated the rebels in 1907. Today the uprising is remembered as a symbol of the common purpose and identity of the people of Tanzania. (*See also* **Colonialism in Africa, Prophetic Movements.**)

Malawi

Malawi, the former British colony of Nyasaland, is a small, landlocked nation in southeastern Africa. One of the most densely populated countries in Africa, many of its people live in desperate poverty. Since gaining independence in 1964, the nation has struggled to develop its economy and meet the needs of its people.

Geography. About 500 miles from north to south and a little more than 100 miles across at its widest point, Malawi is a narrow, curving land on the western edge of Africa's Great Rift Valley. It is bordered on the east by Lake Malawi (formerly Lake Nyasa), one of the largest lakes in Africa. The lake takes up more than one-fifth of the total area of the country. The people of Malawi have both historic and economic links to the lake.

Malawi is a spectacular land of high mountains covered with lush forests, sparkling lakes, and rolling plateaus. The nation's plateau regions enjoy some of the most fertile soils in east Africa, a feature that has attracted settlement throughout Malawi's history. The nation's climate is generally temperate, with a rainy season between November and April. Temperatures vary with the seasons, but because of the high altitude in much of the country they average between 55° and 85°F.

History and Government. The first Bantu-speaking inhabitants of Malawi arrived in the area nearly 2,000 years ago. Around the 1400s more Bantu peoples began migrating into the region from the north. Some only passed through Malawi and continued moving into southern Africa, but many stayed and eventually established a number of chiefdoms and kingdoms. Among the most important of the kingdoms were Kalanga, Lundu, and Undi, which dominated different parts of the region from the 1500s to the 1700s.

When Portuguese traders reached the region in the 1500s, they established commercial relations with various groups. Competition for trade became a key factor in political power, and some kingdoms declined in importance as trade went to other groups. During the 1800s other Bantu peoples invaded the region. These invasions were linked directly to the IVORY TRADE and the growing SLAVE TRADE.

Religion and Protest

The migration of workers from Nyasaland to other parts of Africa contributed to the growth of protest movements against colonial rule throughout the region. One of these was the Watchtower movement of the Jehovah's Witnesses. Originating in northern Nyasaland, the movement took root in the mining centers of Northern and Southern Rhodesia. Protests continued after the colonial period ended. In the 1970s the government of Malawi harassed Jehovah's Witnesses because of their activities, causing thousands to flee into exile in neighboring countries.

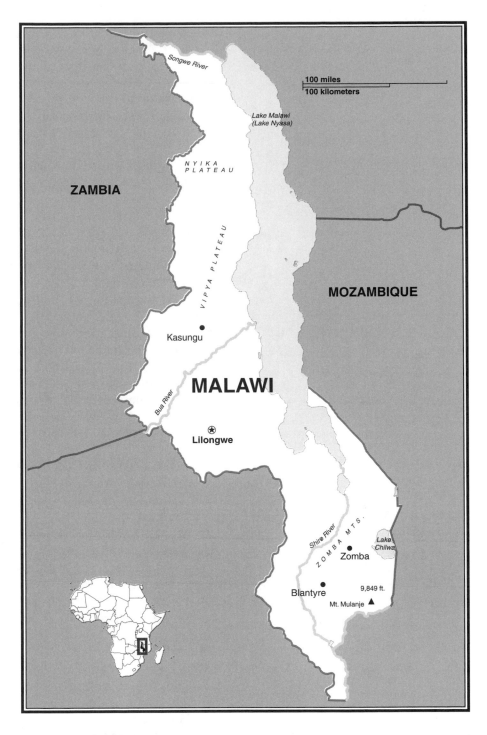

European missionaries became active in Malawi in the mid-1800s and established numerous missions and schools. British missionaries dominated and played a key role in the establishment of a colonial administration. One of the most famous missionaries in the region was David LIVINGSTONE.

In 1889 the British South Africa Company received a royal charter to develop its economic interests in a large area of southern Africa, including the region near Lake Malawi. To ensure control, British officials

Malawi

* **protectorate** weak state under the control and protection of a strong state

* **federation** organization of separate states with a central government

* **autocratic** ruling with absolute power and authority

made a series of treaties with chiefs in the region. As a result of these treaties, the region became a British protectorate* in 1891. In 1907 the territory was renamed Nyasaland.

As white settlers moved into Nyasaland they took much of the best agricultural land, leaving many Africans without land to farm. Unable to work and feed their families, many Africans migrated to Northern Rhodesia (present-day ZAMBIA), Southern Rhodesia (present-day ZIMBABWE), and SOUTH AFRICA to work as laborers in gold, diamond, and copper mines. Continued migration of laborers from Nyasaland in the early 1900s contributed to the growing poverty of many rural areas.

The growth of the European-controlled PLANTATION SYSTEM contributed to the outbreak of rebellion in Nyasaland in 1915. Thousands of plantation workers rose up to protest the policies and brutality of their white employers. The rebellion, brief but intense, failed to win wide support before being crushed. Despite its failure, the revolt began a tradition of resistance to colonial rule.

In 1953 Britain joined its Rhodesian colonies and Nyasaland into a federation*. Colonial authorities believed that this would lead to more efficient administration and contribute to long-term economic and political development of the region. Africans, however, saw the federation as reinforcing white rule and opposed it bitterly. During the 1950s, protests against colonial rule in Nyasaland became increasingly forceful, leading to widespread arrests and a crackdown on opponents in 1959. In the face of growing unrest, Britain granted Nyasaland internal self-government in 1963. The following year it gained full independence as Malawi.

From independence until 1994, Malawi was ruled by Hastings Kamuzu BANDA. Prime minister from 1964 until he became president in 1966, Banda was named life-president of Malawi in 1971 under a one-party political system. Under his autocratic* rule, Banda extended his powers from governmental matters to such things as regulating hair styles and dress and censoring books, magazines, and films. Intolerant of any dissent, he dealt ruthlessly with opponents, who were either imprisoned, sent into exile, or killed.

Attempts at revolt in 1965 and 1967 were crushed, and Banda faced no serious challenge to his rule until the 1990s. By that time he was coming under increasing criticism for HUMAN RIGHTS abuses. In 1992 Banda reluctantly agreed to hold multiparty democratic elections, and in 1994 he was voted out of office. The following year he was arrested and charged with killing political opponents. Banda was acquitted in 1995 and died two years later.

Malawi president Bakili Muluzi, elected in 1994, worked to improve his nation's economy, expand its infrastructure, and increase foreign investment. While his reforms led to modest improvements, they have had little effect on most rural areas of the country, which remain mired in poverty.

Economy. Although more than half of Malawi's land area is suitable for agriculture, much less than that is actually farmed. Nevertheless, agriculture is the nation's primary economic activity, employing more than 80 percent of the people and generating nearly 90 percent of

Ngwazi Hastings Kamuzu Banda served as president of Malawi from 1966 to 1994. During this time, he established a strict one-party government.

---

* **subsistence farming** raising only enough food to live on

* **cash crop** crop grown primarily for sale rather than for local consumption

* **infrastructure** basic framework of a society and its economy, which includes roads, bridges, port facilities, airports, and other public works

Malawi's export income. Many of Malawi's people engage in subsistence farming*, and rural poverty is widespread. Cash crops*, such as tobacco, tea, and sugar, also play a significant role in the nation's economy.

Malawi has very little industry and few mineral resources of any commercial value. The nation's primary industries include cement factories, sawmills, shoe factories, tobacco processing, and the manufacture of textiles, chemicals, and fertilizers. Most industrial activity occurs in the southern part of Malawi, particularly around Lilongwe, the nation's capital. Although Malawi's most important mineral resource is bauxite, an ore that contains aluminum, little has been done to extract and use this resource. Malawi's lakes and rivers provide a rich source of fish, but most of the catch reaches only local markets.

The development of Malawi's economy is hindered somewhat by the lack of an extensive infrastructure*. The country's rail network is confined to the southern part of the country, where railways link the nation with ports on the coast of neighboring MOZAMBIQUE. The country's

Malawi

The Republic of Malawi

POPULATION:
10,385,849 (2000 estimated population)

AREA:
45,747 sq. mi. (118,484 sq. km)

LANGUAGES:
English, Chewa (both official); Tonga, Yao, Tumbuka, Lomwe

NATIONAL CURRENCY:
Kwacha

PRINCIPAL RELIGIONS:
Protestant 55%, Muslim 20%, Roman Catholic 20%, Traditional 5%

CITIES:
Lilongwe (capital), 395,500 (1994 est.); Blantyre, Zomba, Mzuzu

ANNUAL RAINFALL:
30–40 in. (760–1,010 mm)

ECONOMY:
GDP per capita: $940 (1999 est.)

PRINCIPAL PRODUCTS AND EXPORTS:
Agricultural: tea, tobacco, sugar, cotton, corn, potatoes, cassava, sorghum, goats, peanuts
Manufacturing: agricultural product processing, cement, sawmill products, consumer goods
Mining: lime, coal, bauxite

GOVERNMENT:
Independence from Britain, 1964. Multiparty democracy with president elected to five-year term. Governing bodies: National Assembly (legislative body) and cabinet appointed by president.

HEADS OF STATE SINCE INDEPENDENCE:
1964–1994 President Hastings Kamuzu Banda
1994– President Bakili Muluzi

ARMED FORCES:
5,000

EDUCATION:
Compulsory for ages 6–14; literacy rate 56%

reliance on foreign investment and variations in foreign demand for Malawi's agricultural exports have often created serious financial problems for the nation.

People and Culture. Most of Malawi's people are Africans of Bantu origin, although a few Europeans and Asians also live in the country, primarily in the cities. The major ethnic groups are the Chewa, Yao, Nyanja, Chipoka, Tonga, Tumbuka, and Ngonde. The Chewa, the largest single group, occupy the central region of Malawi and areas in the far south. Among the most distinctive aspects of Chewa culture are ritual masked dances and the SECRET SOCIETIES associated with them. Masked dances are a cultural feature shared by several of the other peoples of Malawi as well. In fact, Malawi is known throughout East Africa for its dance societies, which were used in the past as a tool in social and political control.

The country's ethnic groups share other cultural features. One of these is a matrilineal social system in which descent in traced through the female rather than the male line. Despite cultural similarities, the various groups in Malawi clearly regard themselves as different from one another. Yet the country has not faced the serious ethnic conflicts that plague other African nations.

Although Malawi is one of the most densely populated countries in Africa, it is also one of the least urbanized. Nearly 90 percent of the people live in rural areas. Rural villages are generally quite small and are organized around extended families and kinship groups. Most of the nation's cities are located in the southern part of the country. (*See also* **Bantu Peoples, Central African Federation, Colonialism in Africa, Masks and Masquerades, Missions and Missionaries.**)

Mali

* **coup** sudden, often violent, overthrow of a ruler or government

Large but thinly populated, the West African nation of Mali is one of the poorest in Africa. However, its early history includes a number of powerful and wealthy empires. Conquered and colonized by the French in the late 1800s, Mali gained its independence in 1960. Its modern history has involved a series of dictators and military coups*, but the recent trend has been toward developing a democratic society.

GEOGRAPHY

The largest country in West Africa, Mali is about twice the size of Texas. Its land is mostly flat and rocky and covered with poor soils that make agriculture difficult. The only mountain range, the Adrar des Isforas, lies in the northeast.

The NIGER RIVER flows through the middle of this landlocked country, providing its only access to the sea. But the river cannot be navigated in all seasons, and it passes through other nations before reaching the sea. Part of the middle Niger Valley is a vast inland delta, where the river has deposited soil and dirt. The Niger floods its delta regularly. When the waters recede, they leave behind shallow lakes, and farmers work the land that emerges.

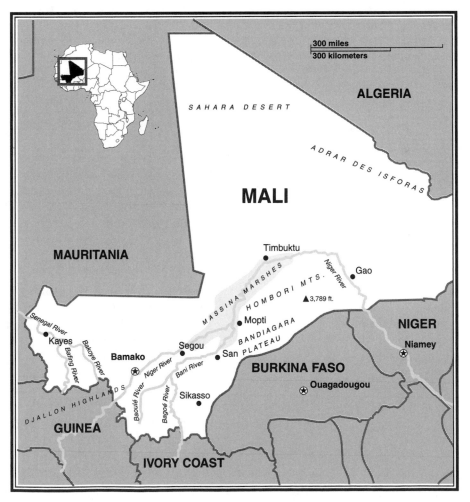

Mali

Children at Work

Families in Mali work hard to provide for themselves, and that includes the children. About half of the country's children aged 10 to 14 work, mostly at farming. Mali has few job opportunities for people with an education, so few parents have a reason to send their children to school. Only about 20 percent of Mali's school-age population actually attends school—one of the lowest rates in the world.

* **savanna** tropical or subtropical grassland with scattered trees and drought-resistant undergrowth

* **Islamic** relating to Islam, the religion based on the teachings of the prophet Muhammad

* **indigenous** native to a certain place

* **exploit** to take advantage of; to make productive use of

Though generally hot and dry, the climate of Mali varies considerably from north to south. The northernmost region lies within the SAHARA DESERT and endures extreme heat with little rain or plant life. To the south is the SAHEL, a somewhat less dry region with a milder climate but also periods of severe drought. Mali's southernmost region enjoys the mildest temperatures and the most rainfall, from 20 to 59 inches per year. The south contains small areas of forest, extensive savannas*, and most of Mali's wildlife.

Mali has two distinct seasons, dry and wet. The dry season begins in November when a cool wind lowers temperatures throughout the country. In February a hot, dry wind called the harmattan blows out of the Sahara, pushing temperatures to their highest levels. The rainy season starts in late May or early June and lasts until October.

HISTORY AND GOVERNMENT

Inhabited since prehistoric times, Mali has seen the rise and fall of several powerful empires. Trade in slaves and gold brought wealth to these states. The kingdom of Ghana (unrelated to the modern nation of GHANA) flourished between about A.D. 800 and 1100. After Ghana came the empire of Mali, founded by SUNDJATA KEÏTA in 1235. The magnificent MANSA MUSA ruled Mali from 1312 to 1337. He built mosques and palaces in the city of TIMBUKTU and made it a center of Islamic* culture. In the 1460s, SUNNI ALI established the empire of Songhai, which fell to Moroccan armies in 1591.

Following the Moroccan conquest, numerous small kingdoms emerged in Mali and West Africa. One of them, Segu, was started in the early 1700s by a group of young bandits and was based on slavery and war. Macina and the Tukulor Empire, both Muslim states, flourished in the 1800s.

French Colonial Rule. French interest in the region began in the late 1850s. Twenty years later France launched a series of military campaigns against Tukulor and the other indigenous* states, crushing them easily. In 1892 it established a colony known as French Sudan over what is now Mali. The colony underwent several name and border changes in the following decades.

Life was somewhat less difficult for Africans in French Sudan than for those in other French colonies. This was mainly because the area had fewer resources the French wanted to exploit*. Still, though the French had abolished slavery, they sometimes recruited forced labor for special projects such as building a railroad. They also drafted nearly 50,000 Africans to fight in World War II.

Independence. Soldiers returning after the war played a key role in the political struggle for independence. Workers, intellectuals, religious leaders, and ethnic leaders were also involved. The colony gained a degree of self-government in 1956 and some more two years later under the name Republic of Sudan. In June 1960, the republic joined Senegal in the independent Federation of Mali. Senegal withdrew two months later, and the Republic of Sudan became the Republic of Mali. Soon afterward, the new nation cut all its political ties to France.

The first president, Modibo Keita, governed Mali as a one-party state. He introduced socialism* and nationalized* the economy. However, Keita's policies led to an economic disaster in Mali. Dissatisfaction with his rule grew throughout the 1960s as the nation's economic crisis deepened.

In the late 1960s, Keita began to reorganize the government and to reduce the political power of the army. In response a group of young officers, led by Lieutenant Moussa Traoré, launched a coup in November 1968. Although promising to return Mali to civilian government, Traoré ruled Mali through the military for more than a decade. A new constitution created a presidency and a legislature in 1979, but Traoré dominated this government as well.

Meanwhile, a long drought brought terrible suffering to northern Mali during the 1970s and 1980s. Traoré ignored the people most affected, the nomadic* TUAREG, and opposition to his rule grew. The drought also worsened Mali's staggering economic problems. Two international bodies, the World Bank and the International Monetary Fund, offered loans and aid if the government sold the national industries and cut

* **socialism** economic or political system based on the idea that the government or groups of workers should own and run the means of production and distribution of goods

* **nationalize** to bring land, industries, or public works under state control or ownership

* **nomadic** referring to people who travel from place to place to find food and pasture

The mudbrick buildings of Timbuktu rise from the edge of the desert. Once a great center of Islamic culture and trade, Timbuktu is one of Mali's most popular destinations for tourists.

Mali

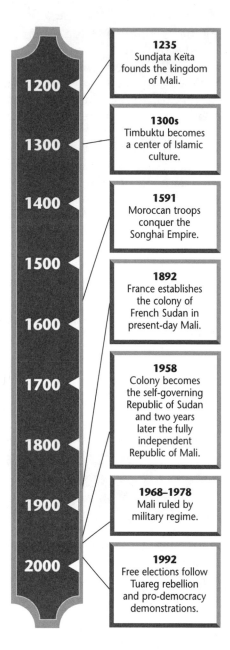

1235
Sundjata Keïta founds the kingdom of Mali.

1300s
Timbuktu becomes a center of Islamic culture.

1591
Moroccan troops conquer the Songhai Empire.

1892
France establishes the colony of French Sudan in present-day Mali.

1958
Colony becomes the self-governing Republic of Sudan and two years later the fully independent Republic of Mali.

1968–1978
Mali ruled by military regime.

1992
Free elections follow Tuareg rebellion and pro-democracy demonstrations.

* **infrastructure** basic framework of a society and its economy, which includes roads, bridges, port facilities, airports, and other public works

See color plate 11, vol. 4.

funding for public programs. The government agreed despite fierce protests by many people.

Another crisis hit in 1990, when the Tuareg launched a rebellion. That same year, students and workers began organizing a pro-democracy movement that led to violent demonstrations in March 1991. Days later, the military staged another coup, led by Lieutenant Colonel Amadou Toumani Touré. The new ruler soon replaced the military with a plan for a multiparty democracy. Free elections in 1992 led to the election of Alpha Oumar Konaré as president, and the Tuareg gradually reached a peace agreement with the government.

Since taking power, Konaré's government has actively encouraged the development of democratic institutions, including a free press and independent radio stations. Konaré was reelected in 1997, but the elections were so poorly managed that many opponents cried foul and took to the streets. Doubt and instability have continued to plague Konaré's efforts, but he has persisted with reforms. His approach has been to give local communities the power to govern themselves and create their own schools. Meanwhile, foreign investors have begun to see Mali as a generally stable and profitable opportunity, bringing new money into the economy.

ECONOMY

Although Mali has little fertile farmland, agriculture and livestock are the foundation of its economy. The best land is found in the southern region and along the Niger River. Between 80 and 90 percent of the people work in agriculture. Most of them grow food crops for their own use. Few use modern machinery.

Commercial agriculture and livestock are important sources of foreign income. The main export crops are cotton, peanuts, and sugarcane. Cotton is the most important export crop, as it produces about half of Mali's total export earnings; livestock is the second greatest source of foreign money. However, periodic droughts damage both crops and livestock. Mali also exports fish from its lakes and the inland delta of the Niger River. Though a landlocked country, Mali is the largest producer of fish in West Africa.

Mali's abundant mineral deposits include iron, tin, petroleum, uranium, manganese, bauxite, and diamonds. Most of these resources remain undeveloped, however, because money, technology, and infrastructure* are lacking. By comparison, gold mining has attracted considerable foreign investment. In the past salt was the country's most important mineral resource. For hundreds of years, camel caravans carried salt across the Sahara to the Mediterranean world—and they still do. Though less important today, salt mines still operate in northern Mali.

A tiny manufacturing industry produces canned foods, household goods, and textiles. Most manufacturing takes place in Bamako, the capital and largest city. In manufacturing as in mining Mali suffers from a lack of investment, transportation, and infrastructure. Despite its vast size, the country has only a single rail line and few roads, most of which are unpaved.

The Republic of Mali

POPULATION:
10,685,948 (2000 estimated population)

AREA:
478,767 sq. mi. (1,240,007 sq. km)

LANGUAGES:
French (official); Bambara, numerous others

NATIONAL CURRENCY:
C.F.A. Franc

PRINCIPAL RELIGIONS:
Muslim 90%, Traditional 9%, Christian 1%

CITIES:
Bamako (capital), 919,000 (1999 est.); Mopti, Ségou, Kayes, Gao, Kimparana

ANNUAL RAINFALL:
Varies from 20–60 in. (500–1,500 mm) in the south to 0–7 in. (0–175 mm) in the Sahara region

ECONOMY:
GDP per capita: $820 (1999)

PRINCIPAL PRODUCTS AND EXPORTS:
Agricultural: cotton, millet, rice, peanuts, corn, vegetables, sorghum
Manufacturing: food processing, consumer goods, construction products
Mining: gold, phosphates, kaolin, bauxite, iron ore

GOVERNMENT:
Independence from France, 1960. Republic with president elected by universal suffrage. Governing bodies: Asemblee Nationale (legislative body), Council of Ministers and prime minister appointed by the president.

HEADS OF STATE SINCE INDEPENDENCE:
1960–1968 President Modibo Keita
1968 Lieutenant Moussa Traoré and Captain Yoro Diakité
1968–1991 Colonel Moussa Traoré, president after 1979
1991–1992 Lieutenant Colonel Amadou Toumani Touré
1992– President Alpha Oumar Konaré

ARMED FORCES:
7,400

EDUCATION:
Compulsory for ages 7–16; literacy rate 31%

PEOPLE AND CULTURE

* **sub-Saharan**   referring to Africa south of the Sahara desert

For more than 600 years, Mali has been a crossroads of western Africa, where people from North Africa met those from the sub-Saharan* region. Over the centuries, economic and cultural exchanges among these groups have created a web of social relations and commercial networks based on KINSHIP, political alliances, and regional homelands.

The population of Mali includes several major ethnic groups, each with its own language and cultural practices. In any given region, however, the differences have blurred through trade and migration. As a result, people tend to emphasize their family name, clan*, or place of origin more than their ethnic identity.

* **clan**   group of people descended from a common ancestor

Black Africans dominate southern and central Mali and are the major force in the political life of the country. Speaking languages of the Mande family, these people combine indigenous black cultures with Islamic traditions. The largest and most important Mande group is the BAMBARA; related groups include the Malinke, Dyula, and Soninké. They make a living mostly by farming, ranching, and trade.

In these societies the families are patrilineal—that is, property and power pass through the male side of the family. Authority, especially in rural areas, remains with the eldest male of the family. Some ethnic groups within these societies also divide people according to social origin, with nobles at the top and descendants of slaves at the bottom. A separate caste* includes hunters, craftsworkers, artists, and mystics who perform special, sometimes sacred, services for the nobles. What sets this caste apart is that they are believed to control a powerful—though potentially destructive—spiritual or magical force.

* **caste**   division of people into fixed classes based on birth

The main ethnic groups of the northeast are the Songhai and the FULANI. Descended from the people of the ancient Songhai Empire, the Songhai farm and raise livestock. Their traditions have been strongly shaped by Islam. The Fulani, originally nomadic herders, have been forced to establish permanent communities after severe cattle losses in the droughts in the 1970s and 1980s.

The population in northern Mali consists primarily of nomadic peoples. The Tuareg are part of the ancient BERBER people, with a strong Islamic heritage, though they speak a Berber tongue. Driving herds of livestock and trading goods, the Tuareg range over vast areas of the Sahara and northern Sahel. The Tuareg were fierce opponents of French colonial rule and still resist efforts of others to intrude on their land or traditions. However, in recent times many young men have migrated to Bamako and urban areas in foreign countries to find work. (*See also* **Arabs in Africa, Colonialism in Africa, Deserts and Drought, Ethnic Groups and Identity, French West Africa, Islam in Africa, Sudanic Empires of Western Africa.**)

See color plate 9, vol. 4.

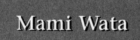

MALI, KINGDOM OF

See *Sudanic Empires of Western Africa.*

Mami Wata

Mami Wata is a female figure important to religious and social life in many parts of Africa. In some cultures she is a goddess. In others, the term *Mami Wata* refers to women who have the qualities of Mami Wata, including exceptional beauty and great power.

Throughout western and central Africa, Mami Wata is a beautiful river goddess with long flowing hair and fair skin. During colonial times, prints from Europe or India of light-skinned women and female deities were often used to represent Mami Wata. In other images, she is shown with the tail of a fish to indicate her connection with the world of water spirits.

Mami Wata is believed to be powerful and seductive. She may bring good fortune to those who worship her, but she may cause terrible misfortune to those who anger her. Her wild, free, and independent nature is associated with the modern lifestyle of urban women. She also represents irresistible female sexuality.

* **deity** god or goddess

* **cult** group bound together by devotion to particular person, belief, or god

The worship of Mami Wata as a deity* appears to have arisen in the early 1900s in southern NIGERIA and then spread to other parts of Africa. Men and women join the cult* of Mami Wata for a variety of reasons, including physical and spiritual sickness. To please her, they make offerings of sweet drinks and food, perfume, powder, and other luxury goods used by women.

In CONGO (KINSHASA), Mami Wata is represented as a mermaid in the west and as a crocodile person, known also as Mamba Muntu, in the east. Images of Mami Wata are found in murals, paintings, and other forms of popular ART. The idea of a being that is half woman, half aquatic animal combines elements of local culture, including traditional beliefs in water sprits, a colonial-era belief that whites were ghosts who came from beyond the sea, and aspects of West African folklore.

As African nations gained independence from their European rulers in the mid-1900s, Mami Wata became an important social and political symbol in the Congo region. Many people displayed a painting of Mami Wata in their homes because she was said to provide guidance on how to succeed in the modern world. However, such paintings often showed her accompanied by a snake, which represented evil. The snake reminded the viewer that the knowledge, power, and wealth offered by Mami Wata and modern urban life could be harmful if misused. After the 1980s, Christian symbols and paintings took the place of most Mami Wata images in city homes. (*See also* **Gender Roles and Sexuality, Popular Culture, Religion and Ritual, Women in Africa.**)

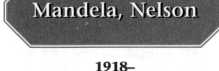

Mandela, Nelson

1918–
President of South Africa

* **apartheid** policy of racial segregation enforced by the white government of South Africa to maintain political, economic, and social control over the country's blacks, Asians, and people of mixed ancestry

See color plate 11, vol. 1.

Nelson Mandela is one of the best-known and most influential political leaders in Africa. Imprisoned for many years because of his activities against apartheid*, he later became the first black president of SOUTH AFRICA. For many South Africans, Mandela symbolized the hope for black equality.

Born in the Transkei region of South Africa, Mandela was the son of a XHOSA chief. Although a member of a royal family, he could not inherit the chieftainship because his mother was his father's third wife. After his father's death, the nine-year-old Mandela was sent away to school. When he finished his primary education in 1938, he gained admission to Fort Hare College. However, he was expelled two years later for taking part in a strike.

In 1941 Mandela moved to the city of JOHANNESBURG, where he worked as a policeman and took correspondence courses to complete his college degree. He then studied law at Witwatersrand University. In law school, Mandela met Indian and white students and came in contact with many radical ideas. In 1944 he joined the African National Congress (ANC), a black political movement, and eventually became one of its leaders.

When the South African government began to establish its apartheid policies after 1948, the ANC became an important source of opposition. The group organized work stoppages and other activities to protest and defy the racist laws. Following an outbreak of violence in 1952, the government banned several ANC leaders, including Mandela. He was not allowed to move about the country freely or to associate with other people. The government placed banning orders against Mandela again in 1953 and in 1956.

In 1955 the ANC adopted a document called the Freedom Charter, which called for the establishment of a nonracial, democratic South Africa. The South African government declared the charter to be treason and arrested Mandela and more than 150 other ANC leaders. However, when they were brought to trial, all were acquitted.

Racial tensions led to violence in 1960, when police killed 69 protesters during a peaceful demonstration against apartheid in the

Johannesburg suburb of Sharpeville. In response to the killings, black South Africans held a massive work stoppage. The government declared a state of emergency, banned the ANC, and arrested thousands of blacks. Mandela was again among those arrested, but he was soon released. He resumed participation in antiapartheid activities, working in secret to avoid another arrest.

Mandela decided that stronger action was needed to oppose apartheid. In 1961 he founded a group called Umkhonto we Sizwe (Spear of the Nation) to organize acts of sabotage* against the government. By the end of 1961, the group was bombing government sites. Mandela left South Africa secretly and traveled to other African nations to raise money and to set up training bases for Umkhonto members.

* **sabotage**   act designed to interfere with work or damage property

When Mandela returned to South Africa in the summer of 1962, he was arrested and brought to trial on charges of leading a strike and leaving the country illegally. He received a sentence of five years in prison. Two years later, the government sentenced him to life imprisonment for sabotage and for attempting to overthrow the government through violent revolution. Mandela spent 28 years in prison. Yet black South Africans and people in other countries continued to support him and his struggle against apartheid.

Unrest and threats of revolt, as well as international criticism, shook the South African government. In 1988 it began negotiating with Mandela over the conditions of his imprisonment. Two years later, South African president Frederik Willem DE KLERK released Mandela from prison. The two men then worked together to dismantle the apartheid system and prepare South Africa for a nonracial democracy. Because of their efforts to bring about peaceful change, de Klerk and Mandela shared the Nobel Prize for peace in 1993.

In 1994 South Africa held the first elections in its history in which all races could vote. Mandela became the nation's first democratically elected president. He worked to improve the economic and educational conditions of blacks and to root out the last elements of apartheid. In 1999 Mandela chose not to run for a second term as president and retired from active politics. (*See also* **Apartheid.**)

Mansa Musa

Early 1300s
Emperor of Mali

* **pilgrimage**   journey to a shrine or sacred place

* **Islam**   religion based on the teachings of the prophet Muhammad; religious faith of Muslims

Mansa Musa was the most famous ruler of the ancient West African empire of MALI. During his reign the Mali empire reached its greatest size, extending hundreds of miles from north to south and from east to west. However, Mansa Musa is best remembered for his pilgrimage* to Mecca, the holy city of Islam*, in 1325. The magnificence and riches he displayed on this trip dazzled people along the way.

Thought to be a descendant of SUNDJATA KEÏTA, the founder of the Mali empire, Mansa Musa took the throne in about 1312. He was educated in Arabic and followed the tradition of Malian rulers in making a pilgrimage to Mecca. To support his journey, Mansa Musa required contributions from the towns and provinces of his empire. In this way he amassed a treasure of gold and other riches to take with him.

Emperor Mansa Musa of Mali, shown at the lower right hand corner of a map, traveled to Mecca in 1325. The great wealth he displayed and distributed during his trip brought him great fame.

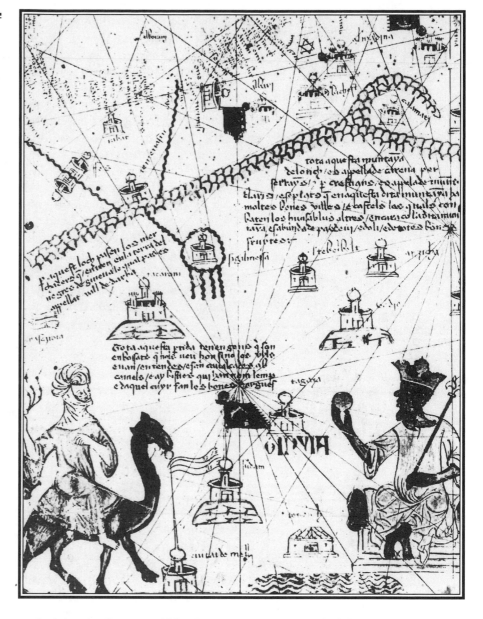

* **mosque**   Muslim place of worship

* **patron**   special guardian, protector, or supporter

Arriving in CAIRO in 1324, Mansa Musa astounded the inhabitants and the royal court of Cairo in EGYPT. According to accounts of the time, he came on horseback, superbly clothed, and followed by a procession of more than 10,000 followers. His camels carried bags of gold and jewelry that were distributed as gifts. Mansa Musa gave away so much gold in Cairo that the price of that precious metal dropped.

Mansa Musa returned home from his pilgrimage with a famous Arab architect, who constructed several magnificent buildings. One of them, Djinguereber mosque*, still stands in the city of TIMBUKTU. A patron* of the arts, Mansa Musa attracted poets and artists to his royal court. He also built several libraries and supported education in the Qur'an, the holy book of Islam. (*See also* **Islam in Africa, Kings and Kingship, Sudanic Empires of Western Africa.**)

Mansur, al-

1549–1603
Ruler of Morocco

* **dynasty** succession of rulers from the same family or group

* **diplomacy** practice of managing relations between nations without warfare

* **mercenary** hired soldier

Mulai al-Mansur was the sixth, and perhaps greatest, ruler of the Sa'di dynasty* of MOROCCO. During his reign (1578–1603) Morocco enjoyed a long period of peace and prosperity, highlighted by its conquest of the ancient city of TIMBUKTU, now part of present-day MALI.

A master of diplomacy*, al-Mansur managed to balance relations with many competing foreign powers including France, Portugal, Spain, and England. He also kept Morocco largely independent of its official ruler, the Ottoman sultan in Turkey. Al-Mansur reorganized and centralized the government of Morocco, developed the country's industry and agriculture, and encouraged foreign trade.

Al-Mansur assembled a highly trained army consisting largely of foreign mercenaries* who used European firearms. In 1590 he sent the force south to invade the Songhai empire in West Africa and captured the rich cities of Gao and Timbuktu. The cost of the campaign was very high, however, and it provided few long-term benefits for Morocco. After al-Mansur's death, Morocco went into a decline. (*See also* **Sudanic Empires of Western Africa**.)

Maps and Mapmaking

* **cartographer** person who practices cartography, the science of mapmaking

If Africans had a mapmaking tradition before the coming of Europeans, no traces of it survived. The mapping of Africa was carried out largely by Europeans until independent African nations began producing their own maps in the late 1900s.

The Greeks created the earliest maps of Africa, and they dealt mainly with the northern and eastern coastlines of the continent. Later, Arab cartographers* added to these maps. Although the Arabs devoted little attention to the interior of Africa, their knowledge of the eastern coast was appreciated by Chinese cartographers, who used it in drawing their world maps.

Beginning in the 1400s, Portuguese navigators charted the west coast of Africa. They launched a wave of exploration, and for several hundred years Italian, Dutch, French, English, and German mapmakers recorded the information that explorers brought to Europe. At first, maps of Africa dealt only with the outline of the continent. Details about the interior of Africa came from written texts and were based largely on guesswork.

The oldest known printed map of the whole continent was published in Italy in 1508. Gradually, African maps began to include names of places in the interior. From the late 1700s through the 1800s, travelers and explorers published a vast body of material on Africa, including maps. For the most part, these maps were concerned with locating the main physical features of the continent, especially rivers and lakes, and with drawing attention to areas that held valuable economic resources. Europeans felt that producing scientific maps was part of the process of "civilizing" Africa. Cartography helped justify their penetration into the continent and their growing involvement in its affairs.

Beginning in the late 1800s, the mapping of Africa was driven by the needs of the European powers that controlled most of the continent. These colonizers wanted maps recording boundaries and property ownership. After the 1940s, governments and organizations involved in planning social and economic development programs required large-scale maps showing land features and resources. Cartographers used new techniques such as aerial photography—taking images from planes with special cameras—to produce highly detailed maps.

Independence had little immediate effect on mapmaking in Africa. The former colonial powers continued to provide cartography as a form of foreign aid. In the late 1900s, however, many African countries loosened their ties with former colonial powers, and cartography became the responsibility of African national mapping agencies. Economic difficulties, however, have limited their activities. As a result, some nations are more thoroughly mapped than others. (*See also* **Travel and Exploration.**)

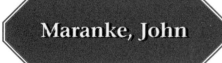

Maranke, John

**1912–1963
African religious leader**

John Maranke was the founder of a successful independent church called the Apostolic Church of John Maranke. Today the church claims over 500,000 members in Africa, and many European converts outside the continent.

Maranke was born Muchabaya Ngomberume in Southern Rhodesia (now Zimbabwe). His mother was the daughter of the Shona chief Maranke, whose clan name he adopted when he founded the church. Little is known of his early life, but church tradition says he had the first of several spiritual visions at age five. It is reported that he suffered mysterious illnesses throughout his adolescence and had a near-death experience. Maranke claimed a voice told him to take the name John the Baptist and to preach to many nations. In July 1932, he held his first religious ceremony, at which approximately 150 people joined the new Apostolic Church of John Maranke.

* **indigenous**   native to a certain place

The practices of Maranke's church, a mixture of Jewish, Christian, and indigenous* Shona religious elements, were inspired by his visionary experiences. As the church grew, Maranke gave some followers—including family members—leading positions. After his death, control of the church passed to his sons. (*See also* **Prophetic Movements, Religion and Ritual.**)

Markets

* **barter**   exchange of goods and services without using money

The open-air market is an important feature of African life in both rural and urban areas. As centers of commerce where cash and barter* transactions take place, they play a key role in the economy. Most African agricultural products and craft goods enter the system of exchange at local markets, alongside imported products. Tailors, barbers, carpenters, and other tradesmen come to market to sell their services. Markets also serve as community centers where people socialize and share news and information.

Markers

In small settlements, they are often located next to important buildings such as the chief's house or the court.

Traditional Markets. Across sub-Sarahan* Africa, nearly every community has a market of some kind. Most take place outdoors in open spaces. Sellers squat behind their baskets of goods or display their wares in temporary shelters made of branches roofed with palm leaves or grass thatch. Only in some large towns do markets contain permanent, concrete vendors' stalls.

Though generally crowded, markets are usually well organized. Authorities charge fees to vendors and supervise the pricing of goods. Certain areas of the market may be devoted to particular kinds of products, such as vegetables or cloth, so buyers can easily find and compare all available wares. The number of buyers and sellers at a market ranges from a handful in tiny rural settlements to thousands in the bustling marketplaces of Africa's great cities. Resembling strips of open shops, large urban markets often develop into permanent shopping streets.

See color plate 8, vol. 1.

Most commerce in rural North Africa takes place in traditional markets called *suqs*. Each *suq* is held on a specific day of the week and takes its name from the day and from the group on whose territory it is held. In larger towns, the *suq* is a more permanent feature. It serves as a meeting-place for nomads, townspeople, and traders bringing goods that are not produced locally.

Market Cycles and Traffic. Large urban markets are busy every day. However, most rural markets operate on a periodic schedule, which ranges from opening every other day to opening every seventh or eighth day. In any given district, a group of periodic markets may function as a ring or cycle. An eight-day ring, for example, might include seven markets in different locations, each open on one day. A day on which there is no market completes the cycle. When markets are set up in an eight-day ring, markets held on successive days are usually far apart in the market region. For example, the first market might be in the center of the region, the second in the far south, and the third in the far north. This ensures that no town in the market area ever goes more than three days without having a market open nearby.

On market day, streams of vendors and traders move to and from marketplaces, walking or riding on bicycles or in trucks. Many are women, carrying goods on their heads. A study of one market ring showed that on each market day, as many as 5,000 women—30 percent of the total population of the region—visited that day's market. In a week, a woman might travel a total of 50 miles to various markets.

Changes in African life may alter the market's role. As increasing numbers of Africans move into urban centers, they obtain more of their goods from stores and European-style shopping centers. Improvements in the mass transport of goods have made local markets less important in the selling of major cash crops* such as coffee. However, with their unique combination of social and economic functions, it is unlikely that open-air markets will ever disappear from African cities and towns. (*See also* **Trade**.)

Marriage Systems

* **Islamic**   relating to Islam, the religion based on the teachings of the prophet Muhammad

M arriage takes many forms in Africa. Throughout the continent, the diversity of systems reflects the traditions, religions, and economic circumstances of a wide variety of distinct cultures. Islamic* laws and customs have shaped the institution of marriage in North Africa and in some nations of western and eastern Africa. In recent years, modern life, industry, and cities have brought changes to African marriages and to the roles of men and women.

African marriage systems do share several characteristics. They almost always involve the transfer of bridewealth—cash, goods, or services—from the groom or his family to the bride's family. This exchange is both real and symbolic, as it marks the woman's passage from one social group to the other. Thus, for Africans, marriage is a matter between families as much as between the bride and groom, and many families arrange the marriages of their members.

The Western attitude that marriage is the union of two people drawn together by love has had some influence in Africa, especially in the cities. But African cultures emphasize that the union of two individuals must fit into the larger picture of social networks known as KINSHIP groups. Each marriage creates an alliance between or within kinship groups, and the children of the union will inherit property, rights, and responsibilities from their kin.

Types of Marriage Systems. In Africa the institution of marriage varies as widely as the many thousands of ETHNIC GROUPS and cultures. Although some cultures forbid certain types of marriage, all the traditions are designed to promote kinship ties, to safeguard land and wealth through an orderly transfer, and to create a social order in which members of the community clearly understand their roles and relationships to others. Polygamy* is common in much of sub-Saharan* Africa, and it is the privilege of men, not of women. Polygamy enlarges a family and increases its ability to work and earn a living. It also demonstrates the power and status of the head of the household. In addition, polygamy gives men more freedom in selecting partners. If a man follows certain rules and traditions for his primary marriage, his others may be guided by personal choice or feeling.

* **polygamy**   marriage in which a man has more than one wife or a woman has more than one husband

* **sub-Saharan**   referring to Africa south of the Sahara desert

Africans practice four other main types of marriage. Each is defined by whom a man or woman is allowed, expected, or encouraged to marry. One common type of marriage involves unions between close relatives. A man may marry his niece, his cousin, or even his half sister or granddaughter. A second type consists of marriages between in-laws, people already related from previous marriages. A man might marry his wife's brother's daughter, his niece-in-law. A third type, called the levirate, occurs when a man marries the widow of his older brother. Finally, a sororate union is a man's marriage to his wife's younger sister, either after his wife's death or while she is still alive.

Many societies in central and southern Africa favor marriage between cousins. Since cousins' parents are brothers and sisters, the marriage of two cousins means that bridewealth is transferred among siblings and their families. This system of marriage, with several variations, strengthens the bonds between brothers and sisters and ensures that the

Marriage Systems

The wide variety of marriage traditions and systems in Africa reflects the continent's diverse ethnic groups and cultures. Here, on the Comoro Islands, wedding guests wear traditional dress and body paint.

bridewealth stays within the extended family. Such arrangements are especially common among pastoralist* peoples who offer cattle, vital assets* for them, as bridewealth. However, some ethnic groups prefer bridewealth paid in service, not money or cattle. For instance, among the Bemba, farmers in a poor region of ZAMBIA, a man earns his bride by working for years for her family.

Some marriage systems circulate women instead of wealth. Among some peoples of central NIGERIA, women must marry many men from different kinship groups. They change their residence each time they go to a new husband or return to an earlier one. Young children follow their mother at first, but when they get older, they join a male member of the family—their father, their mother's brother, or one of their mother's other husbands. Other Nigerian groups expect a man who marries to give a sister in marriage to a male in his bride's family. In this way, the two families exchange women through marriage. If the man has no sister to offer, he must give his wife's family custody of his children instead.

African men rarely seek to divorce their wives because divorce means that they must give up the marriage's material goods as well as its social alliances. Women do sometimes seek a divorce. In some cases, they may

Ghost Marriages

Some unions in Africa are called "ghost marriages." People who marry in this way hope to have children, sometimes on behalf of the dead. For example, a widow may have children by her husband's male relatives, and the dead man will be considered their father. When an unmarried man dies, another man may marry a woman in his name and father offspring who are regarded as his children. Other nontraditional marriages are unions between two women. The "wife" has children who are regarded as the offspring of the "husband" woman. In this way, a rich or powerful woman may take a wife and obtain children without losing her property or position to a man.

* **dowry** money or property that a woman brings to the man she marries

wish to end a traditional first marriage and to make a second marriage based on personal choice. Generally, however, the courts do not allow women who divorce to keep their children.

Islamic Marriage and Divorce. Islam, the major religion of North Africa, encourages marriage as the proper way of regulating sexuality and organizing families. Many groups regard marriages between cousins as ideal because they strengthen family ties and keep property within the extended family. When families arrange marriages, the selection process may begin with the women, but the final decision comes from the elder men of the family. The groom or his relatives pays bridewealth to the bride's family, which in turn provides a dowry* for the bride. The wedding ceremony usually takes place at the groom's family home.

Islamic law—based on the Qur'an, the holy book of Islam—gives men and women different rights and privileges in marriage and divorce. A man can divorce his wife whenever he wishes to do so, whether she agrees to the divorce or not. A woman can only divorce her husband under certain conditions. The practice of polygamy is limited to men, who may have as many as four wives at the same time. Women are not permitted to have more than one husband. Polygamy has never been universal among North Africans, and the practice has dropped sharply in modern times.

Marriage in Modern Africa. Modern life in Africa's growing cities has distanced people from their traditional rural kinship groups. Men and women in urban areas are becoming more likely to insist on their personal wishes in arranging a marriage, though they may still seek approval from their families in the countryside. African women now have greater opportunities for jobs and education, and they have gained more power to make choices and be independent. They are generally marrying at a later age and having fewer children.

Modernization has brought other changes to marriage systems. Many families now accept money instead of the more traditional forms of bridewealth such as cattle. In urban areas this change has made it easier for employed young men to marry. In addition, media such as television and film in urban areas have exposed more people to Western models of relationships. Like other forms of social organization in Africa, marriage systems are changing as people combine the demands of modern life with those of tradition. (*See also* **Family, Gender Roles and Sexuality, Islam in Africa.**)

Masks and Masquerades

Many African societies have a rich tradition of masquerades, which are plays, ceremonies, or dances by masked performers. Masquerades provide entertainment, define social roles, and communicate religious meaning. The masks used in such performances may be treasured as works of art. They are also important symbols of ancestors, spirits, or even the history and culture of whole peoples.

This Bamileke folk dancer in Cameroon performs in a mask and costume. The mask features a pair of prominent eyes.

Masks. Masks take many forms. Some are made of carved wood, such as the towering masks of the Dogon people of Mali. Engraved with designs telling the history of generations, the intricate Dogon creations represent multistory family houses. Other groups make masks from bark, animal skins, plant fibers, and woven cloth. Not all masks are worn on the head or over the face. The traditional rulers of western African states such as Benin wore special masks on their chests or hips that symbolized royalty.

In most societies, only certain people are allowed to own or wear masks. With a few exceptions, women may not wear them. Groups of men—usually members of a community, kinship group, professional organization, or club—own most masks. Masks are also linked with SECRET SOCIETIES. They are symbols of the special knowledge held by those within the society and of their authority. Members of some secret societies wear miniature masks of wood or ivory as badges of membership or symbols of their rank.

Masquerades. Masquerades play a central role in many cultures in western and central Africa. They are less common in northern, eastern, and southern Africa, although they occur among a few groups in these regions. Several BERBER groups in Morocco, for example, hold masquerades in connection with Muslim festivals. The Chewa people of rural Malawi hold ceremonies with individuals wearing spirit masks when a new village headman takes office.

See color plate 5, vol. 3.

People in many societies believe that spirits become visible and perform through masquerades. Groups such as the YORUBA of Nigeria and the Chokwe of Congo (Kinshasa) hold masquerades in which ancestral spirits appear. The Dan of Ivory Coast and the Ibo of Nigeria believe that the spirits of the forest act out masquerades. Powerful water spirits perform during yearly masquerades in other Nigerian communities.

Important social events, such as INITIATION RITES, or coming-of-age ceremonies, often include masquerades. Spirits acting through masked performers oversee the symbolic rebirth of adolescents into adults. They also may appear in the public ceremonies that present the new adults to the community. Masks also play important roles in funeral customs. Among the Hemba of the Congo region, for example, a figure masked as death appears in two funeral masquerades. The first illustrates the social disorder brought by death; the second shows order restored.

In modern Africa, masquerades are taking on new forms and purposes to meet new needs and conditions. One example is the urban, multiethnic masked associations called Ode-Lay that sprang up in Sierra Leone in the 1950s. Developed in response to social unrest, Ode-Lay associations helped unite people by drawing on the masquerade rituals of various hunting groups and secret societies. In other countries, masquerades have been incorporated into the routines of national dance troupes. Some traditional masquerades, such as Dogon funerals, are occasionally performed for tourists. (*See also* **Art, Dance, Festivals and Carnivals, Music and Song, Mythology.**)

Mau Mau

* **guerrilla** type of warfare involving sudden raids by small groups of warriors

Mau Mau began as a movement by Africans against British rule in KENYA in the 1950s. Eventually the movement became a guerrilla* war. With complex political, economic, and social roots, Mau Mau has been interpreted in various ways. To the fighters and their supporters, Mau Mau was a struggle for liberation. To European settlers and British officials, it was an outbreak of terrorism and primitive violence. Although the British ended the rebellion with military force, Mau Mau forced them to change their role in Kenya and opened the way for majority rule by black Africans in 1963.

Origins of Mau Mau.

The origin of the term *Mau Mau* is unknown, but it had come into use by 1947. The British colonial administration in Kenya soon associated it with an underground antigovernment movement. This movement arose at the end of a long period during which Africans had tried without success to change the policies of land ownership, government, and social organization that made them second-class citizens in their own country.

Many of the Africans' grievances concerned land. In the early 1900s, the British began establishing white settlers in Kenya. They created an economy based on export crops such as coffee. More than 7.5 million acres of land once inhabited by the MAASAI, GIKUYU, and other peoples were set aside for about 4,000 European-owned plantations and farms. The desire to reclaim these "stolen lands" became a powerful force in Mau Mau.

Before the late 1930s, Africans were not allowed to grow coffee and other high-income crops. In order to raise money to pay for taxes, schooling, and medical care, many black men became migrant workers on white-owned farms, docks, and railways. African laborers received low wages, and those who worked in cities lived in poor housing. The result was a tension-filled society divided by race into unequal classes.

Although Africans were not represented in the Kenyan legislature, they organized a number of political and social welfare associations to promote their goals. The Gikuyu people founded the Kikuyu Central Organization (KCA) in 1924. At the outbreak of World War II in 1939, colonial authorities banned the KCA, fearing it might form an alliance with Germany, Britain's enemy. The KCA went underground, becoming secretive and militant*. Other African groups did the same, even after the war ended in 1945. Trade unions of African laborers called many strikes in the late 1940s and early 1950s. The sense of militancy and unrest felt by many Kenyans, especially young people, was channeled into Mau Mau.

Activities and Effects.

Mau Mau began with threats and acts of violence among the Gikuyu, both in rural areas and in urban centers such as NAIROBI. The government banned Mau Mau in 1950, but the violence continued, directed against both Europeans and Africans who were believed to be opposed to the movement.

A key element in establishing Mau Mau was the use of secret military-style oaths to bind members in a pact against the colonial government. The nature of these oaths made it clear that Mau Mau leaders expected a military confrontation with the government. In 1952 Mau Mau fighters assassinated an African chief who supported the British. The government responded by declaring a state of emergency and arresting more than 150 black political and labor leaders. Authorities also questioned and imprisoned thousands of Africans, mostly Gikuyu.

The Kenyan fighters rejected the label "Mau Mau" and used other names, such as the KCA or the "Kenya Land and Freedom Army," to refer to themselves. Among them were peasants, urban workers, the unemployed, and World War II veterans, as well as a few educated individuals and some women. The lifeline of their movement consisted of

* **militant** aggressive, willing to use force

the men, women, and children who did not actually belong to Mau Mau but provided food, medical supplies, ammunition, and information. Not all Africans aided or approved of the movement, however, and Mau Mau support varied from region to region.

The British viewed Mau Mau as something from Africa's past, and they regarded the group's often violent practices as a sign of breakdown among Africans. Yet the authorities used equally brutal methods to crush the movement. By 1956 British forces had defeated Mau Mau. The war left at least 12,000 Africans and about 100 Europeans dead. It also changed the social and political landscape of Kenya forever. Although the Mau Mau leaders had not provided a clear plan for the future, most who supported the movement sought return of the "stolen lands" and political independence for Kenya. The British had put down the rebellion but could not ignore its message. Mau Mau shocked Britain into beginning the reforms that led to black majority rule and to the return of land to Africans. (*See also* **Colonialism in Africa, Independence Movements.**)

Mauritania

* **sub-Saharan** referring to Africa south of the Sahara desert

A former French colony, the Islamic Republic of Mauritania is a large, thinly populated nation that borders the Atlantic Ocean in western Africa. Geographically, it connects the MAGHREB in North Africa and the coastal regions of West Africa. It also forms a link between the cultures of Arab North Africa and of sub-Saharan* Africa.

Geography and Economy. The northern, central, and eastern regions of Mauritania—more than half of the country's land area—are part of the SAHARA DESERT. These arid regions consist of vast stretches of sandy plains and dunes occasionally broken by rocky peaks and plateaus. South of the Sahara region is the SAHEL, a semidesert area of scattered grasses, low-growing bushes, and stunted trees. The most fertile and inhabitable region of the country is a small area in the extreme southwest along the Senegal River.

Mauritania's dry climate makes agriculture very difficult, except in areas along the Senegal River and at oases in the desert. Fertile soil and water from the river support farming, although much of it is merely subsistence farming*. Among the major food crops are rice, corn, dates, sorghum*, and millet*. At oases, scattered throughout the desert, groups of nomadic peoples who move from place to place with their livestock sometimes grow a few crops. The economy of Mauritania's Sahel region is based primarily on the raising of cattle, sheep, goats, and camels.

* **subsistence farming** raising only enough food to live on

* **sorghum** family of tropical grasses used for food

* **millet** family of grains

Small-scale trading has always been an important economic activity in Mauritania, with goods generally moving between North Africa and the coastal regions of West Africa. Mining and fishing are the most important of the nation's industrial activities. Much of the mining occurs in the Sahara region, which has plentiful deposits of iron ore and copper. The fishing industry, based along the Atlantic coast, accounts for about half of the country's export income.

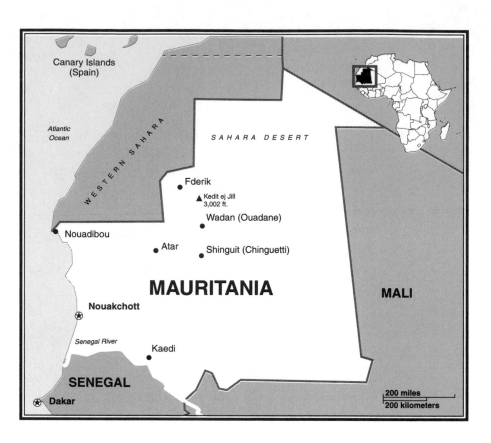

In recent years Mauritania's traditional agricultural and livestock activities have failed to support the nation's population. Moreover, much of the country suffers from periodic droughts, which have had a severe impact on agriculture. Since the 1970s Mauritania has been largely dependent on food imports to feed its people. The nation also relies heavily on other types of foreign aid and assistance.

History and Government. Mauritania was originally inhabited by BERBERS in the north and black Africans in the south. When the Muslim Arabs conquered North Africa, they established trade routes across Mauritania and spread Islam* throughout the region. In the A.D. 1000s the center of the empire of Ghana was located in Mauritania, and in the 1300s and 1400s Mauritania was part of the empire of MALI.

The first Europeans to visit Mauritania were the Portuguese, who established forts and trading posts along the Atlantic coast in the mid-1400s. Later the Dutch, French, and British joined in the competition for trade in the region. France finally gained control of Mauritania in the 1800s, and in 1903 it became a French protectorate*.

At first Mauritania was governed as part of the French colony of SENEGAL, and the Senegalese town of St. Louis served as the colonial capital. In 1920 Mauritania became a separate colony within the administrative federation* of FRENCH WEST AFRICA. Throughout the colonial period, the French did little to develop the economy of Mauritania or to educate its people.

* **Islam** religion based on the teachings of the prophet Muhammad; religious faith of Muslims

* **protectorate** weak state under the control and protection of a strong state

* **federation** organization of separate states with a central government

After World War II INDEPENDENCE MOVEMENTS arose in Mauritania, and in 1958 France granted the colony self-government. Two years later Mauritania gained full independence from France and adopted a system of government headed by a president. The nation's first president, Mokhtar Ould Daddah, ruled from 1961 until his overthrow by the military in 1978. Between 1978 and 1992 Mauritania was governed by a succession of military regimes*. Some attempts at political and social reform

* **regime** current political system or rule

The government of Mauritania has promoted Arab culture and ties to the Arab world. This man in Chinguetti reads an ancient copy of the Qur'an.

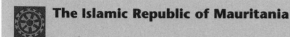

Mauritania

The Islamic Republic of Mauritania

POPULATION:
2,667,859 (2000 estimated population)

AREA:
397,953 sq. mi. (1,030,700 sq. km)

LANGUAGES:
Hasaniya Arabic, French (both official); Wolof, Pular, Soninke

NATIONAL CURRENCY:
Ouguiya

PRINCIPAL RELIGIONS:
Muslim, nearly 100%

CITIES:
Nouakchott (capital), 735,000 (1995 est.); Atar, Zouérate, Kaédi, Nouadhibou

ANNUAL RAINFALL:
Varies from less than 20 in. (500 mm) in the south to less than 4 in. (100 mm) in the northern desert region

ECONOMY:
GDP per capita: $1,910 (1999 est.)

PRINCIPAL PRODUCTS AND EXPORTS:
Agricultural: dates, millet, sorghum, root crops, livestock, fish, corn, rice, beans
Manufacturing: fish processing, petroleum refining, textiles, plastics and chemicals production
Mining: iron ore, copper, gypsum, gold

GOVERNMENT:
Independence from France, 1960. Republic with president elected by universal suffrage. Governing bodies: Senate and National Assembly (legislative bodies), Council of Ministers and prime minister appointed by the president.

HEADS OF STATE SINCE INDEPENDENCE:
1960–1978 Prime Minister Mokhtar Ould Daddah (elected president in 1961)
1978–1979 Lieutenant Colonel Mustapha Ould Mohammed Salek
1979–1980 Prime Minister Lieutenant Colonel Mohammed Khouna Ould Haidalla and Lieutenant Colonel Mohammed Mahmoud Ould Louly
1980–1984 Lieutenant Colonel Mohammed Khouna Ould Haidalla
1984– President Colonel Maaouya Ould Sid'Ahmed Taya

ARMED FORCES:
15,700

EDUCATION:
Compulsory for ages 6–12; literacy rate 38%

took place during this period, but for the most part the nation's rulers pursued harsh policies that restricted freedoms.

In the 1960s and 1970s, Mauritania faced several problems, including tensions between black Africans in the south and the Arab-Berber population in the north. These tensions arose primarily from a rivalry between the two groups as each sought to dominate the country's government and its economy. In the 1970s Mauritania became involved in a conflict over the fate of Spanish Sahara (now known as WESTERN SAHARA). Mauritania and MOROCCO each laid claim to different portions of the former Spanish colony, provoking a highly destructive guerrilla* war. Armed by ALGERIA, groups fighting for the region's independence waged a devastating campaign across Mauritania. Focusing their attacks on the country's iron mines and railroads, the rebels effectively crippled the nation.

Beginning in the 1970s, a source of great conflict in Mauritania has been the policy of "Arabization," by which the government took steps to strengthen Arab culture and increase links with Arab nations in North Africa. This policy has been bitterly resisted by the nation's black population. It contributed to growing political unrest that erupted in violence several times in the 1980s and early 1990s. In 1989 the racial and ethnic tensions in Mauritania spilled over into a crisis with neighboring Senegal. Several hundred Mauritanians and Senegalese were killed and tens of thousands of people fled the two countries to avoid the violence.

* **guerrilla** type of warfare involving sudden raids by small groups of warriors

Increasing demands for political reform led to the adoption of a new constitution in 1991 and to multiparty elections the following year. The newly elected government began taking steps to bring greater political and economic stability to the nation and to improve its relations with Senegal and other neighboring countries. Despite these efforts, many problems remain and Mauritania still faces political and social unrest as well as economic uncertainty. The country's Arabization policies continue, and Mauritania remains more closely linked to the Arab nations of North Africa than to the countries of sub-Saharan Africa.

People and Culture. More than two-thirds of Mauritania's population are Moors*. Half of them are of mixed Arab and Berber ancestry; the other half are black Africans. Traditionally, the Moors have been nomads, moving from place to place with their cattle, camels, and other livestock. The remainder of Mauritania's people are black Africans, including members of the FULANI, Tukulor, Soninke, and WOLOF groups. Most live in the southernmost part of the country. For the past few decades, Mauritania has faced serious racial and ethnic conflicts between Moors and black Africans. These conflicts grew out of a history of blacks being held as slaves by the Moors, which ended only in the 1960s.

* **Moors** North African Muslims who conquered Spain in the A.D. 700s

Nearly 80 percent of Mauritania's population live in the southwest, where the capital city of Nouakchott is located. About one-quarter of the people are still nomads. Traditionally, the nomads, farmers, and ranchers have depended on one another for trade and food. Several factors, including changes in agricultural patterns and serious droughts in the Sahel, have caused the number of nomads to decline in recent years, and many have settled permanently in farming villages, towns, and cities. (*See also* **Colonialism in Africa, Deserts and Drought, Islam in Africa, Livestock Grazing, North Africa: History and Cultures, Sudanic Empires of Western Africa.**)

Mauritius

The small island nation of Mauritius lies about 500 miles east of MADAGASCAR in the Indian Ocean. It consists of Mauritius and several small islands off to the north and east. Once heavily dependent on the production of sugar, Mauritius has developed a strong economy that includes a variety of manufacturing industries.

Of volcanic origin, the island of Mauritius measures only 38 by 29 miles. Its high central plateau is broken by gorges and small rivers and by peaks that remain from an ancient volcanic crater. Mauritius has a subtropical climate with fairly even temperatures throughout the year. The central plateau receives more rain per year than other areas.

Sugar, first introduced to Mauritius in the 1600s, remains the island's leading export. Since the 1970s the country has diversified its economy by establishing the Mauritius Export Processing Zone, an industrial center focusing on producing goods for export. Among the most important manufactured goods are textiles and clothing. The tourist industry is also growing.

Mauritius

* **indigenous**   native to a certain place

* **cede**   to yield or surrender

* **Creole**   person of mixed European and African ancestry

The first people to reach Mauritius were probably seafarers from the Arabian peninsula. (The island had no indigenous* population.) The Portuguese explored the area in the early 1500s. Between 1638 and 1710, the Dutch made several attempts to colonize the island, which they named Mauritius. However, it was the French who established the first permanent colony there in 1721. Renamed Île de France, Mauritius remained a French colony until 1810 and was used as a naval base to defend French interests in India. Its main port and capital city, Port Louis, became a major commercial center.

Located along the shipping routes between Europe and Asia, the island had great strategic importance and attracted the interest of other nations, including Britain. In 1810 the British captured the island and reinstated the name Mauritius. France formally ceded* the island to Britain in 1814. Mauritius remained a British colony until it gained independence in 1968. Originally a constitutional monarchy, with Queen Elizabeth II as head of state, Mauritius became a republic with an elected president in 1992.

Mauritian society and culture are very diverse. Many of the people are either Creole* or of French ancestry. Those of Indian descent make up the single largest group. Many Indians came to Mauritius in the 1800s as indentured laborers—people who agree to work in another country for a specific length of time in return for transportation. Mauritius also has a sizable Chinese population. The three main religions on the island are Hinduism, Christianity, and Islam. The official language is English, but French, Hindi, and other languages are widely spoken. (*See also* **Colonialism in Africa, Indian Communities.**)

Mboya, Tom

**1930–1969
Kenyan labor and political
leader**

Tom Mboya was a labor leader who played a key role in the early government of KENYA after independence. At age 22 he founded a government workers' union and later became general secretary of the Kenya Federation of Labor. At the time, labor organizations had considerable power in Kenya (then a British colony) because African political parties were not allowed.

In the mid-1950s, Mboya went to England to study. On his return, he was elected to Kenya's Legislative Council, where he fought for and won a new constitution for the colony. He also helped form the Kenya Africa National Union (KANU). When Kenya gained independence in 1963, KANU became the country's governing party.

Mboya, a member of the LUO ethnic group, served in the government of Kenya's first president, the GIKUYU leader Jomo KENYATTA. As minister of economic planning and development, Mboya promoted a program in which Western nations would assist African nations with economic development. As Kenyatta aged, some Gikuyu became concerned about holding onto power after their leader's death. Mboya was considered a likely successor, but as a Luo he raised alarm among the Gikuyu. On July 5, 1969, a Gikuyu man assassinated Mboya. (*See also* **Unions and Trade Associations.**)

Mengistu Haile Mariam

ca. 1942–
President of Ethiopia

* **coup** sudden, often violent, overthrow of a ruler or government

* **socialist** relating to an economic or political system based on the idea that the government or groups of workers should own and run the means of production and distribution of goods

Mengistu Haile Mariam led a military coup* that removed Ethiopia's emperor HAILE SELASSIE I from power in 1974. As head of state, Mengistu hoped to modernize Ethiopian society and unify the country by lessening ethnic rivalries.

Mengistu's military career began when he joined the Ethiopian army at the age of 14. After attending officer training school, he rose to the rank of colonel.

As president, Mengistu tried to limit the influence of the AMHARA people in Ethiopia's government. Following socialist* policies, he brought many of the country's private industries under state control and also took over vast tracts of land. However, a series of attempted coups, failed governmental programs, and an independence movement in the province of ERITREA led to his downfall. Mengistu fled the country in 1991 and was given refuge in ZIMBABWE. (*See also* **Ethiopia, Independence Movements.**)

Menilek II

1844–1913
Emperor of Ethiopia

* **protectorate** weak state under the control and protection of a strong state

Menilek II was the son of the heir to the kingdom of Shewa in what is now central ETHIOPIA. In 1856 TÉWODROS II used modern weapons to conquer Shewa and many other parts of Ethiopia. Menilek was captured and taken to Téwodros's court, where he was raised and educated. Nine years later, he escaped and returned to Shewa. After Téwodros died in 1868, Menilek tried to win the Ethiopian throne but lost out to Yohannes IV. Menilek then worked to make Shewa the center of Ethiopian political and economic power by expanding his control over lands to the south and east.

In 1889 Yohannes died in battle, and Menilek succeeded him as the emperor of Ethiopia. That same year, Italy declared Ethiopia a protectorate*. Menilek led the Ethiopians to war to defend their independence, eventually defeating the Italian forces in 1896. Later, he expanded Ethiopia to its present size and promoted economic growth by building a railway from ADDIS ABABA to DJIBOUTI. Under his rule, Addis Ababa became the country's first modern city. When Menilek suffered a severe stroke in 1909, his grandson took over as emperor.

Meroë

Located on the Nile River about 120 miles north of present-day KHARTOUM, the royal city of Meroë was the capital of the ancient kingdom of Kush. The kingdom arose in the region known as NUBIA (in what is now southern Egypt and northern Sudan) about 750 B.C. and flourished until the A.D. 300s. Although strongly influenced by Egypt, the Kushites eventually developed their own culture.

Meroë was inhabited by the 700s B.C., but at that time the Kushite rulers lived and were buried in the city of Napata to the north. Later, perhaps in the 600s B.C., the royal residence and administrative center of Kush moved to Meroë, which became the new capital. However, the city did not become the burial site for Kushite royalty until around 300 B.C.

* **deity**   god or goddess

* **hieroglyphics**   ancient system of writing based on pictorial characters

Scholars know little about the organization of the Meroitic state. They do know that its monarchy was similar to that of Egypt and that its rulers—some of them women—were closely identified with gods. Many of the deities* pictured on the walls of temples and pyramid chapels were Egyptian in origin, but there were also purely Meroitic gods, such as the lion-headed Apedemek.

Meroë was an important urban center. In its heyday it was the largest city in Africa south of Egypt, with elaborate stone palaces and temples as well as areas where the common people built their mud-brick dwellings. The city was noted for its industries, especially for ironworking. Meroitic craftspeople also produced pottery in a variety of Nubian, Egyptian, and Mediterranean styles and made glass and cloth. The earliest inscriptions in the city were Egyptian hieroglyphics*, but by the 200s B.C. the people of Meroë had developed a version of Egyptian script in which to write their own language. Scholars have not succeeded in translating these texts.

The last royal burials at Meroë date from around A.D. 350. Archaeologists think that the Meroitic state came to an end at that time, perhaps as a result of war campaigns in Meroitic territory by Aezanes Aksum, king of Ethiopia. (*See also* **Aksum; Egypt, Ancient; Sudan.**)

METALS

See *Minerals and Mining.*

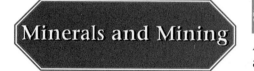

Deep in the ground of the African continent lies a wealth of minerals, metals, and gems. But few African countries—and few Africans—receive the benefits of these resources. The lack of technology and investment money have limited mining operations, and not all countries have significant resources. However, even countries with major deposits have seen most of the profits go to foreign corporations or small groups of privileged Africans. Meanwhile, mine workers labor under harsh conditions for little pay. The explanation for Africa's abundant resources and limited benefits begins with the European quest for riches in colonial times and continues with the modern plague of corruption.

MINERAL RESOURCES

Africa's mineral wealth takes many forms thanks to its long history of geology—the activities of mountains, rivers, volcanoes, lakes, and forests. Ancient woodlands have been transformed over millions of years into fossil fuels such as petroleum, natural gas, and coal. The courses of rivers and the upheavals of landforms have produced deposits of metals such as uranium, iron, copper, zinc, and tin, as well as rock minerals such as phosphates. Africa's rocks, soil, and volcanic activity are the source of some of the world's greatest treasures—from gold and

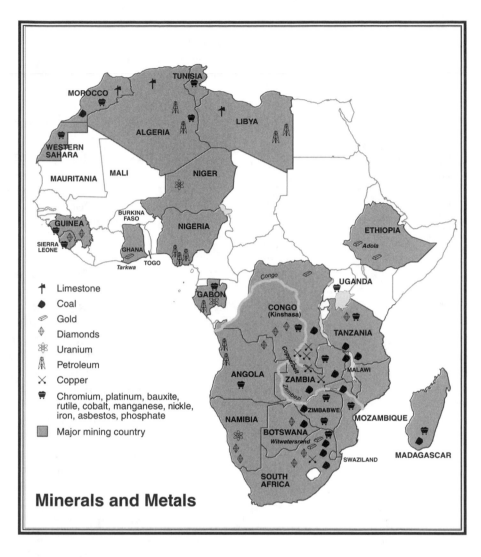

Minerals and Metals

Limestone
Coal
Gold
Diamonds
Uranium
Petroleum
Copper
Chromium, platinum, bauxite, rutile, cobalt, manganese, nickle, iron, asbestos, phosphate
Major mining country

platinum to diamonds of all sizes. Unfortunately, mining operations have also damaged the environments that yielded these resources.

Although abundant, Africa's mineral resources are not evenly distributed. North Africa's reserves of petroleum and iron ore may run out in a few decades. In sub-Saharan* Africa, metals and minerals are concentrated in a few major areas, and about half of the region's mineral production comes from two countries: SOUTH AFRICA with its gold and diamonds and NIGERIA with petroleum.

Fossil Fuels. Africa produces petroleum for the global market. ALGERIA and LIBYA together possess about 3 percent of the world's known petroleum reserves, and North Africa earns much of its foreign income from its petroleum and natural gas. However, the continent's largest petroleum producer is the West African country of Nigeria. Coal deposits exist in limited quantities in MOROCCO and in large reserves in the sub-Saharan nations of MOZAMBIQUE, MALAWI, TANZANIA, ZIMBABWE, and South Africa.

* **sub-Saharan** referring to Africa south of the Sahara desert

See color plate 13, vol. 4.

Minerals and Mining

Industrial Metals and Minerals. North Africa's nonpetroleum resources are fairly limited. The region's deposits of iron ore have been greatly reduced over the last 2,000 years, but small deposits remain of lead, zinc, manganese, copper, and other metals.

Industrial metals are a major industry in some African countries, making them key players in the global economy. ZAMBIA and CONGO (KINSHASA) produce more than half of the world's cobalt and a significant amount of its copper. Other leading suppliers of industrial metals include GUINEA and GHANA, of the aluminum ore bauxite; Zimbabwe, of asbestos; and GABON, of manganese. Uranium—an essential ingredient in nuclear reactors and weapons—is also produced in Africa, mainly by Gabon, NAMIBIA, and NIGER.

Rock minerals are another major African resource. Phosphates, a mineral used to manufacture detergents and fertilizers, come from Morocco, TUNISIA, and elsewhere. North Africa also contains abundant deposits of limestone used in cement.

Precious Metals and Gems. More than half of all the world's diamonds and platinum are mined in Africa. South Africa's vast gold field, the Witwatersrand, is rivaled by important deposits in Ghana, ETHIOPIA, and Zimbabwe. South Africa's diamond mines are world famous, but major diamond deposits exist in ANGOLA, Guinea, BOTSWANA, Tanzania, and Congo (Kinshasa) as well.

MINING

Mining has a long history in Africa. In North Africa, people have mined for iron ores and other metals for more than 2,000 years. Iron mining began in sub-Saharan Africa by around 500 B.C. and had spread through the region by the A.D. 200s. Iron played a crucial role in the improvement of agricultural tools and weapons.

During the colonial period, Europeans eager to profit from Africa's mineral wealth made developing mining a priority. Since the 1950s and 1960s, when most African states won their independence from Europe, mining has remained an important but troubled part of the national economies.

Early Mining. The ancient Egyptians, and later the Romans, launched substantial mining operations in North Africa thousands of years ago. Between the A.D. 700s and 1500s, gold mining provided the major item of trade in the former western African kingdoms of Ghana, MALI, and Songhai. In eastern Africa, the ancient civilization of MEROË (in present-day SUDAN) mined iron ore. Later, gold from what is now Zimbabwe was shipped across the Indian Ocean to Arabia and India, and inhabitants of central Africa mined copper long before the arrival of Europeans.

Mining in these early periods had different forms and meanings than it would later have. With limited technology, Africans could not dig deep into the earth and could only exploit* fairly shallow deposits. They also had no way of emptying water from mines filled with groundwater.

* **exploit**   to take advantage of; to make productive use of

78

Much of the revenue from African mines goes to foreign corporations, leaving local communities with few benefits. Here workers dig for diamonds at a mine in Liberia.

* **ritual**   religious ceremony that follows a set pattern

* **taboo**   religious prohibition against doing something that is believed to cause harm

When Africans reached the limits of their skills, they had to abandon mines. Mining took place only in the dry seasons. In addition, mining had an almost sacred meaning. Many groups had rituals*, ceremonies, and taboos* surrounding these resources and the process of bringing them out of the earth.

The Colonial Period. The fabled gold mines of south-central Africa lured Portuguese explorers into the continent's interior in the late 1400s and 1500s. But the Portuguese failed to establish any effective mining operations, and by the 1700s most European colonizers preferred making their money in the SLAVE TRADE.

By the 1880s, however, Europeans were involved in a frantic race to conquer all of Africa and to exploit its natural riches. Surveyors in South Africa had found astonishing sources of copper in 1854, diamonds in 1867, and gold in the 1880s. For the next few decades, Europeans established mines throughout Africa. In south-central Africa, a chain of major copper mines stretched from what is now Zambia to present-day Congo (Kinshasa). In western Africa miners produced diamonds and gold in Ghana and SIERRA LEONE, and tin and coal were found in Nigeria.

Mining supported many colonial African economies, but the profits went back to the mining industry and its owners. European corporations invested their money mainly in mining, ignoring the development of

Minerals and Mining

* **infrastructure** basic framework of a society and its economy, which includes roads, bridges, port facilities, airports, and other public works

transportation or other infrastructure* except to exploit mining. Railroads were built to carry minerals to ports on the coasts—not to link major cities, populations, or other industries. Like the minerals themselves, the profits from mining were taken out of Africa to make Europeans wealthy.

Meanwhile, the people who worked in the mines suffered severe hardships and upheavals. Many thousands of rural Africans left their families and moved into large settlements owned by the companies. Together with white workers, their movements and behaviors were strictly controlled. Even after slavery was abolished, the companies subtracted the costs of rent, equipment, and other expenses from workers' wages—little remained. Furthermore, accidents and diseases killed and injured workers at a frightening rate, leading to many major labor strikes. The companies responded in some cases by raising the white workers to supervisory jobs with higher pay, separating them from the black workers and fueling racial prejudice.

The Postcolonial Period. The impact of colonial control on the mining industry continued after African nations won independence in the mid-1900s. Mines and miners kept working and producing. However, now European owners often granted a share of the profits, as well as taxes, to African governments.

See color plate 11, vol. 4.

In some nations, the new governments seized ownership of the mines. But the results were often disastrous. The industries suffered from poor management, lack of investment money, low selling prices, political turmoil, outdated machinery, and general neglect. Labor disputes remained common. As African economies faltered in the 1970s and 1980s, their governments fell in debt to Western banks and international institutions such as the World Bank and the International Monetary Fund. These bodies pressured African nations to sell their mines and other industries to private investors, mainly international corporations.

Several other factors limited the profitability of African mining in the late 1900s. For the most part, the continent's raw ores are exported to other countries for manufacturing. The ores sell for much less than the goods made from them. Furthermore, changes in industrial processes worldwide have reduced the demand for copper, iron ore, and other metals. In Africa, the mining industry continues to be poorly connected to other industries and methods of transportation. In addition, diamond smuggling is widespread in illegal markets, drawing taxes and other profits away from African governments and companies.

Most mining operations in Africa today are on a large scale, and small companies find it hard to compete. Even so, small-scale mining—often for local use and not for profit—does exist in more than 30 African countries. It is estimated that small-scale mining operations account for more than $800 million a year in the African economy and employs more than one million people. Africa still contains vast mineral riches, but for the present, much of that potential is not being tapped. (*See also* **Colonialism in Africa; Development, Economic and Social; Economic History; Energy and Energy Resources; Labor; Slavery; Trade; Unions and Trade Associations.**)

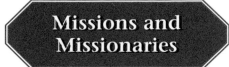

Missions and Missionaries

* **indigenous**   native to a certain place

* **secular**   nonreligious; connected with everyday life

* **sub-Saharan**   referring to Africa south of the Sahara desert

Christian missionaries have played an important, yet inconsistent, role in African history. While the goal of missions has remained the same—to convert indigenous* peoples to CHRISTIANITY, methods and attitudes have changed dramatically over time. During the last 1,500 years, the focus of missionary activity in Africa has shifted from the people in power to the average African. As a result, African Christianity has gone from a religion strongly supported by the state and serving its needs to one that addresses the concerns of the African people and finds its leaders from among them.

EARLY MISSIONARY ACTIVITY

In the past the nature of missionary activity in Africa has reflected the social and political conditions in which Christianity developed. As the secular* influences on Christianity changed, so did the way in which missionaries approached their task in Africa.

Initial Successes.   Africa's connection to Christianity began soon after the founding of the church. According to the Bible, Christian missionaries visited Africa before going to Italy. The apostle Philip is said to have converted a member of the royal court in ETHIOPIA. Although early Christian missionaries in Africa sought converts among ordinary folk, they worked mainly through traditional power structures. They hoped to convert rulers, who would then force their subjects to adopt the new religion.

By the A.D. 500s, Christian missionaries had succeeded in bringing their faith to EGYPT, MEROË, AKSUM, and Ethiopia. The monastic movement, based on the founding of isolated monasteries that served as centers of Christian faith and learning, developed in Egypt. However, the monastic movement had its earliest successes in Europe, where monasteries became the main means of missionary activity. By the time monastic Christianity finally reached sub-Saharan* Africa, it had become entangled in European politics and served the interests of commercial expansion as well as of faith. With the age of European exploration, missionary activity became closely linked with conquest.

The Age of Exploration.   Beginning in the early 1400s, European explorers carried European culture, including Christianity, to the farthest points on the globe. The primary motives for these voyages of discovery were financial profit and the creation of large empires. The church saw the voyages as an opportunity to bring Christianity to new converts in distant lands. Thus, priests and monks often accompanied explorers and conquerors as they sailed to America, Africa, and Asia.

The goals of conquest and accumulating riches clashed with the ideals of Christianity. However, by this time the success of the church was tied directly to the success of the kingdoms and rulers that embraced and supported the faith. To bring the faith to people in other lands, missionaries had to cooperate in the conquest of those lands. A church decree called the *Padroado*, issued by Pope Nicholas V in 1455, was typical of the type of arrangement the church made with the state. The

Missions and Missionaries

Padroado authorized Portugal to seize land and enslave indigenous peoples wherever Portuguese authority extended.

Conquest was not always necessary to spread Christianity. In Ethiopia and other early centers of African Christianity, the rulers willingly embraced the new faith. Notable among them was King Afonso I of the kingdom of KONGO in central Africa. Afonso made his subjects adopt Christianity, and by 1491 his kingdom had been converted. European nations recognized Kongo as a Christian kingdom, and Kongo officials who visited Lisbon and Rome received warm welcomes.

Despite the acceptance of Christianity in Kongo and a few other African kingdoms, the popularity of the faith eventually declined in many of those states. Local peoples went back to their traditional beliefs and abandoned Christianity, which survived only among foreigners and their agents and slaves. By the 1800s, Christianity had vanished almost without a trace in many places.

The Influence of Slavery. The decline of Christianity in much of Africa was a sign of the weakness of missionary policies. By the late 1700s, most local Africans saw missions as centers of unwanted foreign influence. Missionaries became associated with the merchants and soldiers who killed and enslaved Africans. As it turned out, however, the SLAVE TRADE provided the motivation for a new, more successful missionary effort in Africa.

In 1807 Great Britain outlawed the slave trade and soon afterward began a campaign to end the trade among other nations. To influence public opinion, antislavery forces recruited former slaves to tell their stories. Besides generating antislavery sentiment among Europeans, such activities also marked the beginning of African participation in the missionary enterprise. It became clear that this participation would play a vital role in missionary success in Africa. Christianity would come to Africa only through indigenous involvement.

MISSIONARY EFFORTS AFTER 1800

Shortly after 1800 various new missionary orders were founded that would lead the effort in Africa. Both Catholics and Protestants adjusted their policies with the aim of producing an indigenous clergy*. In this way, members of local populations, rather than Europeans, would be responsible for spreading Christianity in Africa.

Toward an Indigenous Clergy. In 1845 Pope Gregory XVI issued a decree that called for establishing overseas seminaries, or religious schools, to train indigenous clergy in lands conquered by European Catholic powers. At the same time, Protestant missionaries began following a similar path, with missionary organizations such as the Church Missionary Society seeking to enlist African clergy to lead Africans.

In 1861 Henry Venn, a leader of the Church Missionary Society, transferred nine parishes* in SIERRA LEONE to indigenous clergy. Many more would come under African control over the next several years.

* **clergy** ministers, priests, or other religious officials

* **parish** church district

These events occurred at the same time as the formation of the Niger Mission in Nigeria, headed by Samuel Ajayi CROWTHER, the first African bishop. Such changes marked a turning point for African Christianity, and Crowther played a crucial role in the African missionary enterprise.

Crowther translated the Bible into his native YORUBA language, the first time the Scriptures appeared in an African tongue. He also produced works in the IGBO, HAUSA, and Nupe languages. These efforts stimulated Christian missionaries to compile the first written versions of many African languages.

The Bibles, prayer books, dictionaries, and other works that appeared in African languages transformed the spread of Christianity and secular knowledge in Africa. With access to written languages, Africans began to master their own history, and materials written in African languages gave European readers a chance to understand the African point of view. As missionaries and church authorities came to see the importance of an indigenous clergy and African-language scriptures, Africans took a larger role in planning and carrying out missionary policy.

A philosopher and devout Christian, Dr. Albert Schweitzer founded this medical mission in Lambarene, Gabon, in the early 1900s. In 1952 Schweitzer received the Nobel Peace Prize for his work on behalf of "the Brotherhood of Nations."

Missions and Missionaries

During the late 1800s, a number of independent African churches and movements emerged, many led by charismatic* figures such as William Wadé Harris of IVORY COAST. These churches reinterpreted European Christianity in an African environment and redirected growing social unrest into religious channels. Harris and other African prophets also interpreted political events in religious terms, such as seeing the outbreak of World War I as a sign that the end of the world was near.

Most of the new churches and prophetic movements split off from Protestant missions; few developed in areas dominated by Catholic missions. Because Protestant missionaries preached that only those who could read the Bible themselves could be converted, a steady stream of Africans left the church to begin their own sects. The approach of Catholic missionaries was different. They baptized all who entered the church. African Catholics thus had less compelling reasons to leave the church than African Protestants.

Missions in Modern Africa. World War II disrupted missionary work in Africa, as the attention of Europeans was focused on the battle at hand. When the war ended, European leaders assumed that missionary ties in Africa would be renewed and strengthened. However, the struggle to restore freedom and liberty to nations conquered by Germany and Japan inspired Africans to seek the same freedom for themselves. Africans were no longer willing to accept European authority without question.

Independent churches flourished in the new environment in which Africans not only called for, but fought for, political freedom. Although these churches took a number of different forms, they shared a reforming zeal and continuity with traditional African religious belief and practice. The coming of independence for African nations in the 1960s removed other barriers to the development of indigenous churches. It also contributed to a process that resulted in the development of a "world" Christianity partly defined by the values of non-Western cultures and languages.

Established Christianity indicated its acceptance of these trends in 1995 when the first African Synod, a meeting of Catholic bishops, was held in CAMEROON. Pope John Paul II attended the meeting, which confirmed the church in Africa as a new, indigenous movement committed to addressing the political, economic, and social needs of African peoples.

The acceptance of an "Africanized" Christianity was the logical result of the long period of missionary activity in Africa. Once a distant continent with only a few isolated Christian outposts, Africa now boasts some 300 million Christians. With its large Christian population and vibrant local traditions, the continent has produced an important new form of Christianity. (*See also* **Braide, Garrick Sokari; Colonialism in Africa; Equiano, Olaudah; Ethiopian Orthodox Church; Kingsley, Mary Henrietta; Livingstone, David; Prophetic Movements; Tutu, Desmond Mpilo.**)

Mobutu Sese Seko

1930–1997
President of Zaire

* **regime**   current political system or rule

* **nationalize**   to bring land, industries, or public works under state control or ownership

* **coup**   sudden, often violent, overthrow of a ruler or government

President of Zaire—now known as CONGO (KINSHASA)—from 1965 to 1997, Mobutu Sese Seko ruled as a dictator. His regime* gained a reputation for corruption and mismanagement. Despite Zaire's rich natural resources, the nation suffered a serious economic decline under Mobutu's rule.

Born Joseph Désiré Mobutu in the Belgian colony of Congo, Mobutu was educated in missionary schools and entered the army in 1950. When the Congo gained its independence in June 1960, he was appointed head of national defense. During a struggle between the nation's top leaders, Joseph Kasavubu and Patrice LUMUMBA, Mobutu seized power. After a few months Mobutu turned the government over to Kasavubu, who named him commander in chief of the nation's armed forces.

In November 1965, Mobutu seized power again. This time he declared himself president and began establishing tight control over the country. He outlawed opposing political parties, set up a centralized government, and nationalized* certain industries. He took steps to "Africanize" the nation by renaming it Zaire, and changed his own name to Mobutu Sese Seko.

For a time it appeared that Mobutu had stabilized Zaire's economy and was encouraging development. However, by 1975 the nation had begun a long and steady decline. Groups opposed to Mobutu staged coups* to remove him from office, but they were unsuccessful. As opposition grew in the early 1990s, Mobutu was forced to allow multiparty elections in Zaire. In 1997, seriously threatened by rebel forces, he finally relinquished power and fled the country.

Mogadishu

Mogadishu, the capital of SOMALIA, is the nation's largest city and major seaport. During the long civil war that ravaged Somalia in the 1980s and 1990s, large parts of the city were destroyed, and hundreds of thousands of its inhabitants fled to other towns and to the countryside.

Mogadishu was founded in the A.D. 900s as a Swahili and Arab outpost on the Indian Ocean. By the 1200s it had become the most important town in East Africa. A major trading center, the town grew considerably during the 1300s and had a large population of rich merchants. After visiting Mogadishu about 1330, the famous Arab traveler IBN BATTUTA wrote about its great size and its wealth.

For centuries Mogadishu was an independent city-state ruled by its own sultans. In the mid-1800s, however, it came under the control of the sultans of Zanzibar. They rented the city to the Italians in 1892 and sold it to them in 1905. The Italians made Mogadishu the capital of Italian Somaliland. The city remained under Italian control until after World War II, and then the British took it over.

When Somalia gained its independence in 1960, Mogadishu became the capital of the new nation. The city grew rapidly, nearly doubling in size between 1965 and 1974. Many of Somalia's exports, primarily fruits and animal hides, passed through the city, and it supported a number of industries, including food processing, textiles, and cosmetics.

85

Mogadishu suffered tremendous damage in Somalia's civil war. A three-month struggle in 1991 left burned-out buildings and dead bodies scattered throughout the city. At least 400,000 people fled to the countryside. International peacekeeping forces were unable to bring order to Mogadishu. In 1994 they pulled out, leaving the city still in a shambles. (*See also* **Colonialism in Africa.**)

Moi, Daniel arap

1924–
President of Kenya

In 1978 Daniel Toroitich arap Moi succeeded Jomo KENYATTA as president of KENYA. Moi has managed to remain in power since then, despite a growing opposition and accusations of corruption.

A member of the Kalenjin people, an ethnic minority in Kenya, Moi worked as a teacher as a young man. In 1955 he was one of the first Africans chosen to serve on the colony's Legislative Council. Five years later he became assistant treasurer of the Kenya African National Union (KANU), which became the country's governing party after independence. For a while, he belonged to a rival party consisting of politicians who feared that ethnic GIKUYU and LUO were dominating KANU. This second party was later absorbed by KANU.

After Kenya won its independence, Moi served as minister of home affairs and, later, as vice president. When Kenyatta died in 1978, Moi assumed the presidency. Moi began his administration by launching an anticorruption campaign and releasing various political prisoners. However, his reform program soon stalled, and by 1982 Kenya was a single-party state. That year the air force attempted to overthrow the government, but Moi's forces defeated and jailed the rebels.

Moi's rule has been marked by a lack of political freedom and a poor record on HUMAN RIGHTS. During the 1988 elections, he did away with secret balloting and opponents accused him of rigging the vote. Two years later the murder of a respected member of the government led to calls for a multiparty political system. Moi allowed the formation of an opposition party, the Foundation for the Restoration of Democracy, in 1991. Moi was reelected in 1992 and 1997, but his victories were tainted with charges of fraud.

Mondlane, Eduardo Chivambo

1920–1969
Mozambican anticolonial leader

Eduardo Mondlane established the freedom movement known as FRELIMO that eventually won MOZAMBIQUE's independence from Portugal. Educated in South Africa, Portugal, and the United States, Mondlane became heavily involved with the movement for Mozambican independence. He concluded that Portugal's inflexible attitude probably meant that war was inevitable for Mozambique. However, he was determined to avoid devastating the country in the process.

After founding FRELIMO in 1962, Mondlane oversaw the expansion of military action against the colonial government. In 1969 he was killed by a package bomb sent from either a Portuguese or South African source. Mondlane is remembered as one of the founders of an independent Africa. (*See also* **Colonialism in Africa; Independence Movements; Machel, Samora Moises.**)

Money and Banking

* **precolonial** referring to the time before European powers colonized Africa

frican societies had many types of money in the precolonial* period, but no banking systems. As Europeans established colonies in Africa in the late 1800s and early 1900s, they introduced uniform systems of money and established banks to handle the exchange of money and other financial transactions.

MONEY

Money has three distinct functions. It can serve as a medium of exchange, a way of storing wealth, or a standard of value. In Western cultures, money combines all three of these functions. However, traditional African cultures generally have different forms of currency for each function. For example, gold jewelry might serve as a store of wealth, glass beads as a medium of exchange, and copper bars of a certain size and weight as a standard of value.

Traditional African Money. People in Africa relied on a variety of materials to serve as money, including metals, cloth, coins, gold, beads, seashells, cows, salt, and slaves. Africans used these "currencies" as a medium of exchange and lent or borrowed them as a form of credit.

Brass and copper—usually in the form of wires, rods, or handcrafted objects—served as money in many areas of Africa. Wires were usually worth less than metal in other forms. Some of the metal "currency" was produced in Africa, but a substantial amount came from Europe. Iron was also used as money, mostly in the form of bars and rods but in a variety of objects such as hoes, knives, and axes as well.

Cloth woven into strips or made into mats served as money in some regions of Africa. Beginning in the 1700s, cloth imported from Europe or other regions replaced locally made cloth currencies. The most valuable imported cloths came from India, in particular a blue cloth made from an indigo dye. Such cloth was a major form of currency in MAURITANIA.

A variety of coins from Europe, the Middle East, and the Americas served as money in Africa, although silver and gold coins were considered too valuable for everyday use. In West Africa, however, silver dollars—particularly those from Latin America—were used in trade along the coast. Gold dust functioned as money in some areas, especially among the ASANTE people of West Africa. The state controlled the production of gold dust, and those who used this currency weighed it very carefully.

Certain types of beads served as currency as well. In general, the societies that used bead money were small and poor. Seashells were also in wide circulation. In West Africa, cowrie shells were important. Most of these brightly colored shells originated in the Maldive Islands in the Indian Ocean and reached West Africa by way of caravan routes across the SAHARA DESERT. Later, cowrie shells traveled in the cargo holds of ships as ballast, which provided stability for the ships in rough seas.

Several groups, particularly those in East Africa, used cows as money. East Africa had many pastoralist* societies that valued cattle highly. Salt existed as a form of currency in many parts of Africa. It usually circulated in the shape of blocks, cakes, cones, or bundles. In all areas of Africa, people used slaves as money in major transactions.

* **pastoralist** related to or dependent on livestock herding

87

Money and Banking

Paper currencies, introduced in Africa in the early 1900s, are now used throughout the continent. These 10, 20, 50, and 100 Rand notes come from South Africa.

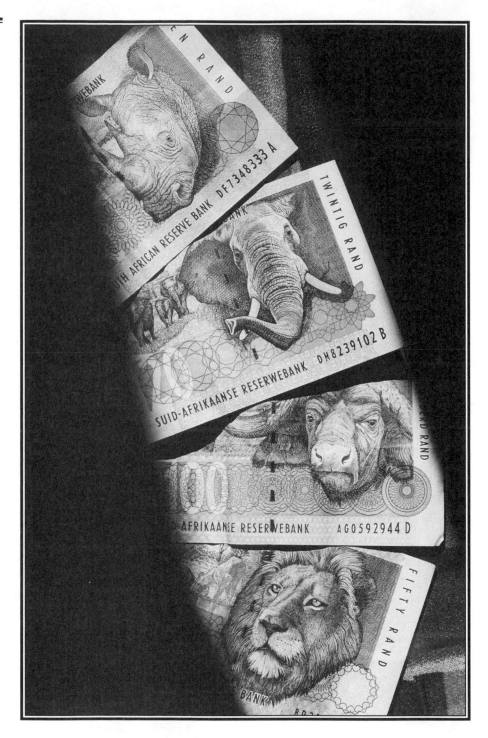

Characteristics of Precolonial Currency. While taking a wide variety of forms, precolonial currencies in Africa shared several characteristics. Most were informal, or unofficial; that is, neither introduced nor controlled by governments. The currencies were usually put into circulation by producers, merchants, and traders, and their value was determined by supply and demand. They could serve as money because people accepted them as a common means of exchange.

In some areas, more than one type of money might be in circulation at any given time. Such places usually had fixed rates of exchange for different types of currencies. With multiple currencies in circulation, the type of money in use frequently changed, with moneys of lower value replacing those of higher value. Frequent changes of currency, however, led to periods of considerable instability.

Generally, one form of precolonial money could be substituted for another, and some—such as salt or cloth—had other functions. For example, gold, silver, and cowrie shells could serve as money or as decoration and display. No matter how they were used, they maintained their monetary value. However, salt lost value if used to flavor food, and cloth cut for clothing became less valuable.

Unlike domestically produced currency, coins came from distant places. Coins came to Africa through the export trade—for example, in payment for slaves. Foreign coins were also acquired in exchange for African goods such as mineral resources, cotton and other agricultural products, and ivory and gold.

Colonial and Modern Currency. Colonial rule led to the replacement of informal African currencies with coins and paper notes. Each colonial power issued its own coins and paper money, which were usually backed by treasury reserves in the home country. These formal colonial currencies were standardized. They consisted of silver coins for high-value transactions and copper, bronze, and nickel coins for low-value exchanges. In general, paper notes came into circulation in Africa in the early 1900s.

The transition from traditional to colonial money was slower in some areas of Africa than in others, and in many cases local currencies remained in use as well. The colonial powers took steps to undermine traditional currencies in favor of their own money. Sometimes they simply banned the use of local currency. They also required that tax payments be made in colonial money.

All modern African nations have their own formal currencies of coins and paper notes. Urban areas also have electronic money—various forms of credit and debt without the exchange of actual coins or paper currency. In many rural areas, however, traditional currencies are still in use as a means of exchange and a sign of wealth.

BANKS AND BANKING

No formal system of banks and banking existed in Africa before the arrival of Europeans. Colonial officials established banks to handle the financial transactions of the government as well as those of individuals and businesses. European commercial banking practices penetrated Africa very unevenly, with banks set up primarily in urban areas. Even today many rural Africans have little connection with banks or banking.

After gaining independence, African nations retained the banking systems established by the colonial powers. In some cases, private banks owned by Europeans continued to operate as foreign-controlled businesses. In others, African governments nationalized* the banking sys-

* **nationalize** to bring land, industries, or public works under state control or ownership

tem, taking control of all the banks in the country. The banking systems in Africa today consist of a mixture of private and government-controlled banks.

Every African nation today has a central bank that supervises its banking system. These central banks usually issue currency, maintain foreign currency reserves, control the credit supply, oversee the specialized lending institutions of the government, and regulate the commercial banking industry. In the Muslim nations of Africa, Islamic* law governs various financial and banking practices.

* **Islamic**   relating to Islam, the religion based on the teachings of the prophet Muhammad

Most African nations also have development banks, which help finance economic development projects and provide technical assistance for such activities. Several countries in North Africa, for example, have branches of the Arab Bank for Economic Development in Africa, which has its main headquarters in SUDAN.

In addition to central and development banks, African nations have a variety of commercial and savings institutions. Such banks may be owned and operated by the government or by private companies; most have branch offices throughout the country. Although commercial and savings banks have been established in many parts of Africa, only a small percentage of Africans use them frequently. For rural Africans especially, money remains something to use before it loses value, is stolen, or is taken by beggars—not to put in the bank. (*See also* **Colonialism in Africa, Development, Economic and Social, Economic History, Ivory Trade, Slave Trade.**)

Morocco

Morocco lies at the northwest corner of Africa, on the southern side of the Strait of Gibraltar. On a clear day, it can be seen from the Spanish coast, a mere nine miles away. At the crossroads between Africa and Europe, Morocco has always been a melting pot of people and ideas, a country influenced by many cultures.

THE LAND

Geographically, Morocco is divided into three major regions: the ATLAS MOUNTAINS, which run diagonally across the country; the Atlantic coastal plains (northwest of the mountains); and the SAHARA DESERT (southeast of the mountains). Four ranges make up the Atlas Mountains: the Rif, along the Mediterranean coast; the Middle Atlas, south of the city of Fez; the High Atlas; and the Anti-Atlas, which runs southwest to the sea. Beginning as small hills at the edge of the Atlantic, the Atlas Mountains rise rapidly and reach 13,665 feet at Mount Toubkal. With an average elevation of 2,600 feet, most of Morocco lies at high altitudes.

Morocco's landscape, climate, and economy are affected by its geography. Northern Morocco, especially along the coast, enjoys a Mediterranean climate—mild, rainy winters and hot, dry summers. The annual rainfall ranges from 8 to 32 inches in the northern coastal plains

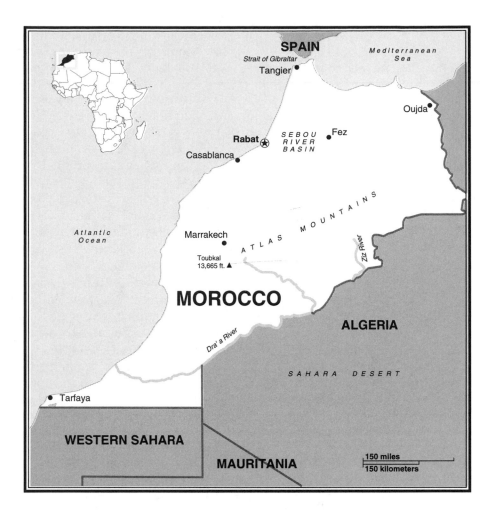

and from 30 to 80 inches in the mountain regions. Devastating floods sometimes occur during the rainy season.

The Sebou River basin, a vast plain between Fez and the capital city of Rabat, is heavily populated and includes the fertile Gharb (or Rharb) Plain. South of the Sebou basin, the country rises gradually to a number of less populated, but agriculturally important, plains. The major city of the high plains is Marrakech, an oasis nourished by water from the Atlas Mountain springs. Between the High Atlas and Anti-Atlas ranges is the Sous Valley, where many of Morocco's political movements have begun.

The southern regions of Morocco depend on the water from several streams that flow down the eastern slopes of the Atlas Mountains into the Sahara. These streams form the Dadès, Ziz, and Dra'a Rivers. Farmers in the region use complicated irrigation systems to carry water from the streams to their fields.

HISTORY AND POLITICS

BERBER peoples from the Sahara and Southwest Asia arrived in Morocco between 4000 and 2000 B.C. The earliest reports of the region and its people come from ancient Greek and Phoenician records. The

 See map in Archaeology and Prehistory (vol. 1).

Morocco

Phoenicians, who originated in the eastern Mediterranean, founded the first Moroccan towns on the southern side of the Strait of Gibraltar. By A.D. 100, Rome had annexed* most of North Africa.

Arab Rule.   North Africa was invaded by Arabs in the 600s and loosely incorporated into the Islamic* world by the early 700s. A large Arab army passed through Morocco to conquer the Iberian Peninsula, but Arab interest in Morocco remained slight until 789. In that year Idris I, a descendant of the prophet Muhammad, established a small independent state in the region. In 809, his son, Idris II, moved the capital to the newly established city of Fez. The Idrisid dynasty* transformed Morocco into an Islamic, Arabic-speaking society. The Idrisids were succeeded by several other dynasties: the Almoravids and Almohads (from the 1000s to the 1200s), the Merinids (from the 1200s to the 1400s), the Sa'adis (in the 1500s), and the Alawids (from the 1600s to the present).

During these centuries, Morocco was divided into many principalities, or emirates. The most important of these was the Merinid emirate of Fez. The emirates struggled constantly to keep the indigenous* peoples under control and to defend Moroccan ports against Portuguese and Spanish invaders. In 1664 the Alawids seized power and began a vigorous program of modernizing the country. Opposition from rural peoples, however, led to the downfall of this program. Morocco fell into political decline, which lasted until 1912, when most of the country became a French protectorate*.

European Colonization.   Europe's interest in Morocco began in the late 1800s. By 1900 the French had begun building a commercial port in the fishing village of Casablanca. A treaty between France and Spain divided the country into two protectorates, with the Spanish controlling the northern part of the country. The rest of Morocco, governed by the French, was effectively a colony. Large numbers of Europeans settled in the most fertile regions of the country. Both France and Spain spent much time and money putting down rebellions among the Berbers of the Rif and Atlas Mountains, who objected to European rule.

Independence.   After World War I, French forces began a campaign to end the Berber rebellion. In 1934 they finally brought the rebels under control. About ten years later, members of a Moroccan nationalist* movement founded the Istiqlal (Independence) party with the support of Sultan MUHAMMAD V (later King Muhammad). After World War II, Istiqlal began to demand independence, which France granted in March 1956. An agreement between Morocco and Spain a month later ended the Spanish protectorate. The following year Muhammad changed the Sultanate of Morocco to the Kingdom of Morocco. European settlers were forced to leave the country, and a new era in Moroccan history began.

In 1959 Istiqlal split into two parts—a larger group representing the older, more traditional members, and a smaller group representing younger members who favored socialism*. King Muhammad ruled until

* **coup** sudden, often violent, overthrow of a ruler or government

* **Soviet Union** nation that existed from 1922 to 1991, made up of Russia and 14 other republics

* **gross domestic product (GDP)** total value of goods and services produced and consumed within a country

1961, when his son, Hassan II, came to power. The following year, Morocco became a constitutional monarchy.

The governments of Muhammad V and Hassan II introduced modest and cautious modernization programs to the country. Clashes developed between the new urban population and the traditional leaders over issues such as providing funds for basic food products and introducing democracy. During the early years of King Hassan's reign, his inexperience led to some serious mistakes and two coup* attempts. Officials linked these threats to Berbers in the military, who were subsequently removed.

In the mid-1970s, King Hassan sought to gain control of Spanish Sahara (now Western Sahara). The large Spanish colony lay south of Morocco along the Atlantic Coast. It was mostly desert but contained valuable deposits of phosphates. Spain eventually withdrew its claim to the region, but a Saharan independence movement, known as Polisario, declared its opposition to Moroccan rule. In the 1990s negotiations about holding an election on the question of independence stalled, leaving the fate of the Western Sahara unresolved.

By the early 1980s, poor harvests and a sluggish economy had drained Morocco's resources, causing riots in Casablanca. In recent years, international lending agencies and human rights organizations have pressed the nation for political and economic reform.

Unlike most of its Arab neighbors, Morocco has generally sided with the West rather than with the former Soviet Union* and its allies. King Hassan helped pave the way for the Camp David Accords (1978) between Israel and Egypt and continued to press both Israelis and Palestinians to seek a peaceful resolution of their disagreements.

By the end of the 1990s, King Hassan was the longest-reigning monarch in the Arab world. He introduced various democratic reforms to Moroccan politics but at the same time kept a firm hold on the government and the legislative process. In his role as the religious head of state, he gained widespread support among the urban poor and rural people. Remembered for his political savvy and appealing personality, Hassan was succeeded by his son, Muhammad VI, in 1999.

ECONOMY

With about 33,000 square miles of good farmland and a generally temperate climate, Morocco has better conditions for agriculture than most African countries. About 40 percent of the people are engaged in farming. Agricultural activities account for nearly 20 percent of the nation's gross domestic product (GDP)*. Moroccan farms produce grains and meats for domestic use and fruits and vegetables for export. The production of commercial crops, such as cotton, sugarcane, and sunflower seed, is expanding. Nevertheless, the danger of drought is constant—generally occurring every third year and devastating crops.

Manufacturing in Morocco consists mainly of the production of phosphates, which are used in fertilizers. When Morocco acquired the Western Sahara, it also gained about two-thirds of the world's phosphate

See color plate 10, vol. 2.

reserves. Higher fuel costs and decreased demand for phosphates, however, have reduced export earnings.

The waters off Morocco's west coast contain abundant supplies of fish. Because the country lacks modern fleets and processing plants, however, it is unable to benefit from the rich fishing grounds. A trade agreement between Morocco and the European Union allows Spain to fish in Moroccan waters, for an annual fee.

Morocco's sandy beaches, comfortable climate, and cultural heritage account for its appeal to tourists. Tourism has grown rapidly, providing jobs and a source of hard currency.

A well-maintained network of roads links the regions of Morocco. Built during the colonial period, the roads have been gradually expanded since that time. In addition, railroads connect the major cities of the north to the Western Sahara. Morocco has more than 20 ports along its coastline.

The government spends about 20 percent of its budget on education, mostly to build schools. The country also has many clinics and other medical facilities, although the rural population has little access to health care. Infant mortality remains high and about one-third of the population is malnourished.

As in other parts of North Africa, many of the older towns in Morocco were once protected by a massive outer wall and defensive fort called a Casbah. The well-preserved Casbah of Ait Benhaddou, shown here, has been featured in several major films.

Kingdom of Morocco

POPULATION:
30,122,350 (2000 estimated population)

AREA:
178,620 sq. mi. (446,550 sq. km)

LANGUAGES:
Arabic (official); French, Berber dialects

NATIONAL CURRENCY:
Dirham

PRINCIPAL RELIGIONS:
Muslim 98.7%, Christian 1.1%, Jewish 0.2%

CITIES:
Rabat (capital), 1,496,000 (2000 est.); Casablanca, Marrakech, Fez, Oujda

ANNUAL RAINFALL:
Varies from about 32 in. (800 mm) to less than 8 in. (200 mm) in the northern coastal lowlands, and 30–80 in. (760–2,030 mm) in the southern mountain regions

ECONOMY:
GDP per capita: $3,600 (1999 est.)

PRINCIPAL PRODUCTS AND EXPORTS:
Agricultural: grain, citrus, wine grapes, olives, fish
Manufacturing: food and beverages processing, textiles, leather goods
Mining: phosphates, iron ore, manganese, lead, zinc

GOVERNMENT:
Independence from France, 1952. Constitutional hereditary monarchy. Governing bodies: elected legislative body consisting of Chamber of Councilors and Chamber of Representatives, and Council of Ministers and prime minister appointed by the monarch.

HEADS OF STATE SINCE INDEPENDENCE:
1952–1961 Sultan Muhammad V (adopted title of king in 1957)
1961– King (Moulay) Hassan II
1999– King Muhammad VI

ARMED FORCES:
196,300

EDUCATION:
Compulsory for ages 7–13; literacy rate 44%

PEOPLE AND CULTURE

The people of Morocco live mainly in cities. They are mostly Berber and Arab in origin, and centuries of intermarriage between the two groups have erased most of their cultural differences.

The main distinguishing feature that remains between ethnic groups is linguistic. Berber-speaking Moroccans are divided into three groups: the Riffi of the Rif Mountains, the Tamazight of the Middle Atlas, and the Shluh of the High Atlas and Sous Valley. The remainder of Moroccans speak Arabic, the national language, with French as a second language used in commerce, education, and government. Radio broadcasts can be heard in Arabic, French, Berber, Spanish, and English. Newspapers are written in both Arabic and French. Despite a recent boost in Berber culture, Berber languages remain largely unwritten.

Islam is the state religion and most Moroccans belong to the Sunni tradition. King Hassan II, a descendant of the prophet Muhammad, was the symbol of Islam throughout his long reign. Hassan was also responsible for expanding Morocco's territory. Beginning in 1975, he extended the country's borders by moving to the south and incorporating territories that were formerly part of the Spanish colonial empire. This included land held by the Sahawari Arab Democratic Republic, which at the time claimed independence. In 1993 he constructed the world's largest mosque in Casablanca. Morocco also has a small Jewish community. (*See also* **Arabs in Africa, Colonialism in Africa, Independence Movements, Islam in Africa, North Africa: Geography and Population, North Africa: History and Cultures.**)

Moshoeshoe I

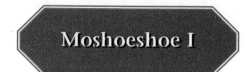

Moshoeshoe I

**1786–1870
Founder and king of
Basutoland**

* **diplomatic** involved with conducting relations with other nations

Founder and king of the Basotho nation (present-day LESOTHO), Moshoeshoe I was noted for his military skill and diplomatic* abilities. He played a major role in protecting Lesotho from conquest by European settlers, and he helped the country achieve independence.

Originally named Lepoqo, Moshoeshoe was the son of a Koena chief. While a young adult, Moshoeshoe gained a reputation as a leader by making daring cattle raids. Yet he was impatient and hot-tempered, and he killed followers for minor offenses. A local wise man told him that being just and humane would make him a more successful leader. This advice helped Moshoeshoe to realize that peace, not war, would gain him more faithful followers. Using this approach, he united various small groups to form the Basotho nation by the early 1830s. During that time, Moshoeshoe studied the complex relationships between African and European populations and learned to deal with them in a positive manner. By showing he was a strong and intelligent leader, Moshoeshoe earned the respect of other African leaders and colonial officials, which would prove to be an important factor in his struggles to maintain an independent Basotho nation.

The greatest challenges facing Moshoeshoe during his reign were attempts by European settlers to conquer the Basotho people and seize their land. At first Britain sided with the settlers. In 1852 a British force invaded Lesotho, but Moshoeshoe defeated them. Over the next 15 years, the settlers tried to overpower Moshoeshoe and his followers but failed. Through his diplomatic skill, Moshoeshoe earned the respect of colonial officials and brought the British government over to his side. By forging an alliance with Britain and gaining its protection, he helped save the Basotho from European control. As a result, the people of Lesotho consider Moshoeshoe the father of the country. (*See also* **Southern Africa, History.**)

Mossi

* **dynasty** succession of rulers from the same family or group

* **hierarchical** referring to a society or institution divided into groups with higher and lower levels

The Mossi are the largest ethnic group in BURKINA FASO, making up almost half of the population. They speak Mooré, which is used as a common language throughout the country. The Mossi arose from the merging of many different ethnic groups and formed several competing empires. Soldiers known as Mossi conquered the city of TIMBUKTU during the reign of Emperor MANSA MUSA of MALI in the 1300s. However, the modern Mossi may not be descended from these warriors.

In the 1400s, warriors on horseback arrived from the south and founded the first Mossi dynasty* in what is now northern Ghana. Mossi nobles called *nakombse* led small groups out to conquer new areas. All later Mossi empires trace their origin back to the *nakombse*, who founded several major kingdoms, including Ouagadougou. Mossi empires had strong central governments and a hierarchical* social structure. After the French colonized the region in the late 1800s, the *nakombse* rulers lost most of their power and privileges. Nevertheless, modern Mossi leaders are still respected in Burkina Faso both by political leaders and the population as a whole.

Mozambique

*****exploitation** relationship in which one side benefits at the other's expense

A large country on the east coast of Africa, Mozambique has had a long and violent history. After 450 years of exploitation* by the Portuguese, Mozambicans fought a ten-year war for independence, then a civil war that lasted into the 1990s. Today the people of Mozambique have begun to put their violent past behind them. But drought, flooding, and a crushing national debt have made it one of Africa's poorest countries.

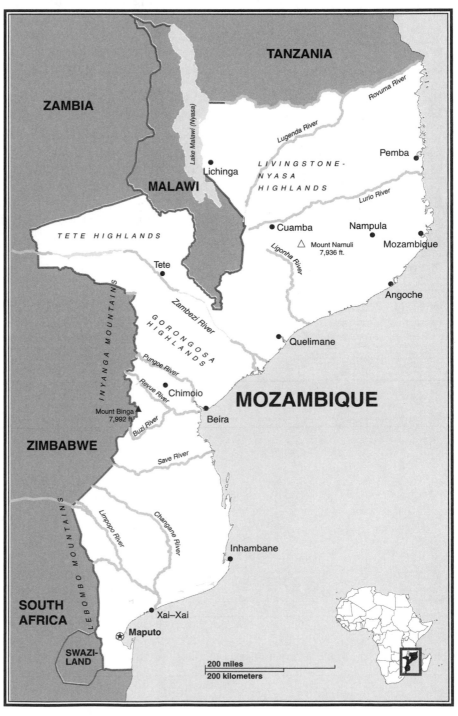

Mozambique

* **mangrove**   tree found in coastal areas that grows in dense clusters

* **savanna**   tropical or subtropical grass-land with scattered trees and drought-resistant undergrowth

GEOGRAPHY

A land of great contrasts, Mozambique is nearly twice the size of California. The country has hundreds of miles of coastline along the Indian Ocean, with some of the best natural harbors in Africa. The Mozambique Channel separates the country from the large island nation of MADAGASCAR.

The country's terrain consists mainly of a low plain along the ocean coast, rising westward to a high central plateau and mountains. The ZAMBEZI RIVER divides the country from west to east. North of the river, the coastal plain is narrow and rises steeply to the highlands. South of the river, the plain is much broader and the change in elevation more gradual. In the far northwest, Mozambique borders the waters of Lake Malawi.

The northern two-thirds of Mozambique has a rainy season from November to April, with annual rainfall between 39 and 55 inches. The southern third sees less rain, only about 23 to 31 inches, and sometimes suffers from long periods of drought. Although Mozambique lies not too far from the equator, its temperatures generally remain moderate because of the country's high elevations. The hottest weather is found in the low-lying coast and the Zambezi River valley.

Mozambique has a rich diversity of forests, waters, and wildlife. Along the coast, shrimp and other marine creatures thrive in the marshy mangrove* forests. Tropical forests are shrinking but still exist in coastal areas and in the north-central region, while savanna* grasslands cover much of the plateaus.

Mozambique's natural resources hold great promise for the country's future. Geologists believe that a wealth of metals and minerals lie below the surface. However, the country has little capacity for mining, and many forests and wildlife habitats are being destroyed for short-term profits. Mozambique's greatest resource may be its rich soils, which can support a wide variety of farming. Many people live in the most fertile areas.

HISTORY AND GOVERNMENT

From the earliest known hunters and gatherers to the politicans and bankers of modern life, Mozambique's history spans thousands of years. The region has experienced a long series of migrations, invasions, conquests, and struggles.

Early History. By about A.D. 70, people living in what is now Mozambique had established some stable settlements where they farmed, fished, processed iron, and crafted pottery. Around 250 small groups of BANTU PEOPLES began migrating into the region from the north and west. Over the next 150 years, waves of Bantu displaced or absorbed much of the indigenous* population. They laid the foundation for a shared Bantu heritage that still can be felt in the languages and social customs of Mozambique.

* **indigenous**   native to a certain place

After about 1000, Arab, Swahili, and Indian traders began to settle along the coast. They founded small chiefdoms that grew into independent states. The port of Sofala became a major center for exporting gold and ivory.

These coastal traders had contact with several African states that lay farther inland. The kingdom of Mutapa, also known as Mwene Mutapa, controlled the gold trade south of the Zambezi River, and by the 1500s it was probably the largest and most powerful state in central and southern Africa. The kingdom of Malawi controlled the ivory trade north of the river.

Within Mutapa and Malawi, chiefs and councils of elders ruled over small local areas. They distributed land to their subjects and called on the spirits of ancestors to make the land flourish. In return, the people paid taxes to the chiefs in food and labor, and the chiefs were entitled to the larger tusk of any elephant that died in their territory. The chiefs, however, had to pay tribute* to the larger state. The local economies of Mutapa and Malawi rested mainly on farming, along with cattle raising, hunting, fishing, and mining. Trade in gold and ivory linked both Mutapa and Malawi to the Arab and Swahili merchants on the coasts.

* **tribute** payment made by a smaller or weaker party to a more powerful one, often under the threat of force

The Portuguese Invasion. Portuguese sailors first landed on the coast of Mozambique in 1498, while searching for a sea route to India. Other explorers followed, and within a few years the Portuguese had several small settlements and trading posts on the coast. During the 1500s the Portuguese challenged the Swahili and eventually succeeded in taking control of the coast.

From their strongholds on the ocean shores, the Portuguese sent their armies and diplomats inland. In 1607 they forced the rulers of Mutapa to give up all their mines, and in 1632 they defeated Malawi. The king of Portugal gave out *prazos,* large estates in the interior, to Portuguese settlers. These settlers, *prazeiros,* often formed alliances and marriages with local African families, producing a mixed Afro-Portuguese culture. As a result, the influence of Portuguese authority declined. Indian traders moved in on Portuguese commerce, and several Arab and African groups revolted. In 1692 Mutapa and its allies drove the Portuguese from the interior.

The Slave Trade. In the mid-1700s, however, the Portuguese regained power and wealth through the slave trade, which grew to terrifying proportions. As many as 1 million Africans from the region were forcibly taken to work in the Americas, the Caribbean, India, and Madagascar. Although Portugal outlawed the slave trade in 1836, the trade continued to dominate commerce throughout the century.

Slave raiders destroyed and captured entire communities in Mozambique. The rural economy was ruined as productive workers were taken away, and the remaining people could not grow enough food or protect against droughts. Indigenous societies were deeply disrupted and divided as a new, small class of Africans profited from enslaving other

Soldiers from the Mozambique Liberation Front (FRELIMO) on parade in Maputo, the capital of Mozambique. In the 1960s FRELIMO launched a guerrilla war to free the country from Portuguese rule.

Africans. Southern Mozambique suffered less from the slave trade, but in the mid-1800s the area was conquered by the Nguni, an African people who had fled from South Africa.

Colonial Rule. Although the Portuguese grew rich from the slave trade, they were dependent on the Africans and *prazeiros* who controlled much of it. This situation and the success of the Nguni limited Portuguese influence. In the late 1800s, however, Portugal launched new assaults on the interior. Many Africans took up arms to defend their homelands, and Portugal did not overcome all resistance in Mozambique until 1917.

To increase their control over the country, the Portuguese set up a centralized administrative system with districts divided into European and non-European areas. They forced many African peasants to work for farms and factories owned by Europeans. Large numbers of Mozambican men went to work in South Africa for better pay in the mines and plantations there.

* **infrastructure** basic framework of a society and its economy, which includes roads, bridges, port facilities, airports, and other public works

* **autonomy** independent self-government

* **cash crop** crop grown primarily for sale rather than for local consumption

Portugal also granted private companies the right to rule the lands and peoples of specific areas. In return, the companies were supposed to develop the area's agriculture, trade, and infrastructure*. Most companies, however, merely exploited the natural resources for their own profit.

In 1932 a dictator named Antonio Salazar came to power in Portugal. Mozambique was given a new status, that of province, that seemed to involve more autonomy*. In fact Portugal kept a harsh grip on its Mozambique. The colonial authorities forced the indigenous population to grow cotton, rice, and other cash crops* for export. The workers received little or no pay, so Portuguese companies could obtain these products very cheaply and make enormous profits on the world market.

Portugal also declared that Mozambicans who adopted the Portuguese language and culture could gain citizenship and rights. But in practice very few Africans could qualify, allowing the whites to justify their own dominance. During the 1950s and 1960s, thousands more Portuguese settlers came to Mozambique to claim the opportunities denied to indigenous people.

Meanwhile, the Salazar regime gave the Roman Catholic Church full responsibility for educating and converting black Mozambicans. The church's mission was to provide only a basic education and to instill discipline so that the Portuguese could rely on Africans as a source of cheap labor. As a result, the vast majority of Africans in Mozambique remained illiterate.

These policies continued to devastate black communities in Mozambique. Rural areas lost hundreds of thousands of their most productive members, while the emphasis on growing export crops left little land for food crops. Debt, famines, disease, and other problems all increased. The few Africans who lived in urban areas endured segregation and filthy slums.

Independence and After. By the 1950s a number of black leaders emerged in Mozambique to oppose colonial rule. In 1962, several groups united as the Mozambique Liberation Front (FRELIMO), a political party that spearheaded the movement for independence. Two years later, under its leader Eduardo MONDLANE, FRELIMO took up arms and launched a guerrilla* war. For more than a decade, the rebels fought to liberate areas of the country. They abolished the cash crop system so that people could grow food for themselves and the army, and they helped open free clinics, schools, and orphanages. In 1974, Portuguese officers overthrew the dictatorship in Portugal and ended the war.

* **guerrilla** type of warfare involving sudden raids by small groups of warriors

* **socialism** economic or political system based on the idea that the government or groups of workers should own and run the means of production and distribution of goods

* **nationalize** to bring land, industries, or public works under state control or ownership

Independence came in 1975, but peace and progress did not. Thousands of Portuguese settlers left the country, taking their skills and wealth. Before leaving they killed cattle and destroyed property and machinery, which had a ruinous effect on the economy.

FRELIMO and its leader, Samora MACHEL, established a one-party state based on socialism*. The government nationalized* all industry and abolished private ownership of land. It also provided a safe haven for black rebels who were fighting the white minority governments of SOUTH

101

Mozambique

Republic of Mozambique

POPULATION:
19,104,696 (2000 estimated population)

AREA:
308,642 sq. mi. (799,384 sq. km)

LANGUAGES:
Portuguese (official); Sena, Shona, Makua, Swahili, and others

NATIONAL CURRENCY:
Metical

PRINCIPAL RELIGIONS:
Traditional 50%, Christian 30%, Muslim 20%

CITIES:
Maputo (capital), 3,025,000 (2000 est.); Tete, Beira, Quelimane, Sofala

ANNUAL RAINFALL:
55 in. (1,420 mm) in center, less in the north and south

ECONOMY:
GDP per capita: $1,000 (1999 est.)

PRINCIPAL PRODUCTS AND EXPORTS:
Agricultural: cashews, cotton, sugar, corn, cassava, tea, tobacco, rice, tropical fruits, beef, poultry
Manufacturing: chemicals, petroleum products, textiles, food and beverage processing, cement, glass
Mining: coal, titanium, tantalite, some gold, mineral sands

GOVERNMENT:
Independence from Portugal, 1975. Republic with president elected by popular vote. Governing bodies: Assembliea da Republica (legislature) with 250 seats elected by popular vote; Cabinet and prime minister appointed by the president.

HEADS OF STATE SINCE INDEPENDENCE:
1975–1986 President Samora Machel
1986– President Joaquim Alberto Chissano

ARMED FORCES:
6,100

EDUCATION:
Compulsory for ages 7–14; literacy rate 40%

AFRICA and Rhodesia (present-day ZIMBABWE and ZAMBIA). In 1976 Rhodesia began to supply arms and funding to an opposition movement in Mozambique. With additional backing from South Africa, the Mozambique National Resistance Movement (RENAMO) launched armed strikes against FRELIMO that developed into a bloody civil war by 1982.

In 1986 FRELIMO abandoned socialism. It accepted loans from the World Bank and the International Monetary Fund, international organizations that required Mozambique to change its economic system so that it could produce enough money to pay back the loans. The government sold off many state industries, often to foreign investors. It devalued its currency, which caused the country's poor people to become even poorer. Hardship, unemployment, and unrest grew amid a few economic success stories.

Meanwhile, FRELIMO reached a cease-fire with RENAMO in 1992 and opened elections to other political parties. Although the 1999 elections drew wide protests by RENAMO supporters, FRELIMO managed to cling to power. The government has pursued new goals for industry and tourism and has introduced a program to combat poverty by empowering women.

ECONOMY

Mozambique's economy is still in transition from socialism to capitalism*. The economy has grown and has benefited a few people in business and government. Despite new optimism, Mozambique faces a great challenge to develop its agriculture and industry and overcome the poverty of its people.

* **capitalism** economic system in which businesses are privately owned and operated and where free markets coordinate most economic activity

* **subsistence farming** raising only enough food to live on

* **sorghum** family of tropical grasses used for food

See map in Minerals and Mining (vol. 3).

* **hydroelectric power** power produced by converting the energy of flowing water into electricity

* **Islamic** relating to Islam, the religion based on the teachings of the prophet Muhammad

Agriculture is the primary economic activity in Mozambique. Most people engage in subsistence farming*, growing corn and sorghum* and raising cattle, goats, sheep, and chickens. In the most fertile areas, however, large plantations have replaced family farms since the early 1900s. The plantations employ many laborers to produce cash crops, especially cashew nuts, sugar cane, cotton, and tea. However, this large-scale agriculture did not perform well under socialism and has suffered from a series of droughts.

Mozambique has a large fishing industry, and shrimp is the country's major export. However, the shrimp industry faces a growing threat—the destruction of coastal mangrove forests where most of the shrimp live and breed. Overfishing also poses a danger, although the government has recently set limits on how much fish and shrimp can be caught.

Mozambique currently produces iron ore, titanium metal, oil, and natural gas. Small industries exist to refine oil, process aluminum, and manufacture textiles, machinery, chemicals, and cement. However, these activities employ only a small percentage of the population. Mozambique's industry suffers from corruption, outdated technology, a shortage of roads and rail lines, and a shortage of electrical power.

The nation's many rivers are a great resource that could be used for hydroelectric power*. The giant Cabora Bassa dam on the Zambezi River does produce electricity, but most of this power is sold to South Africa and not used to develop Mozambique itself.

PEOPLE AND CULTURE

Mozambique has a great diversity of ethnic groups and ways of life. From the far corners of the country near Lake Malawi to the bustling cities and shores, Mozambican life is both traditional and in transition.

The great majority of Mozambicans belong to related ethnic groups that speak Bantu languages. The largest Bantu group, the Makua-Lomwe, lives mainly north of the Zambezi River. Along the northern coast, many residents speak Swahili and are part of the Islamic* culture and religion. The Nguni peoples are a smaller group who migrated to Mozambique from South Africa in the 1800s. While more information is being learned about the people of Mozambique, very little historical information exists. Both the Portuguese colonial leaders and native leaders such as ex-president Samora Machel were reluctant to gather information on the different ethnic groups that populate the country. Instead they attempted to present the image of a unified Mozambique in which all people used a common language and shared similar goals. Those attempts at unification largely failed.

Most Mozambicans live in rural areas and follow traditional lifestyles based on KINSHIP relations. Many groups north of the Zambezi River have a matrilineal society in which people trace descent through the female side of the family. Most groups south of the Zambezi have patrilineal descent through the male side of the family. Today, growing numbers of Mozambicans are moving to the capital city of Maputo and other urban areas in search of opportunities. (*See also* **Colonialism in Africa, Ethnic Groups and Identity, Independence Movements, Ivory Trade, Plantation Systems, Southern Africa, History.**)

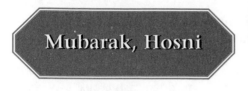

Mubarak, Hosni

1928–
President of Egypt

* **guerrilla** type of warfare involving sudden raids by small groups of warriors

* **Islamic** relating to Islam, the religion based on the teachings of the prophet Muhammad

* **militant** aggressive, willing to use force

Hosni Mubarak became president of EGYPT in 1981 after the assassination of Anwar SADAT. Reelected several times, Mubarak has steered Egypt through a difficult period marked by growing unrest, guerrilla* violence, and threats from Islamic* political groups.

Born in the Nile River delta to a peasant family, Mubarak graduated from the Cairo Military Academy in 1949. He embarked on a career in the Egyptian air force, rising steadily in rank. As commander in chief of the air force, he took charge of Egypt's air preparations for the Arab-Israel War of 1973. Because of Mubarak's outstanding service, President Anwar Sadat appointed him vice president in 1975.

After Sadat was assassinated, Mubarak took over the presidency. He sought solutions to Egypt's economic and social problems and tried to curb the corruption that had marred Sadat's last years in office. Although Mubarak encouraged Western and Arab investment in Egypt, he limited the role of foreign corporations in the country.

In foreign affairs, Mubarak maintained close ties to the United States. He also began repairing Egypt's relations with other Arab countries, which had been damaged when Sadat signed a peace treaty with Israel. In 1990 Mubarak attempted to resolve a dispute between Iraq and Kuwait. When Iraq invaded Kuwait the following year, causing the Persian Gulf War, Mubarak supported the United States and its allies and sent troops to assist in the military campaign.

In the 1990s Mubarak faced rising economic and social unrest in Egypt. In addition, he had to deal with growing political opposition and militant* Islamic groups. He escaped an assassination attempt in 1995 and was slightly wounded in another attack four years later. Throughout his presidency, Mubarak has played an important role in trying to bring about peace in the Middle East. (*See also* **North Africa: History and Cultures.**)

Mugabe, Robert

1924–
President of Zimbabwe

Robert Mugabe has been the leader of ZIMBABWE since the country achieved independence in 1980. Born and educated in a Catholic mission in the British colony of Southern Rhodesia, Mugabe became a teacher. In 1956 he moved to the newly independent nation of GHANA. Several years later, he returned to his home country and entered politics. At the time, white colonists led by Ian Smith controlled the government.

Mugabe founded a political party called the Zimbabwe African Peoples Union (ZAPU). When it split along ethnic lines between SHONA and NDEBELE members, he joined the Shona-dominated Zimbabwe African National Union (ZANU). In 1963 he fled Southern Rhodesia after being charged with speaking out against the government. He returned in 1964 and was jailed for almost ten years. International pressure and civil war finally toppled Smith's government, and in 1980 Mugabe was chosen prime minister in the country's first free elections. However, political rivalry with ZAPU soon led to another civil war. Mugabe and ZANU eventually won the struggle, and in 1987 Mugabe became the first president of Zimbabwe.

Mugabe achieved political success by bringing opponents into his government. He unified the two opposing political parties and named the leader of the former ZAPU party (a member of the rival Ndebele ethnic group) as vice president. He convinced white landowners to join his party to retain their political influence. However, Mugabe's rule gradually became harsher. By 2001, authorities were censoring and arresting those who criticized the government, and support for Mugabe was dwindling both among the people of Zimbabwe and among other nations. (*See also* **Colonialism in Africa; Independence Movements; Southern Africa, History.**)

Muhammad V

1909–1961
King of Morocco

King Muhammad V was the first ruler of MOROCCO after the country gained its independence from France in 1956. Born Sidi Muhammad, the future king was the son of Sultan Moulay Yusuf. When Yusuf died in 1927, the French colonial authorities named the 18-year-old Muhammad as the new sultan. The French hoped to control the young ruler, but he soon attracted followers who demanded Moroccan independence.

During World War II Muhammad angered the French by allowing the formation of a local independence movement. In 1953 the French removed him from office and sent him out of the country. However, support for the sultan grew in his absence. He returned home in 1955 and helped win independence for Morocco the following year. Muhammad officially adopted the title of king in 1957. After his death he was succeeded by his son, who became King HASSAN II. (*See also* **Colonialism in Africa, Independence Movements, North Africa, History and Cultures.**)

Museveni, Yoweri

1944–
President of Uganda

* **pastoralist** someone who herds livestock

* **guerrilla** type of warfare involving sudden raids by small groups of warriors

Yoweri Museveni, a former political activist, became president of UGANDA in 1986. Under his leadership, Uganda has achieved considerable political stability and economic growth. As a youth Museveni organized a movement to prevent pastoralists* from being forced off their lands. He attended the University of Dar es Salaam in TANZANIA, where he led a student group dedicated to African independence. He later worked for Ugandan president Milton OBOTE.

In 1971 Idi AMIN DADA overthrew President Obote. Museveni then formed a guerrilla* group that fought Amin and toppled him in 1979. The following year Obote was chosen president in an election widely seen as fraudulent. Museveni organized another rebel group, the National Resistance Army, to challenge Obote. The rebels eventually seized power and Museveni became president in 1986.

As president, Museveni has created a strong, centralized state and a disciplined army. He has pursued free-market economic policies and has supported opposition movements in several neighboring countries. In 1995 he oversaw the adoption of a new Ugandan constitution. He won the presidential election held the following year and was reelected in 2001.

Music and Song

* **genre**   type of literary or artistic work

* **rite**   ceremony or formal procedure

From the rural farmlands of MOZAMBIQUE to the booming dance halls of NIGERIA, music plays an essential role in the lives of Africans. Many regions have rich, deeply rooted traditions of music and song. But Africans have also incorporated in their music various outside influences—of the Arabs who arrived on the continent long ago, of the Europeans who ruled until well into the 1900s, and of the modern Western media. These influences have brought a tremendous diversity to African music. Swing, jazz, rock, reggae, techno, and other popular forms have exploded into whole new genres* of African music that pour out of concert halls, nightclubs, and radio stations across the continent.

CHARACTERISTICS OF AFRICAN MUSIC

Africans include music in many aspects of their lives, from religious ceremonies to social gatherings to landmarks in the life cycle. For example, some societies hold INITIATION RITES for adolescents when they reach puberty. Boys and girls in these societies learn and perform certain songs as part of the rites*. Music also plays an important role in many traditional methods of healing. Peoples across the continent—from the Hamadsha of North Africa to the !Kung of SOUTH AFRICA—use music and dance to bring on states of meditation, ecstasy, trance, or SPIRIT POSSESSION that are believed to cure illness. In Nigeria, the Hausa play a lute and rattle to summon spirits that heal the sick.

Other kinds of social music include that of the *rebita* clubs of Luanda, ANGOLA, which draw on an urban tradition of ballroom dancing. Many southern Africans enjoy gathering around radios and record players for dancing. In such settings, people may be divided by age, gender, or class. But not all African music is performed with a group or for an audience. People also play instruments or sing to themselves for pleasure and to relieve stress.

Words play an important role in African music. In many African societies, music is closely linked to the ORAL TRADITION of spoken or recited literature. Storytelling frequently includes songs, and some forms of music mimic the spoken word. "Talking drum" music uses drumbeats with different tones to echo the sounds of language. Many musical forms are based on the singing and storytelling, and musicians sometimes use their instruments as voices that speak a language.

African music is rarely just for instruments. Musicians and listeners alike take great interest in the lyrics. Singing styles range from solo performances to large group participation. When singing in a group, individuals may sing the same words together. However, in a style known as polyphonic, each person voices a different phrase or syllable to create a variety of vocal patterns and combinations.

In Africa, music is generally considered inseparable from words, dance, and the occasion for which it is performed. It is not linked to specific notes and rhythms within measured units of time. Instead, African musicians play music based on their own individual sense of rhythm or on rhythmic phrases they have learned. Although a drum or rattle may keep a steady rhythm, other players may not use it as a basis for the beats they play or for how they accent notes in the music.

REGIONAL AFRICAN MUSIC

Students of African music are sometimes puzzled by the striking similarities that can be heard in various parts of the continent. For example, people in Mozambique on the Indian Ocean and IVORY COAST and LIBERIA in western Africa play similar-sounding music on log xylophones. Some songs and dances in western UGANDA and TANZANIA resemble those of the HERERO people in faraway NAMIBIA. These similarities may reflect the complex crisscrossing and migration of peoples and cultures in Africa's history.

North Africa. North African music reflects the long influence of Arab culture. The region shares many songs, musical styles, and instruments with cultures of the Middle East. Yet Arab musical traditions have developed in different ways throughout the region. One example is the *nawba* or *nuba,* a traditional composition in several parts, like a symphony or suite in Western classical music. In recent years, governments and private organizations have sponsored a revival of the *nawba,* which has taken on different regional forms. In EGYPT and LIBYA, it has eight parts and uses the lute, zither, violin, flute, and drum. The different style of *nawba* that appears in ALGERIA, TUNISIA, and MOROCCO may have originated in Spain.

North Africa has also produced its own unique styles. Some popular music draws on the musical heritage of the southern parts of Libya, Tunisia, and Algeria. The extremely popular *rai* began hundreds of years ago in the Algerian countryside. In the early 1900s, young Algerian singers—many of them women—gave *rai* a new twist by composing songs with political lyrics. In time *rai* became the music of rebellious young people, and youth now dance to it in Algerian and Moroccan clubs. *Rai* musicians combine traditional instruments such as clay drums with modern Western ones such as electric guitars and synthesizers. The energetic sound of Cheb Mami, Cheb Khaled, and other *rai* musicians is winning fans around the world.

Not all North African music emerges from Arab culture. The BERBERS of western North Africa have their own traditions. A *rwai* is a group of Berber artists that performs poetry and dance as well as music; an *imdyazn* is a group of four traveling musicians that performs in village marketplaces. Berber, Arab, and Western musical styles sometimes merge, as in Moroccan *chaabi* music, known for songs with a political or social message. People use songs to make political statements in many parts of North Africa. In SUDAN, the two sides in a civil conflict sing the praises of their rival leaders.

Western Africa. People throughout western Africa have developed various types of traditional music to suit different religious, political, and social events. The Songhai perform a style of religious music called *follay,* in which each of their divinities is honored with its own special melodies and rhythms. Songhai teenagers sing to one another during courtship, and music is played at wrestling matches as well as at dances. Among many groups, music plays a central role at funerals. For the LoDagaa of GHANA, funerals include special songs and dances, each spe-

Whisper Songs

The people of Burundi in East Africa perform a unique type of music known as inanga chuchotée. *Its name comes from the instrument it is played on, a wooden zither called the* inanga, *and the French word* chuchotée, *meaning "whispered." While plucking out a melody on the strings of his* inanga, *the performer whispers a text.*

Inanga chuchotée *is performed in quiet, intimate settings where the audience listens carefully to the music. The musician sits on a low stool and keeps his head very close to the face of his instrument. His whispers blend with the soft sounds of the strings, so that the* inanga *itself seems to speak.*

107

Music and Song

* **Islam** religion based on the teachings of the prophet Muhammad; religious faith of Muslims

* **savanna** tropical or subtropical grassland with scattered trees and drought-resistant undergrowth

cific to a certain part of the event. They use one style of performance for funerals of men and another for those of women.

As Islam* spread from North Africa into the savanna* country of western Africa, it carried Arab culture with it. The Hassaniya people of Mauritania have developed music based on instruments and singing styles similar to those of North Africa. In Nigeria, Niger, and Chad, the state music performed at the courts of the Hausa and Kanuri peoples includes drums mounted on horses or camels. It is a rich expression of the North African Islamic tradition.

Elsewhere in western Africa, popular music blends local elements with influences from Europe and the Americas. Ironically, many of the European and American genres that have come to Africa—such as American ragtime and rap and Caribbean rumba and reggae—were developed by people whose African ancestors left Africa as slaves. These blended forms are very popular with the young people of urban areas.

Blended music has a long history. The drum music called *goombay,* which started in Jamaica, reached western Africa around 1800. There local people embraced and adapted it. During the 1800s colonial armies and Protestant missionaries introduced marching band music and new instruments such as trombones. In the 1900s musicians on the West African coast blended African drums with the guitars, banjos, and harmonicas of foreign sailors to create a group of styles known together as "palm wine music." These genres include the *maringa* of Sierra Leone, the *makossa* of Cameroon, and the blues of the Asante people of Ghana.

During World War II (1939–1945), nightclubs flourished in the West African cities where British and American troops were based, exposing local musicians to such foreign styles as jazz, swing, calypso, and Afro-Cuban music. After the war, musicians in Ghana mixed this lively brew into a style called highlife. Played by small swing groups, highlife spread through western Africa, and it often had a rebellious edge. People knew that one of the first and most influential highlife bands, the Tempos, favored independence.

As early as the 1950s, the newly independent nations of western Africa adopted policies that encouraged women to be artists and performers. Some women won fame on their own or with bands, while others had government support, such as the Workers Brigade bands in Ghana. Independence also brought a renewed interest in African cultural roots, and some entertainers began using traditional instruments in their performances or playing traditional music on Western-style electric instruments.

* **indigenous** native to a certain place

West African musicians created powerful fusions of Latin, Afro-Cuban, and indigenous* dance music in forms known as Afro-rock, Afro-soul, Afro-beat, and more. They often turned their talents to political commentary. Alpha Blondy of Ivory Coast had a worldwide hit with his Afro-reggae song, "Apartheid is Nazism," which criticized the South African policy of apartheid—racial segregation to maintain white control over the country's black population. Fela Anikulapo-Kuti, a huge star in Nigeria, was censored, harassed, and jailed by his own government.

African popular music often reflects both traditional sources and foreign influence. Singer Salif Keôta of Mali, shown here in concert, became an international star in the 1980s. His music combines acoustic instruments and female vocal choruses with modern synthesizers and drum machines.

* **clan** group of people descended from a common ancestor

Eastern Africa. Although the traditional music of eastern Africa has been used for many purposes, it played a central role in royal courts. Kings and chiefs of the region carried special drums to symbolize their power. The ruler of Buganda once kept several musical groups in his court, including a private harpist, a group of six flutes and four drums, and a band of trumpeters. In some kingdoms, royal musicians had special privileges, such as the right to own land, and they passed on their skills only within their own family or clan*.

Since the 1930s many styles of popular music have emerged in eastern Africa to entertain audiences in urban dance halls, clubs, and bars. Almost all use the guitar as the main instrument. A Tanzanian dance group, for example, might feature three guitars, a bass, trumpets, saxophones, drums, and percussion. Although such dance music uses modern instruments, it is deeply rooted in local musical traditions.

Some of the most popular and widespread genres of dance music feature songs in SWAHILI, the main local language and one used by traders on the eastern coast. But in recent years, people have been writing songs in other local languages, especially in KENYA and Uganda. The lyrics may comment on everyday life, love, current affairs, or politics. The ruling groups of some countries have recognized that music can serve educational purposes and have used songs to communicate information to their people—though they often portray musicians as loafers or drunkards. Authorities also view many singers and songwriters as social critics and frequently censor or ban their songs.

Not all modern eastern African music comes through the urban dance hall. Some genres belong to social occasions, especially celebrations. The best-known of these is *taarab,* the wedding music of the Islamic Swahili-speaking people of the east coast and nearby islands. *Taarab* is sung poetry, and while the words often speak of love and marriage, they also deal with politics and society in general. Female *taarab* expressing the concerns of women has enjoyed great popularity. *Taarab* groups perform wherever Swahili speakers live, and their music has reached wide audiences through radio and recordings.

See color plate 3, vol. 1.

Southern Africa. As in other parts of Africa, southern Africa has a rich heritage of traditional music, used in religious, political, and social settings. The Sotho of LESOTHO play a unique type of music by blowing on an instrument called the *lisiba,* which is made of a stick, a string, and a feather. They use the music both as an accompaniment to cattle herding activities and as a means of controlling their animals. In Zambia, music takes center stage during an important ritual of the Lozi people. They celebrate the annual rising of the river with a procession to higher ground, carrying a national drum called the *maoma,* which may be played only by royal men. The festival includes two days of dances and drumming.

Western folk, religious, and popular music have had considerable influence in southern Africa, perhaps more so than in other parts of the continent. In addition, musicians in MALAWI, ZIMBABWE, Mozambique, and parts of Angola have been swayed by the jazz style known as *soukous,* which comes from CONGO (KINSHASA). Despite these outside influences, southern Africa has developed distinct local and regional styles, and elements of traditional indigenous music remain alive in the music of today.

In southern as in western Africa, colonial army bands and Christian missionaries introduced new musical instruments and styles. Church hymns had a great impact. In the early 1900s, southern African musicians absorbed foreign ragtime and vaudeville tunes and combined them with rural traditional music to create many local popular genres, often featuring guitars. Beginning in the 1930s, South Africa developed its own version of jazz. Bands blended jazz and swing with a local hymn style called *marabi,* which gives a distinctive flavor to South African jazz, such as the work of pianist Abdullah Ibrahim.

A style called *mbaqanga,* based on the guitar music of Zulu-speaking migrant laborers, dominated southern African popular music from the 1950s through the 1980s. Western rock music and African American soul appeared in the 1970s. More recently, reggae and rap have caught on. Some of the world's best-known reggae artists, such as Lucky Dube of South Africa, now come from southern Africa.

Another important trend has been the growing international interest in southern African song and music. Groups such as the South African choir Ladysmith Black Mambazo have become part of the "world beat" movement, which has introduced Western audiences to popular and traditional music from other cultures.

South Africa's musicians have rarely escaped the effects of the country's racial politics. In the 1960s a number of talented black performers fled the country. Some, such as trumpeter Hugh Masakela and singer Miriam Makeba, became international stars. Others took part in the struggle against apartheid. For example, Johnny Clegg was not only a musical star of the 1980s, but a leading activist against apartheid. His band of both white and black musicians appealed to many people as an image of what South Africa might look like without racial barriers. (*See also* **Dance, Musical Instruments.**)

Musical Instruments

* **savanna** tropical or subtropical grassland with scattered trees and drought-resistant undergrowth

Wall paintings in ancient Egyptian tombs show that the people of Africa have made and played musical instruments for thousands of years. Over the centuries, the many invaders of Africa introduced new instruments. Arabs brought musical instruments and styles that became part of the culture of North Africa, the western savanna*, and the eastern coast. European colonial armies and missionaries introduced Western instruments such as brass horns. Urban musicians of modern Africa have adopted Western electric instruments—guitar, bass, and synthesizer—to create exciting new music.

Yet from the dance halls to the rural farmlands, many musicians still play the traditional instruments of Africa. Some of these instruments are unique to Africa, although they are related to instruments used elsewhere in the world. Their sounds—ancient and deeply rooted in the land—help create the distinctive qualities of African music.

CHARACTERISTICS OF AFRICAN INSTRUMENTS

Most traditional musicians fashion their own instruments. The types of instruments they make—and the sounds produced—depend on the materials available. A person setting out to make an instrument draws on a wealth of knowledge about the properties of local materials.

Wood determines the sound qualities of many instruments. In central and southern Africa, musicians favor *kiaat* or sneezewood, which produce a rich, resonant sound. A xylophone made in southern Mozambique is an environmental masterpiece that uses at least 15 natural materials, including gourds, beeswax, palm leaf, and rubber. Africans have developed great skill in creating special sounds and tex-

Musical Instruments

Popular in parts of West Africa, the *kora* has 20 or more strings stretched over a double bridge. It is commonly referred to as a "harp-lute."

tures by adding assorted objects—from seed pods to bottle caps—to their instruments.

A key feature of African music is that when instruments are played together, each is supposed to be heard separately. Musicians in a group usually value contrast more than the blending of sounds. They choose and tune their instruments carefully so that each has its own recognizable voice contributing to a sort of musical conversation or storytelling.

Musicians in sub-Saharan* Africa frequently increase their instruments' contrast and texture by adding buzzing devices to the instruments. Buzzers can be made of many materials, including loosely attached metal rings, bells, shells, beads, seeds, string, grass, or bottle tops. Some buzzers, called mirlitons, consist of membranes* that vibrate when air moves through an instrument. For example, when a player strikes a xylophone made of gourds, the gourds vibrate and push air against the membrane, which makes a buzzing or humming sound. Africans have made mirlitons from countless materials, including cow intestines, spider egg sacs, carbon paper, and plastic bags.

TYPES OF INSTRUMENTS

African musical instruments can be groups into several large families according to the part of the instrument that vibrates to make sound. These include aerophones—wind instruments; chordophones—stringed instruments; membranophones—drums; and idiophones, which produce sound when the instrument's body or part of it vibrates.

Aerophones are basically tubes. The player blows into or across a hole in the tube to produce the sound. Across the continent, people play simple pipes that produce only one note. When playing in a group, each player inserts his or her note into the total pattern at the right moment. African musicians also use panpipes, several pipes fastened together to give the player a choice of several notes.

In North Africa and regions of Arab influence, some musicians play aerophones with vibrating reeds in the mouthpieces, similar to the oboes and clarinets of the West. Examples include the North African *shawn,* an ancestor of the modern oboe; the Tunisian *mezonad,* a version of the bagpipe; and the Egyptian *arghul,* a type of double clarinet.

Chordophones produce sounds when strings are plucked or strummed. The harps that people play in much of Africa sometimes show a remarkable resemblance to ancient Egyptian harps. Ethiopia and other eastern African countries have long favored the lyre, an ancient instrument with a skin-covered body, two necks, and strings that stretch from the bottom of the body to the ends of the necks. A related instrument, the lute, has only one neck. The lute player may pluck the strings or rub them with a bow. Bowed lutes are widely used in North African and Arab music, as are the *rahab,* a type of fiddle, and the oud, a wooden lute as popular in Arab music as the guitar in Western music.

The most magnificent of all African chordophones may be the *kora* of Guinea and neighboring countries. A large round gourd forms the body, covered in skin, and at least 21 strings stretch down from a tall wooden neck across the body. It is held upright by a seated musician. The *kora* is

* **sub-Saharan**   referring to Africa south of the Sahara desert

* **membrane**   thin sheet of tissue, cloth, skin, or other material

113

the instrument of choice of the griots, professional musicians and storytellers whose long history began in the royal courts of West African chiefs, kings, and emperors.

Struck with hands or sticks, the sounds of drums resonate almost everywhere in Africa. Drummers in western Africa have developed the greatest varieties and specialties of membranophones. Though they come in an enormous range of shapes and sizes, drums are of two main types—closed and open. In closed drums, the airspace within the drum is completely sealed. The drum may have one membrane that the player strikes, or it may have membranes on top and bottom. Open drums have only one membrane and are not completely enclosed. Closed drums have a clearer musical pitch but little variety of sound, while open drums make more sounds possible. The sound of each drum is affected by the shape and materials of the drum body. Tambourines are also membranophones.

African musicians have a long tradition of inventing and making small handheld idiophones such as rattles and bells. Xylophones are also idiophones. They consist of a row of wooden slats mounted on a frame and tuned to produce various notes when struck. Sometimes the maker adds hollow bodies such as gourds to amplify the sounds of the slats or buzzing devices for added textures. Some African xylophones require as many as four players.

The *mbira* is a wooden soundboard with a row of several narrow metal keys mounted on it. A bar fixes one end of the keys to the board, while a bridge raises the other end. The player plucks the ends of the keys with thumbs or fingers. From South Africa to Uganda to Sierra Leone, more than 200 types of *mbira* exist. People often play the *mbira* casually, in public or alone, while walking, at parties, or simply to pass the time. In Zimbabwe and the valley of the Zambezi River, however, the *mbira* is played at all-night religious ceremonies involving ancestral spirits. This ancient instrument may have originated in that region, but today it joins the African musical tradition across a large part of the continent. (*See also* **Dance, Music and Song, Theater.**)

Mutapa

* **dynasty** succession of rulers from the same family or group

Mutapa, or Mwene Mutapa (meaning "Ravager of the Lands"), is the title held by a dynasty* of kings that ruled the area that is now ZIMBABWE and MOZAMBIQUE from the 1400s to the 1880s. Historians also use the term to refer to the state led by these kings. The Mutapa state probably arose from branches of the nearby culture of Great Zimbabwe.

Mutapa rulers were members of the *nzou*, or elephant clan, and were said to be descendants of a legendary king named Mbire. Nyatsimba, who ruled in the late 1400s, was the first to take the title Mwene Mutapa. During the 1500s, the kings attempted to expand their territory. However, in most cases, those who were sent to conquer new lands for Mutapa set up independent dynasties of their own.

The heart of the Mutapa state was the territory of Mukaranga, a region of fertile soil, valuable grazing land, and rich deposits of gold. Although most people lived by farming, some mined gold and hunted elephants for ivory. Half of the gold and ivory collected went to the Mutapa ruler. The rest was used in trading for imported cloth and beads. Trade included expeditions to the Zambezi River and to ports on the Indian Ocean as well as a lively exchange with Muslim and Portuguese merchants living under Mutapa rule.

In the 1570s Portuguese forces invaded the Mutapa state. After conquering the region in the mid-1600s, they quickly exhausted its gold fields. Many of the original inhabitants of Mutapa died or migrated to other areas. Frequent civil wars ravaged the state during the 1600s and 1700s. The power of the Mutapa rulers gradually declined, and by the 1880s the Mutapa state had faded away.

Mutesa II, Frederick

**1924–1969
Ruler of Buganda**

Frederick Mutesa II, known as "King Freddie" by Westerners, was ruler of the East African state of Buganda from 1939 to 1953. Buganda enjoyed special treatment within the British colony of UGANDA until 1953. When the British decided to end Buganda's special status, Mutesa demanded independence for his kingdom. When he also refused to pass along British recommendations to his parliament, the British arrested and deported him.

Bugandan leaders arranged for Mutesa's return in 1955 as king of Buganda, under a more limited system of British control. He served in that role until Uganda won its independence in 1963. President Milton OBOTE tried to appoint Mutesa to a position in the Ugandan government, but the two men argued over Mutesa's role and the status of Buganda within the new nation. Conflict erupted when Mutesa tried to stir up trouble between residents of northern Uganda and those in his southern kingdom. The dispute grew until 1966, when Obote forced Mutesa into exile in Britain. Mutesa died three years later. (*See also* **Kings and Kingship.**)

Mvemba Nzinga

**ca. 1465–1543
Ruler of kingdom of Kongo**

* **polygamy** marriage in which a man has more than one wife or a woman has more than one husband

Mvemba Nzinga, son of the ruler of the kingdom of Kongo, was baptized as a Christian in 1491 and took the name Afonso I. When his father died in 1506, Mvemba Nzinga became king, claiming that he had divine help in gaining the throne. He increased his power by selling ivory, copper, and slaves to Portuguese traders in exchange for exotic European goods. He then gave these valuable items to his officials and allies as rewards. Later, Mvemba Nzinga tried unsuccessfully to bypass local Portuguese merchants and deal directly with traders in Lisbon, Portugal.

An enthusiastic student of Christian teachings, Mvemba Nzinga erected churches throughout the country. He sent young nobles, including his son Henrique, to study in Portugal. Despite his Christianity, though, Mvemba Nzinga continued to practice polygamy*. Some historians believe he allowed himself to be used by cooperating with the Portuguese. Others point out that Mvemba Nzinga used his trade relationship with Portugal to strengthen his own power and expand his kingdom.

115

Mythology

* **deity**   god or goddess

* **Islam**   religion based on the teachings of the prophet Muhammad; religious faith of Muslims

* **sub-Saharan**   referring to Africa south of the Sahara desert

* **ritual**   religious ceremony that follows a set pattern

* **pantheon**   all the gods and goddesses of a particular culture

Conversations with Ogotemmeli

Scholars have long relied on individuals as a source for the stories and themes of African mythology. No informant is more famous than Ogotemmeli of the Dogon people of Mali. A hunter who lost his sight in an accident and was gifted with exceptional intelligence and wisdom, Ogotemmeli spent a month telling French researcher Marcel Griaule about Dogon beliefs and sacred myths. Griaule's 1948 book, Conversations with Ogotemmeli, *describes myths of the creation of the world and the origins of the social order. As Griaule discovered, Dogon traditional beliefs are complex and detailed—it takes seven days, for example, to recite the Dogon cosmology.*

Myths are the stories that define a culture. They tell of the creation or beginning of the world; of deities* and their relations with humans; and of the values, heroes, and histories of a group or society. Cosmological myths—those about the origin, structure, or purpose of the universe—reveal a culture's ideas about the universe. With the passage of time, myths may develop into legends or folk tales. They begin, however, as sacred stories, often intertwined with religious belief. In North Africa, where Islam* has been the dominant religion for centuries, mythology is filled with Islamic elements. In sub-Saharan* Africa, mythology reflects the great diversity of beliefs and cultural traditions that can be found in the region.

Egyptian Mythology. The oldest known mythology in Africa is that of ancient EGYPT. In other parts of the continent, mythologies still form the basis for rituals*, stories, and literature. Ancient Egyptian mythology, however, is no longer part of any living culture, and our knowledge of it comes only from documents and inscriptions that are thousands of years old.

Ancient Egyptian mythology included a large pantheon* of national, regional, and local gods and goddesses. Priests and worshippers devoted to individual deities tended temples regarded as the dwelling places of the gods and goddesses. Many deities were associated with particular animals. The god Horus, for example, was frequently portrayed with the head of a falcon, and the goddess Sekhmet was shown as a lioness or a cat-headed woman.

One group of Egyptian myths concerns the creation of the world and of the gods. In some versions the gods are born from the sweat of the creator spirit, while humans emerge from the creator's tears. Other myths deal with the cycle of day and night. According to these stories, day begins with the birth of the sun god, who crosses the sky in a boat. Each night the sun god travels through the underworld, or land of the dead, where various enemies oppose him, trying to prevent the sun from rising again the next day.

Among the most widely told Egyptian myths were those about the god Osiris, his sister-wife Isis, and their son Horus. Isis's magical restoration of Osiris, who was cruelly butchered by his brother Set, is a mythical treatment of the cycle of birth, death, and rebirth. Battles between Set and Horus, who sought to avenge his father's death, depict the struggle between good and evil. In the end, Osiris travels to the underworld to judge the dead and deal out punishment and reward to souls in the afterlife, an idea that was central to the religious belief of the ancient Egyptians.

Islamic Mythology. North Africa and areas of East and West Africa have been deeply influenced by Islam. The Qur'an, Islam's holy book, is the primary source of Islamic mythology about creation and the afterlife. Muhammad, the Arab prophet who founded Islam in the A.D. 600s, became the focus of many legends, as did members of his family. As these legends and traditions grew, they incorporated elements from the mythology and folklore of the various regions that adopted Islam.

* **monotheistic** believing in only one god

* **supernatural** related to forces beyond the normal world; magical or miraculous

A monotheistic* faith, Islam does not have a pantheon of deities but does include various supernatural* beings, such as angels and demons. Less powerful than demons or angels, but still more powerful than humans, are fire or air spirits called jinn, who appear in many North African folk tales. A jinn (or genie) may be good or evil. Although jinn are tricky and mischievous, many tales tell of people gaining power over jinn and forcing them to carry out their wishes.

Mythological Themes. Africa has a multitude of mythological traditions that developed over thousands of years. Sometimes these traditions have become mixed with elements introduced from outside the continent, such as Islam or Christianity. Even many Muslim and Christian Africans, for example, still hold to the traditional African belief that the spirits of ancestors continue to be part of the community. Until modern times, the myths of sub-Saharan Africa were part of an ORAL TRADITION that passed beliefs and information from generation to generation within each community through the spoken word. Africans have illustrated mythological stories in carvings of wood, ivory, and clay and have acted them out in DANCE.

Among the themes commonly found in African mythology are creation, the idea of a lost paradise, heroes who bring civilization to humans, and the arrival of death in the world. African mythologies contain many deities. Although a creator deity often reigns supreme over the others, he or she may be remote from the world and unconcerned with its daily happenings, leaving humans to interact with lesser gods.

In addition to the deities, the universe is filled with spirits, supernatural beings that are either good or evil. People, animals, plants, elements such as fire and water, and landforms such as mountains and rivers may all possess spirits that must be treated with the proper respect to prevent them from doing harm. Magicians and diviners* are thought to control these spirits.

* **diviner** person who predicts the future or explains the causes of misfortune

Tricksters and Animals. The trickster is a mischievous figure that appears in various forms in African myths and legends. Fond of pranks, sometimes helpful, and sometimes causing harm, the trickster is also quick-witted and usually able to get out of trouble. In African tales, the trickster is often a small, helpless creature, such as a spider or a rabbit, who fools larger and more powerful animals. One African trickster story, for example, tells how Rabbit tricked Elephant and Hippopotamus into tugging on opposite ends of a rope, each thinking that Rabbit was on the other end. Their strenuous game cleared a field so that Rabbit could plant his crops.

Animals are characters in many sub-Saharan myths, often symbolizing human qualities or aspects of African cosmologies. In CONGO (KINSHASA), for example, animals called pangolins—a type of scaly anteater—have great symbolic significance. Though scaled like fish, pangolins have legs and climb trees like animals. Like humans, they give birth to one infant at a time. Some African peoples see these creatures as a symbol of the union of the different cosmic* realms of earth and sky. Another animal with symbolic importance in sub-Saharan Africa is the

* **cosmic** large or universal in scale; having to do with the universe

117

The ancient Egyptian god Horus receives
an offering. Shown here as a tall figure
with the head of a bird, Horus was one
of the most important figures in Egyptian
mythology.

leopard, which is widely associated with kingship. While Europeans may regard the lion as the "king of beasts," Africans place the smaller but more cunning and ferocious leopard in that role. Animals also appear in numerous African fables, many of which teach some moral lesson.

Color has important symbolic meanings as well in African mythology and cosmology. Societies throughout the continent recognize white, black, and red as the three primary colors. White typically represents enlightenment, good fortune, and purity. Red is the color of blood and symbolizes heat, energy, and violent change. Black stands for hidden or secret knowledge—either helpful wisdom and insight or dangerous magic. Color symbolism adds a dimension of meaning to many myths. Stories of the Luba people of Congo tell about the wise hero Mbidi Kiluwe, who is "black like the night," and his opponent, a red-skinned serpent named Nkongolo Mwamba. (*See also* **Art, Divination and Oracles, Masks and Masquerades, Religion and Ritual, Spirit Possession, Vodun, Witchcraft and Sorcery.**)

Mzilikazi

ca. 1790–1868
Founder of Ndebele kingdom

* **clan** group of people descended from a common ancestor

* **Afrikaner** South African of European descent who speaks Afrikaans

For a short time in the early 1800s, Mzilikazi served as a lieutenant in the army of the Zulu ruler SHAKA ZULU. After one battle, Mzilikazi kept the cattle he captured instead of sending them to Shaka. When the chief sent men to investigate, Mzilikazi insulted Shaka by cutting the feathers off their headdresses. Realizing that Shaka would be furious, Mzilikazi led several hundred followers north and established his own kingdom called Ndebele.

Mzilikazi built his kingdom by conquering local groups. His military tactics were devastating: his army surrounded villages at night and attacked at dawn, rhythmically beating their shields, killing all but young men and women, and burning the village to the ground. He incorporated the captive men in his army and gave the women of defeated enemies to his followers as wives. Refugees could join the Ndebele but were not allowed to marry until they had served in the army. Under Mzilikazi, the Ndebele moved often to expand their base of power and to escape the Zulu armies sent to pursue them.

During the 1830s Mzilikazi not only defeated Zulu armies, he also raided white settlements, capturing large numbers of livestock. Around 1840 he founded a capital at Bulawayo in what is now ZIMBABWE. From there, he led military campaigns against both local clans* and white Afrikaner* settlers. He forced the Afrikaners to sign a peace treaty in 1852. By this time, his kingdom included more than 20,000 people and had an extensive law code that covered every aspect of Ndebele life, including farming, war, marriage, and taxation. Mzilikazi controlled the region until the gold rush of 1860, when thousands of immigrants contested his rule. After Mzilikazi's death, his son LOBENGULA lost the struggle with the immigrants over land rights, and the Ndebele kingdom collapsed. (*See also* **Ndebele, Southern Africa, History.**)

Nairobi

Nairobi, the capital of KENYA, is the largest city in eastern Africa south of CAIRO, Egypt. British colonists founded Nairobi in 1899 as a camp for laborers who were building the railroad from the coastal city of Mombasa to Lake Victoria. A railway yard and depot were established, and the camp grew rapidly into a town. In 1905 the British named it the capital of the British East Africa Protectorate* (now Kenya).

Nairobi attracted a wide variety of people: Indian merchants, members of the GIKUYU ethnic group from the surrounding area, and white settlers. As Europeans forced the Gikuyu off their lands, more and more Gikuyu settled in Nairobi. Racial tensions eventually led to the MAU MAU uprising of the early 1950s. During this conflict Kenya's British colonial government imprisoned thousands of Africans in and near Nairobi.

After Kenya achieved independence in 1963, Nairobi prospered. However, the city's rapid growth caused a housing shortage, and people built makeshift homes, which the government often bulldozed. Such slums continue to be a feature of life in Nairobi.

Today Nairobi is a lively, modern city of about two million people whose main industry is TOURISM. A favorite destination of big game hunters from Europe and America in the early 1900s, the city serves as the gateway to East Africa's major wildlife parks. Modern tourists carry cameras instead of guns to the Amboseli, Tsavo, and Masaai Mara parks near Nairobi. Other major industries include food processing, cigarette and beverage production, and light manufacturing. Despite a fairly strong economy, Nairobi continues to suffer from a lack of jobs and adequate housing. (*See also* **Cities and Urbanization, Houses and Housing, Wildlife and Game Parks.**)

Namibia

The Republic of Namibia, which achieved independence in 1990, was the last country in Africa to throw off colonial rule. Although thinly populated and dominated by deserts, its great mineral wealth made it an attractive target for European colonizers. Namibia's natural riches continue to play a significant role in the country's economy. However, many years of colonialism have left deep scars in the social and economic fabric of the nation.

GEOGRAPHY

Namibia lies along the west coast of southern Africa. About twice the size of California, it has fewer than two million people. Its sparse population is due largely to the dry climate, which makes most of Namibia unsuitable for agriculture. However, the rugged and inhospitable terrain contains large deposits of gold, diamonds, uranium, and other valuable mineral resources.

Namibia consists of a high central plateau surrounded mostly by dry grasslands and deserts. The Namib Desert runs the length of the coast and stretches some 60 miles inland, while the KALAHARI DESERT covers

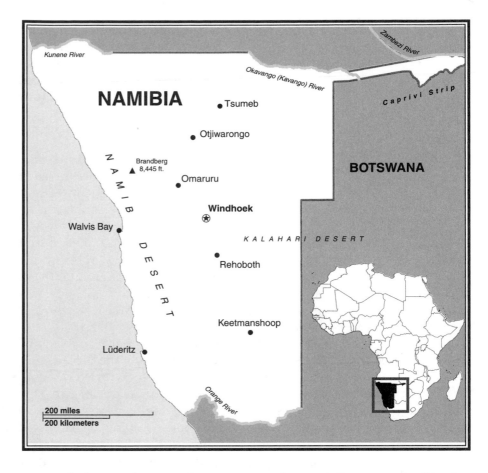

most of the northern and eastern portions of the country. To the south is a vast dry area known as Namaqualand. Wedged between these barren areas is the central plateau, which is home to most of Namibia's people. In the southeast, the Orange River forms Namibia's border with SOUTH AFRICA.

HISTORY AND GOVERNMENT

Before the mid-1800s Namibia was home to KHOISAN hunter-gatherers and some pastoralist* BANTU PEOPLES. By the 1850s, European traders had begun operating from Walvis Bay on the Namibian coast. Local HERERO peoples obtained guns from the traders and overthrew various Namibian states of the Oorlam peoples. As Oorlam power crumbled, settlers from what is now South Africa moved into the region and established a republic in southern Hereroland. This alarmed the Herero, who asked Britain to establish a protectorate* over central Namibia. The British declared a protectorate in 1876, but it included only the area around Walvis Bay.

German Colonization. In the 1880s a German entrepreneur named Adolf Lüderitz acquired some Namibian coastland. Germany set up a protectorate over the land in 1884 and later annexed* the entire coast except for Walvis Bay. In 1889 the Germans seized Walvis Bay and over the next 15 years gradually expanded their control over the interior by cooperating with some local chiefs and fighting others.

* **pastoralist**   someone who herds livestock

* **protectorate**   weak state under the control and protection of a strong state

* **annex**   to take over or add a territory to an existing area

121

Namibia

* **indigenous**   native to a certain place

Tensions between German settlers and indigenous* peoples led to full-scale war in 1904. More than 80 percent of the Herero and some 75 percent of the Nama people died during four years of fighting. Many survivors were placed in concentration camps, sent to other German colonies in Africa, or pressed into forced labor. Meanwhile, colonial officials gave ranch land to German settlers, and the discovery of diamonds and other minerals led to a growing colonial economy.

South African Domination. During World War I, troops from the Union of South Africa invaded Namibia and defeated the German troops there. After the war South Africa received international authorization to oversee Namibia, making it in effect a South African province. During the 1920s the South African government resettled hundreds of white families in Namibia to strengthen its control over the colony. The indigenous peoples rose up against South African rule several times during the 1920s and 1930s, but each revolt was crushed by South African forces.

After World War II South Africa adopted apartheid* laws and policies and applied them to Namibia as well. It also tried to convince the United Nations (UN) that Namibians wanted their country to become part of South Africa, but the UN rejected that claim. During the 1950s and 1960s, apartheid policies forced Namibian blacks off their lands and led to occasional outbreaks of violence. During this period, Namibian nationalists* founded the Southwest African Peoples Organization (SWAPO), which became the leading force in the struggle for independence.

* **apartheid**   policy of racial segregation enforced by the white government of South Africa to maintain political, economic, and social control over the country's blacks, Asians, and people of mixed ancestry

* **nationalist**   devoted to the interests and culture of one's country

* **guerrilla**   member of a fighting force outside the regular army that uses surprise raids against an enemy or government

In 1966 SWAPO guerrillas* in Namibia began an armed struggle against South African rule. The 1970s saw an intensified fight for independence. When neighboring ANGOLA became independent in 1975, it allowed SWAPO guerrillas to operate out of Angolan bases. South Africa responded by increasing the size of its army in Namibia and sending troops into Angola to attack SWAPO bases. The fighting took a toll on both the Namibian and the South African economies and eventually became unpopular with the South African people. In 1989 South Africa agreed to a cease-fire, and the following year it withdrew its troops. Namibia gained independence on March 21, 1990.

Namibia Since Independence. Namibia's president since independence has been Sam Nujoma, a prominent SWAPO leader. He overwhelmingly won elections in 1990 and 1994, but the nation's constitution limited him to two terms in office. In 1997 Nujoma announced his intention to run again in 1999 and called for a constitutional amendment to allow him to do so. His action led to a split in the SWAPO party and charges that Nujoma was trying to establish himself as a dictator. Despite the controversy, the amendment passed and Nujoma enjoyed another sweeping victory in 1999.

* **authoritarian**   relating to strong leadership with unrestricted powers

* **secede**   to withdraw formally from an organization or country

Nujoma has ruled Namibia in an authoritarian* style, rewarding his political supporters but neglecting those areas and groups loyal to his opponents. His policies have resulted in unrest in the Caprivi Strip in northeastern Namibia, which threatened to secede* in the late 1990s. Nujoma has also angered neighboring BOTSWANA by proposing to reroute water from the Okavango River to Windhoek, the Namibian capital.

A colony of Cape fur seals gathers on a sandy beach along the Skeleton Coast of Namibia.

See color plate 14, vol. 2.

Nujoma's persecution of anyone opposing his plans threatens to undermine his attempts to bring stability and prosperity to the nation.

ECONOMY

Northern Namibia is the only area with enough precipitation for intensive agriculture. However, the central plateau receives sufficient rain to produce a groundcover for grazing sheep and cattle, long a major economic activity in the country.

Two industries that show promise in Namibia are FISHING and TOURISM. The cold Benguela Current that runs along the Atlantic coast attracts large schools of fish. This area was overfished in the 1980s, but the government has since passed strict controls to help fish stocks recover. Meanwhile, tourism has been growing at an impressive rate in Namibia since independence.

Namibia

The Republic of Namibia

POPULATION:
1,771,327 (2000 estimated population)

AREA:
317,260 sq. mi. (824,295 sq. km)

LANGUAGES:
English (official); Afrikaans, German, Damara, Herero, Kavango, Ovambo, Nama

NATIONAL CURRENCY:
Namibian dollar

PRINCIPAL RELIGIONS:
Christian 80–90%, Traditional 10–20%

CITIES:
Windhoek (capital), 190,000 (1995 est.); Walvis Bay, Swakopmund, Keetmanshoop, Rehoboth

ANNUAL RAINFALL:
Varies from less than 2 in. (51 mm) in western Namib and lower Orange River valley to more than 19.8 in. (508 mm) in the northern border regions.

ECONOMY:
GDP per capita: $4,300 (1999 est.)

PRINCIPAL PRODUCTS AND EXPORTS:
Agricultural: millet, sorghum, peanuts, livestock, fish
Manufacturing: meat packing, dairy products, fish processing
Mining: diamonds, copper, gold, tin, lead, uranium, salt, cadmium, lithium, natural gas, zinc

GOVERNMENT:
Independence from South Africa, 1990. Republic with president elected by universal suffrage. Governing bodies: National Assembly and National Council (legislative bodies); Cabinet appointed by president.

HEADS OF STATE SINCE INDEPENDENCE:
1990– President Samuel Nujoma

ARMED FORCES:
9,000 (2000 est.)

EDUCATION:
Compulsory for ages 6–16; literacy rate 40%

See map in Minerals and Mining (vol. 3).

* **matrilineal** tracing ancestry or descent through the mother's side of the family

* **forage** to hunt or search for food

The economy of Namibia depends heavily on the export of raw materials such as diamonds, metals, and livestock. In the past South Africa has been the most important market for Namibian goods, but in recent years Namibia has tried to reduce its dependence on that nation.

Despite a relatively high average annual income, Namibia suffers from a large gap between rich and poor. Unemployment stands at about 30 percent of the workforce and more than half of Namibians are illiterate. Fortunately, the country's foreign debt is small and its population is growing at a modest rate. Even so, factors such as unequal distribution of land and ethnic strife severely limit Namibia's potential for economic growth.

PEOPLES AND CULTURES

The population of Namibia is mostly Christian (about 90 percent) and very young (about half of the people are under 18 years of age). The major ethnic groups in the north are those of the Huambo cluster, who practice agriculture and livestock raising. They are one of many matrilineal* societies in this part of Africa. Other matrilineal groups inhabit the Caprivi Strip and the Okavango River in the northeast. Pastoralists and foraging* groups such as the !Kung live outside the towns and mining areas of northern Namibia.

Western, central, and southern Namibia are home to pastoralists such as the Herero and some of the Khoisan. The Herero also have a primarily matrilineal society, although religious items such as sacred cattle are passed through the male side of the family. The Khoisan include both pastoralists and foragers whose societies are noted for their very com-

124

plex KINSHIP systems. Of considerable interest to researchers are the small HUNTING AND GATHERING group called the San, also known as the Bushmen. (*See also* **Colonialism in Africa; Independence Movements; Maherero, Samuel; Southern Africa, History; Witbooi, Hendrik.**)

Nasser, Gamal Abdel

1918–1970
President of Egypt

* **coup** sudden, often violent, overthrow of a ruler or government

* **nationalize** to bring land, industries, or public works under state control or ownership

* **Soviet Union** nation that existed from 1922 to 1991, made up of Russia and 14 other republics

* **socialism** economic or political system based on the idea that the government or groups of workers should own and run the means of production and distribution of goods

P resident of EGYPT from 1956 to 1970, Gamal Abdel Nasser was a leading figure in the Arab world. The son of a postal clerk, Nasser attended primary school in a small village in the Nile Delta. He moved to his uncle's home in Cairo, where he received his secondary education and then attended law school briefly. In 1936 Nasser entered the Royal Military Academy.

Nasser rose quickly in the military and fought in a war against Israel in the late 1940s. With several other officers, he formed a secret revolutionary group known as the Free Officers. In 1952 he led the Free Officers in a coup* that overthrew Egypt's ruler, King Farouk. Egypt became a republic the following year, and Nasser was named its premier in 1954. Middle- and upper-class Egyptians opposed the military coup and Nasser's rule, and one Arab group, the Muslim Brotherhood, attempted to assassinate him. However, Nasser had the protection of the military and police, and his policies earned the support of Egypt's many peasants.

In 1956 Nasser became president of Egypt. Soon after taking office, he nationalized* the Suez Canal, which was controlled by Britain and France. Britain, France, and Israel responded by invading Egypt. Although the Egyptians resisted fiercely, their forces were defeated. Nasser triumphed politically, however, when the United States and the Soviet Union* pressured the invaders into retreating.

Encouraged by his success in gaining control of the canal, Nasser moved to make Egypt the leader of the Arab world. In 1958 Egypt and Syria united to form the United Arab Republic, which was later joined by Yemen. Meanwhile, Nasser attempted to revolutionize life within Egypt. He introduced socialism*, worked to increase the nation's industrial strength, and made improvements in health and education. He also brought about land reform and tried—with little success—to improve agriculture.

Nasser hoped that the entire Arab world might someday unite, but his United Arab Republic lasted only until 1964. The failed union reduced respect for Nasser in the Arab world. Moreover, Nasser's foreign policies had led to conflict with Saudi Arabia and worsened relations with the United States. Partly in response to these setbacks, Nasser adopted a more aggressive policy toward Israel. In 1967 he moved to close the Suez Canal to Israeli ships. Israel declared war and quickly defeated Egypt. Nasser offered to resign, but Egyptians rallied in the streets, demanding that he remain in office.

Nasser ruled for three more years. He refused to accept the terms of peace dictated by Israel and continued to provoke conflict in the canal zone. When he died of a heart attack in 1970, he was succeeded by Anwar SADAT. (*See also* **Arabs in Africa, United Nations in Africa.**)

125

Nationalism

* **clan**   group of people descended from a common ancestor

ationalism is the belief that a group of people have the right to live in and govern their own nation-state. European powers had gained control over most of Africa in the late 1800s and established colonies. In the 1900s, African nationalist movements emerged in many parts of the continent that sought to end colonial rule and European economic power. Eventually, nationalist leaders called for independence and the creation of new nation-states. To achieve this goal, they encouraged Africans to identify themselves as members of national groups, rather than as members of ETHNIC GROUPS, tribes, or clans*.

However, Europeans resisted African demands for freedom with delay and violence. The struggle for African liberation lasted almost 50 years. Success came first with the decolonization—ending European rule—of LIBYA in 1951 and continued across the continent, colony by colony, until ERITREA gained its independence in 1993.

After winning independence, many African nations were racked by internal tensions. The nations' borders were the same as those of the colonies—arbitrary lines that divided ancient ethnic homelands. The institutions of government were often the same as well, keeping power in a few hands and using force to control the nation's citizens. Furthermore, some ethnic groups refused to give up their independence, sowing the seeds of conflict and civil war.

The Character of African Nationalism. The nationalist movement was led primarily by Africans who had recently acquired education, literacy*, and social and economic power. Among the early champions of nationalism was James Africanus HORTON of SIERRA LEONE, a black scientist and businessman. He believed that European models of education would help modernize the continent and pull Africans out of their desperate living conditions. In some ways, leaders like Horton shared the Europeans' racist view of Africans as "backward" and "primitive." These leaders considered nationalism to be a decisive break with traditional African ways of thinking about themselves and their communities.

* **literacy**   ability to read and write

By emphasizing a break with precolonial* cultures, African nationalism lost the opportunity to build on Africa's own achievements. The continent had a centuries-old history of self-rule, including federations* of independent villages and clans. But the nationalists looked instead to the history of Europe and the United States, where people had gained greater independence by forming nation-states in the 1700s and 1800s. African nationalists believed that Africans could gain equality and self-respect in the modern world only by having their own nations. They realized that they might have to keep Africa's indigenous* political and cultural traditions under control. But they saw no other way of ending the abuses of colonial rule. For better or for worse, nation building on the European model became Africa's destiny.

* **precolonial**   referring to the time before European powers colonized Africa

* **federation**   organization of separate states with a central government

* **indigenous**   native to a certain place

Nationalist Movements. African nationalism had its start in World Wars I and II. Africans watched as people fought to break up empires and gain freedom, and as the Japanese, nonwhite people, stood up to

* **guerrilla** type of warfare involving sudden raids by small groups of warriors

* **sub-Saharan** referring to Africa south of the Sahara desert

Europeans and Americans in war. Many Africans gained combat experience after being drafted into colonial armies. Meanwhile, in India, a powerful movement for independence took shape during the 1940s, and India succeeded in throwing off British rule in 1947. This development had an impact on African hopes and plans.

Throughout Africa, nationalist groups found early support in towns and urban areas. There, migrants from rural areas—people seeking jobs and a better life—were an important source of anticolonialism. These displaced people came together in tribal associations based on ethnic group and language. Some of the associations later adopted nationalism and helped spread it to the countryside through networks of family and trade.

In many areas, nationalism led to political competition between different groups. In some respects this competition had its roots in traditional rivalries, although the main disputes were access to power and resources. In many colonies, the tribal associations grew into political parties. Loyal to both the nation and their ethnic groups, these parties helped the privileged groups that were building the nation to gain a wide audience.

The movement for nationhood first gathered steam in North Africa, and in 1951 the former Italian colony of Libya won independence. EGYPT, MOROCCO, and TUNISIA followed in 1956, but ALGERIA had to fight a bloody guerrilla* war against France before gaining its freedom in 1962. West African colonies such as GHANA and LIBERIA also had strong early movements, helped by links to black nationalists in the United States such as Marcus GARVEY. Dozens of sub-Saharan* colonies gained independence in the 1960s, some with little violence, others after long periods of armed struggle. In southern Africa, governments controlled by white settlers won nationhood for SOUTH AFRICA and Southern Rhodesia but were later overthrown by black Africans.

The Hopes of Independence. The goals of national liberation included social, cultural, and economic progress. For millions of Africans, opportunities for education, health care, employment, and other necessities improved with nationhood. Although many new African states had to begin from little or nothing, they made rapid progress. As public education expanded, more graduates could staff the newly built hospitals and medical schools. Towns and cities grew dramatically, and governments worked to meet the basic needs of urban residents.

Nationalism provided new sources of self-respect for Africans who, for decades, had suffered the humiliations of colonial rule. Now citizens rather than servants, Africans found themselves welcomed throughout much of the world. In the United Nations, Africans spoke as confident equals to the representatives of other nations. Great academies elected Africans to honored memberships, and African men and women won medals at the Olympics and other athletic competitions.

As Africans took their place on the world stage, African national identities replaced ethnic identities. Everything from individual people to musical styles became known as Kenyan, Ethiopian, or Nigerian, rather

Eritrea won its independence from Ethiopia in 1993 after a long civil war. Eritrean soldiers guard the country's borders.

than GIKUYU, AMHARA, or IGBO. Nationalism brought Africans dignity and a sense of worth that helped to banish racist stereotypes and notions of inferiority. Instead of seeing "backward" or "primitive" peoples, the world—and Africans themselves—now saw a vivid range of African men and women, politicians and diplomats, scientists and poets.

The Limits of Nationalism. As African colonies gained their independence, leaders began to speak about the possibility of governing in different ways, such as through federations of villages, cities, or regions. In practice, however, the emerging states took over the forms of government that had been designed to meet colonial needs. They found themselves chained to colonial habits, structures, and institutions. Neither the Europeans nor the nationalists offered long-term programs to develop democratic government.

* **bureaucracy** large departmental organization within a government

The nationalist governments thus took shape as bureaucracies* with power concentrated at the top. They often used the media and the armed forces to silence opposition. Some countries, such as ANGOLA and

MOZAMBIQUE, adopted the model of the Soviet Union*, in which the central government also owned the land and controlled the economy. But without the possibility for all people to debate ideas and govern themselves, African nations could not develop true democracy.

The new African governments also faced major economic problems. By the mid-1970s, drought, mismanagement, fuel shortages, poverty, and other factors combined to ruin African economies. The hard times increased unrest. Ethnic groups competed ever more fiercely for ever fewer resources. Centralized governments were vulnerable* to takeovers by small but powerful groups, whether businessmen or military officers. Some countries dissolved into bitter fighting among rebels, criminals, warlords, religious leaders, and ethnic groups. The dreams of the early nationalists for a bright future seemed very dim.

Meanwhile, foreign powers found new ways to control and profit from their former colonies. They provided money or military support to governments or rebels whom they saw as allies. As the economic crises deepened in the early 1980s, many African nations had to take loans from the World Bank and the International Monetary Fund. To qualify for the loans, Africans had to sell national resources to foreign corporations and put in place various social and economic policies. Members of the ruling group sometimes profited from the new loans and policies, but the majority of Africans sank deeper into poverty. Protests and calls for democracy grew louder.

By the late 1990s, disappointment with the promises of nationalism was widespread. Africa gained independence through a nationalism that reflected an imperialist* age. Many Africans realize that in order to survive their nations now must adopt new goals and different political and economic structures. (*See also* **Boundaries in Africa; Colonialism in Africa; Development, Economic and Social; Ethnic Groups and Identity; Government and Political Systems; History of Africa; Independence Movements; Neocolonialism; World Wars I and II.**)

Ndebele

The Ndebele are an offshoot of a group of BANTU-speaking peoples of southern Africa known as the Nguni. The branch of the Ndebele that is centered in ZIMBABWE traces its roots to MZILIKAZI, a former lieutenant under SHAKA ZULU. The other branch, founded by the leader Musi, is located in SOUTH AFRICA. Both branches of the Ndebele at one time fled from Shaka's armies and incorporated other peoples who were doing the same. Both also had encounters with white settlers. Those in South Africa were quickly subdued, but those in Zimbabwe—known to the British as Matabele—offered a much fiercer resistance.

Like other Nguni, the Ndebele are both farmers and herders, raising corn and tending livestock. In recent years some Ndebele have left the land and moved into cities. Today, many work far from home in South Africa's mines. In 1997 the Ndebele elected their first female chief, Singobile Mabhena. The election gained worldwide attention and was perhaps influenced by the emergence of several other female leaders in southern Africa. (*See also* **Ethnic Groups and Identity.**)

Negritude

Negritude was a black literary and cultural movement that spanned the 1930s to 1950s. The movement first took shape among French-speaking writers in Africa and the Caribbean. The leading figure in the Negritude movement was Léopold Sédar SENGHOR, a poet and philosopher who became the first president of SENEGAL when it won independence from France in 1960.

The origins of Negritude can be traced to the shared experiences of Africans who suffered under SLAVERY and colonialism. It developed partly as a response to Western views of Africa as a primitive and savage land and of blacks as an inferior race. These views inspired people in the Negritude movement to emphasize positive African qualities such as emotional warmth, closeness to nature, and reverence for ancestors.

The idea of Negritude was also an outgrowth of political and social movements. Among the most important of these were the "pan-African" movements led by Marcus GARVEY and W.E.B. DU BOIS. These movements encouraged the development of a black identity and sought to unify blacks around the world. Another forerunner of Negritude was the Harlem Renaissance, a literary and artistic flowering that took place in the United States in the 1920s.

* **assimilation** process of adopting the beliefs or customs of a society

As it developed, Negritude came to represent black protest against colonial rule and the assimilation* of Western culture and values by blacks. Many writers in the movement criticized colonialism and Western ideas. Negritude also served as a source of racial pride. Focusing on the richness of black history and culture, it provided a sense of common identity and dignity for blacks in Africa, the Americas, Europe, and other parts of the world. (*See also* **Colonialism in Africa; Diaspora, African; Literature**.)

Neocolonialism

After independence, some African nations declared their political allegiance to their former European rulers—such as Britain, France, and Belgium—and continued to rely on them for economic assistance. This policy became known in the 1960s as neocolonialism.

Not all African nations chose to pursue neocolonial relationships. Those that had gained independence after violent struggles against European powers, such as ALGERIA, usually chose to remain nonaligned, or neutral, or they developed close ties with the Soviet Union* or non-Western countries. In many cases, these African countries adopted economic systems based on socialism* rather than capitalism*. They associated capitalism with the exploitation* they had suffered at the hands of Europeans.

* **Soviet Union** nation that existed from 1922 to 1991, made up of Russia and 14 other republics

* **socialism** economic or political system based on the idea that the government or groups of workers should own and run the means of production and distribution of goods

* **capitalism** economic system in which businesses are privately owned and operated and where free markets coordinate most economic activity

* **exploitation** relationship in which one side benefits at the other's expense

For the most part, the African nations that followed the neocolonialist path, such as IVORY COAST and MALAWI, had been granted independence without conflict. Their relationships with their former colonial rulers remained friendly and often involved financial and technical support. Although the neocolonial nations had also suffered from economic exploitation, they felt that many of the economic and social changes introduced under colonialism were positive. As a result, they followed the path of Western-style capitalism.

The leaders of the neocolonial states proposed to do more rapidly what colonization was supposed to have begun—the creation of a modern economy. Following the colonial model, these states continued to emphasize mining and cash crop* agriculture to increase their export income. Instead of carrying out agricultural reforms, they allowed foreign landowners to hold onto the property they had acquired. They also kept their economic institutions closely linked to foreign capitalist systems. To keep peasant majorities under control, they favored single-party government rather than full democracy.

* **cash crop** crop grown primarily for sale rather than for local consumption

The neocolonialists assumed that economic development would occur in orderly stages. They believed that profits from agriculture and mining would create a market for industry, which would attract foreign and local investors. However, the transition from one stage to the next did not take place as planned. Although certain countries managed to create an illusion of economic success, they soon discovered that the path to prosperity was more difficult than assumed. To survive, many neocolonial governments began to depend on loans from foreign countries and international organizations, and ran up enormous debts. By the 1980s debt payments were draining resources away from programs such as education and health care.

In the long run, neocolonial policies led to a number of unintended consequences: limited political rights for the people, slower economic growth, decreasing food production because of the emphasis on export crops, the collapse of social services, and increasing political corruption. Overall, neocolonialism has been a dramatic failure in Africa, leading to serious political and economic crises throughout much of the continent. (*See also* **Colonialism in Africa; Development, Economic and Social; Economic History; History of Africa; Independence Movements.**)

Neto, Augustinho

1922–1979
President of Angola

* **communist** relating to communism, a system in which land, goods, and the means of production are owned by the state or community rather than by individuals

Augustinho Neto was a leader in the fight against colonial rule in ANGOLA and the country's first president after independence. The son of a pastor, Neto went to Portugal to study medicine in 1947 but soon became involved in the Angolan independence movement and was also involved in communist* activities. After returning to Angola in 1958, he was arrested and exiled, first to CAPE VERDE and then to Portugal. In 1962 Neto escaped, went back to Angola, and assumed leadership of the forces resisting Portuguese control of the country. The fight for independence would not be an easy one, nor would it be quick. For the next thirteen years, Neto's leadership remained constant as his forces struggled to gain power in the face of strong opposition from the Portuguese.

Angola won its independence in 1975 and Neto was elected president. Almost immediately, however, SOUTH AFRICA invaded and tried to take over the country. Only the arrival of Cuban troops saved Angola from defeat. Neto died just a few years after the war ended. In addition to his political achievements, Neto was also a notable poet who published a volume of verse entitled *Sacred Hope*. (*See also* **Colonialism in Africa, Independence Movements.**)

Ngugi wa Thiong'o

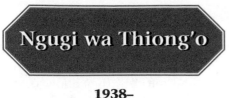

1938–
Kenyan author

* **leftist** inclined to support radical reform and change; often associated with ideas of communism and socialism

Writer Ngugi wa Thiong'o is known not only for his literary work but also for his political protests and his commitment to writing in African rather than European languages. Born into a peasant family of the GIKUYU people near NAIROBI, KENYA, Ngugi received an education at a colonial high school. He began to write while attending Makerere University College in UGANDA. Ngugi also studied at Leeds University in England, where he developed leftist* political views.

In 1967 Ngugi became the first African member of the University of Nairobi's English department. He influenced Kenya's cultural life in two ways: he was the first African to publish creative LITERATURE in English, and he promoted a course of study focused on African subjects, which other African universities used as a model. In 1978 Ngugi was imprisoned for a year because of his protests against government policies. In prison he decided that he would write only in Gikuyu.

The university did not restore Ngugi to his post, but he continued to work in Kenyan THEATER. Still at odds with the government and fearing another arrest, Ngugi left Kenya for London in 1982. He then moved to the United States, where he has taught at Yale University and New York University. Ngugi continues to write about the ways in which Africa and its people are dominated and manipulated by non-Africans.

See map in Mining and Minerals (vol. 3).

* **staple** major product of a region; basic food

* **cash crop** crop grown primarily for sale rather than for local consumption

* **gross domestic product (GDP)** total value of goods and services produced and consumed within a country

A large, landlocked country in north central Africa, Niger is one of the most thinly populated nations on the continent. The SAHARA DESERT covers most of the country, leaving only a small portion of the land suitable for permanent settlement. To make matters worse, long-term drought has devastated Niger's agriculture. A poor economy, combined with political mismanagement, has made Niger one of the world's poorest countries.

GEOGRAPHY AND ECONOMY

Niger is a mostly barren country, dominated by the desert and semi-desert that make up some 80 percent of its total area. Mountain ranges in the center of the country rise to a height of about 6,600 feet, but most of the remaining terrain is flat plains and plateaus covered by rocks and sand dunes. The NIGER RIVER crosses the southwestern corner of the country.

The vast majority of the nation's people live on a thin strip of land along Niger's southern border. Known as "useful Niger," it is the only part of the country with enough rainfall to allow agriculture. The main staple* crops are the grains millet and sorghum, and peanuts are a major cash crop*. In addition, livestock raising is an important activity in this region.

Niger's economy relies heavily on the production of uranium ore, which makes up half of the nation's gross domestic product (GDP)* and 80 percent of its exports. However, the price of uranium dropped steeply in the 1980s and has not recovered. The collapse of the uranium market and the longstanding drought have contributed to a staggering foreign debt and terrible poverty.

Art and Architecture

Plate 1: Sometime before the year 1000, the Shona people of southern Africa built the massive stone structures of Great Zimbabwe. These cone-shaped towers lie within the Great Enclosure, a circular stone wall more than 30 feet high. Archaeologists have found glass beads and Chinese porcelain at the site, suggesting that Great Zimbabwe was connected to trading networks that stretched to the Indian Ocean.

Plate 2: The ancient Egyptians decorated the tombs of kings, queens, and high officials with scenes of family and everyday activities, as well as images of the afterlife and Egyptian mythology. This nobleman's burial chamber is at Thebes.

Plate 3: The Dogon people of Mali have an elaborate mythology and complex rituals related to agriculture and death. This painting on a cliff wall marks the site of Dogon initiation ceremonies.

Plate 4: Heavily influenced by Egyptian civilization, the ancient kingdom of Kush in northern Sudan buried its kings and nobles in pyramid-like structures. Some 70 of these royal tombs, dating from about 750 B.C. to A.D. 350, have been found at the old and new capitals of Napata and Meroë.

Plate 5: The Baule, the largest ethnic group in Ivory Coast, are known for their sculpture and wood carving. The Baule masks shown here play an important role in a ceremony.

Plate 6: The work of West African artisans tends to follow gender lines. Men carve wooden masks and figures and work with iron; women make pottery and textiles. Yoruba figures, such as the head shown here, often have large, protruding eyes. Hairstyles, clothing, and scars are shown with intricately carved lines.

Plate 7: Africans use baskets for storing or serving food or for carrying goods. These woven baskets made of reeds come from Huíla Province in the Central Highlands of Angola.

Plate 8: Traditionally, carved objects were made for functional or ceremonial purposes. This craftsman in Swaziland in southern Africa carves a statue of a man out of a piece of wood. Most of his work is sold to tourists.

Plate 9: Asante weavers of Ghana make the famous kente cloth. To form the complex patterns, they sew together strips of richly colored fabric. Blue and gold, which symbolize power, are often used. Men wear kente cloths on ceremonial occasions.

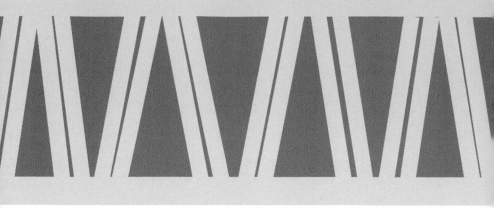

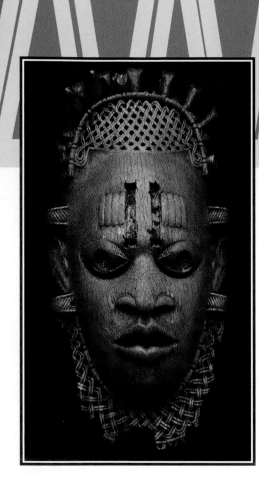

Plate 10: After the British conquered the West African kingdom of Benin in 1897, Benin's bronze sculptures (actually brass) became famous in Europe. The kingdom's artistic tradition also included fine pieces made of ivory and wood. This striking ivory face, probably that of Queen Idia, was carved in the 1500s.

Plate 11: Namibia was a colony of Germany and then of South Africa. This Lutheran church in the Namibian capital of Windhoek was built in 1910 during the German rule.

Plate 12: Beadwork has a long history in Africa, and beads made of bone, ivory, stone, shell, glass, and metal have been found at sites throughout the continent. For the Samburu and other nomadic peoples, beadwork was the main form of visual art. The collar of glass beads worn by this Samburu woman of Kenya tells of her status and her clan.

Plate 13: Geometric designs, flowing patterns of lines and curves, and calligraphy—decorative script—adorn many buildings in North Africa. This colorful door marks the entry to a house in Tunisia.

Plate 14: Abidjan, the economic capital of Ivory Coast, is a major financial center and deepwater port for French-speaking Africa. The modern part of the city boasts sleek skyscrapers and wide shady streets, but Abidjan also has undeveloped areas.

Plate 15: Malangatana, the best-known artist in Mozambique today, specializes in murals. His paintings include scenes from his country's history, including the colonial period and World War II. Shown here is his mural at the University of Western Cape in South Africa.

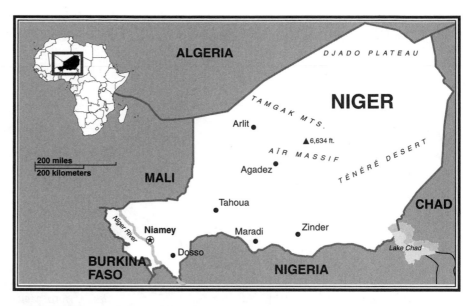

HISTORY AND GOVERNMENT

Before the arrival of Europeans, Niger was controlled by a succession of different kingdoms and empires. Most of these were Muslim states, and Islamic* religion and culture became strongly established throughout the country.

* **Islamic** relating to Islam, the religion based on the teachings of the prophet Muhammad

Precolonial and Colonial History. The Songhai people established the earliest centralized state in Niger in the A.D. 600s. By the 1400s the Songhai Empire dominated the western portion of Niger, while the kingdom of BORNU controlled most of the eastern part of the country. At about the same time, the sultanate* of the Aïr gained prominence in the north. During the 1600s the Djerma peoples migrated from the north, and the HAUSA rose to a position of power in the southwest. Meanwhile, the nomadic TUAREG peoples joined together in the northern desert region.

* **sultanate** territory ruled by a Muslim leader called a sultan

In the 1800s the FULANI swept through the region and established the Empire of Sokoto after conquering much of northwestern Africa. Also known as the Sokoto Caliphate*, the empire incorporated many Muslim and non-Muslim kingdoms, although the Tuareg and several sultanates maintained their independence. In the early 1900s, a British force from Nigeria conquered the Sokoto Caliphate. The French moved into Niger at the same time, forming alliances with some sultanates and attacking the Tuareg. Despite fierce resistance, the Tuareg were finally defeated. Niger became a French colony in 1922. After 38 years of French rule, Niger gained its independence in 1960.

* **caliphate** state in the Muslim empire

Modern History. Niger's first president, Hamani Diori, stifled all political opposition and ruled the country as a single-party state. Diori's inability to improve conditions, along with the effects of drought, led to a military coup* in 1974. The new ruler, Colonel Seyni Kountché, suspended the constitution and restored order, but several coups were attempted during his rule. General Ali Saïbou took over as president in 1987. Under Saïbou, Niger adopted a new constitution, allowed political

* **coup** sudden, often violent, over-throw of a ruler or government

133

Niger

Republic of Niger

POPULATION:
10,075,511 (2000 estimated population)

AREA:
489,189 sq. mi. (1,267,000 sq. km)

LANGUAGES:
French (official); Hausa, Dejerma, others

NATIONAL CURRENCY:
CFA franc

PRINCIPAL RELIGIONS:
Muslim 80%, Christian 10%, Traditional 10%

CITIES:
Niamey (capital), 420,000 (1994 est.); Zinder, Maradi, Tahoua, Dosso, Agadez, Arlit

ANNUAL RAINFALL:
Varies from 20 in. (500 mm) in the south, to 4 in. (100 mm) at Agadez, to almost 0 in. in the far north.

ECONOMY:
GDP per capita: $1,000 (1999 est.)

PRINCIPAL PRODUCTS AND EXPORTS:
Agricultural: millet, sorghum, peanuts, beans, cotton, cowpeas, onions, livestock
Manufacturing: cement, brick, textiles, chemicals, food processing
Mining: uranium, coal, iron ore, tin, phosphates

GOVERNMENT:
Independence from France, 1960. Republic with president elected by universal suffrage. Governing bodies: National Assembly (legislature); cabinet and prime minister appointed by president.

HEADS OF STATE SINCE INDEPENDENCE:
1960–1974 President Hamani Diori
1974–1987 Lieutenant Colonel Seyni Koutché
1987–1993 Colonel (later General) Ali Saïbou, president after 1989
1993–1996 President Mahamane Ousmane
1996–1999 President (Brigadier General) Ibrahim Baré Mainassara; Major Daouda Mallam Wanke, provisional president in 1999
1999– President Mamadou Tandja

ARMED FORCES:
5,300

EDUCATION:
Compulsory for ages 7–15; literacy rate 14%

* **guerrilla** member of a fighting force outside the regular army that uses surprise raids against an enemy or government

* **sanction** measure adopted by one or more nations to force another nation to change its policies or conduct

opposition and protests, and moved for the first time toward a multi-party democracy.

After a period of transition in which Niger was ruled by a National Conference, elections were held in 1993. The new president, Mahamane Ousmane, faced considerable opposition and a chaotic political and economic situation. Among the difficulties he faced was an armed rebellion of the Tuareg in the north. In 1996 Ousmane was overthrown by General Ibrahim Mainassara, who was elected president later that year. Mainassara achieved some successes during his rule, notably the disarming of two groups of guerrillas* that had opposed the government for years. However, Niger's continuing economic problems resulted in strikes, rebellions, and growing instability. Mainassara's reelection in 1999 was marked by fraud and violence and led to widespread protests and unrest.

On April 9, 1999, Mainassara was shot and killed by his presidential guard. The guard's commander, Major Daouda Mallam Wanke, assumed the presidency and announced that there would be no investigation of Mainassara's death. Many countries expressed outrage and threatened economic sanctions* unless democracy was quickly restored.

Under pressure, Wanke scheduled elections for the fall of 1999, and Tandja Mamadou was chosen president. Tandja's party also gained a majority of seats in the national assembly, giving the new president some hope of maintaining a stable government. However, bringing order and a measure of prosperity to this desperately poor country promises to be a difficult task.

PEOPLE AND CULTURES

Niger contains many ethnic groups, including the Hausa, Zerma-Songhai, Dendi, Tuareg, and Fulani. The first three of these are agricultural peoples, while the last two are pastoralists*. These groups all share many Muslim beliefs and practices, although many have kept certain elements of pre-Islamic culture as well.

Under French rule, Nigerois who spoke Zerma achieved positions in the colonial government, and they continue to dominate Niger's political life. The Tuareg and Fulani, however, have struggled. The nomadic lifestyle of the Tuareg was disrupted by the French takeover, and the Tuareg have benefited little from Niger's commercial economy or from Western education.

Social and economic differences tend to be more important in Niger than differences between ethnic groups. Before the colonial era, sharp distinctions existed between nobles and commoners, herders and farmers, warriors and producers. Under French rule, people in the same classes held similar positions in the workforce, government, and military. As a result, people of similar social and economic backgrounds tend to share common interests regardless of ethnic group. (*See also* **Colonialism in Africa, Deserts and Drought, French West Africa, Islam in Africa, Sudanic Empires of Western Africa.**)

Niger River and Delta

The Niger River flows in a great arc through West Africa. The continent's third longest river, after the NILE RIVER and CONGO RIVER, it has carried travelers, traders, and explorers for hundreds of years. The Niger still serves as a highway for people and goods, but it also supplies water for agriculture and hydroelectric power*. The delta at the river's mouth in NIGERIA was an early center of European trade and now yields oil and natural gas.

Geography. The Niger River is navigable* for most of its 2,585 miles. Its source lies in the Kouranko Mountains on the border between SIERRA LEONE and GUINEA. Although the Atlantic Ocean is just 200 miles west of that source, the shape of the land makes the river flow east and north for a long distance before finally turning south toward the Atlantic. Along the way the Niger passes through Guinea, MALI, NIGER, the northern edge of BÉNIN, and Nigeria.

Descending from the Guinea highlands into Mali, the river broadens and moves slowly. Two major tributaries, the Sankarani and Bani Rivers, join the Niger in Mali and add to its flow. Entering a flat plain, the Niger then branches out into a network of waterways called the Inland Delta. During the rainy season, which begins in late August, these channels overflow their banks and form a shallow lake 150 miles wide and 300 miles long. This yearly flood deposits fertile soil, making the inland delta an ideal agricultural zone. In especially wet years a branch of the river reaches the city of TIMBUKTU, seven miles from the river's main channel.

For centuries the Niger River has been a major trade route through West Africa. Boats like this one still carry passengers and cargo along the river's winding course.

The Niger curves to the south at Kabara in Mali and narrows as it passes through a gorge. Flowing through Nigeria it receives another major tributary, the Benue. The river empties into the Atlantic Ocean after passing through a sprawling delta created by soil deposits from the river. Over thousands of years, the Niger has extended this delta out into the Atlantic.

History and Ethnic Groups. Long used for communication and commerce, the Niger River has played an important role in the history of West Africa. It contributed to the rise of the SUDANIC EMPIRES OF WESTERN AFRICA and later offered Europeans a route into the interior.

During the period of the Songhai Empire in the 1400s and 1500s, large canoes carried grain downstream from the Inland Delta to the cities of Timbuktu and Gao. Military and court officials traveled from one end of the empire to the other on the river. The river helped make Timbuktu a busy and prosperous trade center, where the caravan routes that crossed the SAHARA DESERT connected with the Niger's river traffic.

Beginning in the late 1400s, the Ijo people of the Niger Delta formed various city-states that became the focus of European trade. However, archaeological* evidence—including pottery and copper bracelets once used as money—shows that the delta peoples were involved in long-distance trade with the interior well before the Europeans arrived.

European knowledge of the Niger River began with Arab maps of the Middle Ages, which mistakenly suggested a link between the Nile and the Niger Rivers. The maps also indicated that the Niger began in what

* **archaeological** referring to the study of past human cultures and societies, usually by excavating ruins

is now CHAD and flowed west. Scottish explorer Mungo Park disproved this notion in 1796 when he traced part of the river's course. By 1830 Europeans had mapped the full course of the Niger and knew that it emptied into the Atlantic through the Nigerian delta.

European explorers, missionaries, and merchants—mostly British—advanced up the Niger River from the sea to trade and establish settlements. Their expeditions paved the way for the Royal Niger Company, founded in 1886, which not only gained control of European trade along the lower Niger but also expanded Britain's political and military power in the region. British rule of Nigeria soon followed. Meanwhile, far upstream, the French moved east along the river from their colony in SENEGAL, and took over Guinea, Mali, and Niger.

Many diverse ethnic groups live along the Niger and in its delta. The largest are the BAMBARA and Songhai in Mali, the Jerma in Niger, the Nupe in central Nigeria, the IGBO (Ibo) in southern Nigeria, and the Ijo (Ijaw) in the Niger Delta. The Niger River is central to the way of life of a number of these peoples, including the Sorko, a Songhai-speaking group that travels along the river from Nigeria to the Inland Delta, fishing and hunting hippopotamus.

During the 1900s Europeans and Africans used the Niger River for economic purposes. In the 1930s French colonial authorities began digging irrigation channels in Mali to bring the river's water to fields of cotton, rice, and sugarcane. A large hydroelectric dam at Kainji in Nigeria, completed 30 years later, harnessed the power of the river for economic development and is a major source of electricity for Nigeria and Bénin. In the Niger Delta region, oil and natural gas have been exploited* since the 1950s, providing significant revenue for Nigeria. (*See also* **History of Africa, Irrigation and Flood Control, Transportation, Travel and Exploration.**)

* **exploit**   to take advantage of; to make productive use of

Nigeria

With a large and enterprising population and a wealth of natural resources, the West African nation of Nigeria has enormous potential. However, since shortly after independence the country has been troubled by ethnic rivalry, religious strife, and violence. Furthermore, government corruption has hindered progress in many areas. After more than 40 years of unfulfilled promise, the country is still struggling to make the most of its rich heritage.

GEOGRAPHY

Located on the Guinea Coast of West Africa, Nigeria is bordered by the nations of BÉNIN, NIGER, and CAMEROON. The landscape is largely flat and low with few areas above 3,000 feet. The marshy coast is dominated by a wide belt of swamps that give way to thick tropical rain forest inland. Beyond the forest, the land rises gradually until reaching the Jos Plateau, the highest part of the country. This region is covered with savanna*; semiarid and desert areas are found farther north. A series of mountain ranges mark Nigeria's border with Cameroon.

* **savanna**   tropical or subtropical grassland with scattered trees and drought-resistant undergrowth

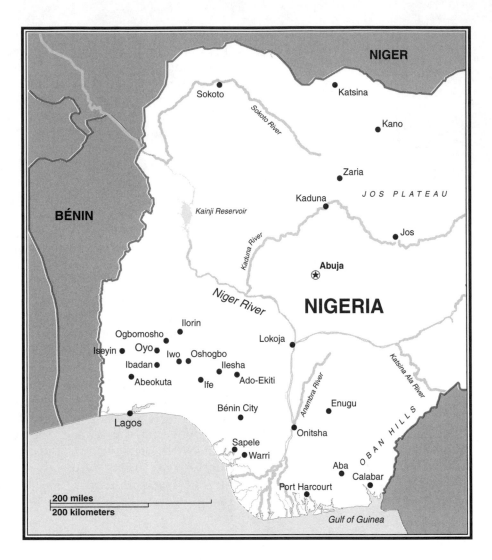

Climate changes dramatically in Nigeria as one moves from south to north. The south is hot and wet, receiving up to 150 inches of rain per year. Precipitation decreases significantly in the upland savanna area and drops to 25 inches or less per year in the hot, dry north. Nigeria has a rainy season and a dry season. Dry weather lasts about a month in the south but up to seven months in the northeast. The NIGER RIVER and its main tributary, the Benue, are the two most important rivers in the country. Together this river system divides Nigeria into three main areas—the north, southeast, and southwest—the homelands of Nigeria's main ethnic groups.

With varying growing conditions, each of the country's regions produces different crops. People in the south grow mainly root crops such as yams and cassava*, while those in the north cultivate grains including millet, sorghum, and rice. Cattle are raised widely in the north but not in the south because of the tsetse fly, which carries a disease that is deadly to large mammals. The middle region of Nigeria can support both root crops and grains and is rapidly becoming the nation's breadbasket.

* **cassava** starchy root plant; source of tapioca

HISTORY AND GOVERNMENT

The modern nation of Nigeria was created by joining two separate British colonies in 1914. These colonies contained three main ethnic and political divisions: Hausaland to the north, Yorubaland to the southwest, and Igboland and the kingdom of Benin (an ancient state unrelated to modern Bénin) to the southeast.

Precolonial Hausaland. Before the colonial era, northern Nigeria was divided into a number of independent states of varying size and wealth. This region, known as Hausaland, lay between two great trading centers—the ancient kingdom of BORNU to the east and the powerful empires of Mali and Songhai in the west. Since at least the 1300s, merchants from these two areas competed for control of the rich HAUSA region.

Bornu, a Muslim state, had considerable influence in Hausaland and received tribute* from many Hausa states. When Mali began expanding, Bornu set up its own trading centers in the Hausa region. At this time the inhabitants of Hausaland were not Muslims, and few spoke the Hausa language. However, trade brought Islam* to the region and led to the establishment of large urban centers in which people of different ethnic groups came together. It was from this mixing of traditions in a Muslim setting that the Hausa culture first emerged.

While some of the region's original inhabitants left the new Muslim states, others remained and converted to Islam. Still others continued to follow indigenous* religions and became minorities within the Hausa states, providing food and protection for the trading caravans of Muslim merchants. Over time Hausa developed as the common language of the urban military and merchant population and their farming allies. It eventually replaced the various other languages spoken in the countryside.

Around 1500 a series of Muslim kingdoms emerged in Hausaland. They enjoyed power and prosperity until about 1650, when a severe economic turndown in North Africa spread to West Africa. After 1650 large-scale invasions of people from the non-Muslim south, combined with a period of unrest and uprisings in several Hausa states, caused the region to splinter politically, and various new kingdoms emerged.

In the early 1800s, the FULANI launched a jihad* against the Hausa kingdoms. Led by Shaikh UTHMAN DAN FODIO, they crushed Hausa political power, set up their own rulers, and replaced traditional religious practices with Islam. The resulting division between the Hausa and the Fulani had a lasting effect on northern Nigeria.

Precolonial Yorubaland. In precolonial* times the YORUBA-speaking peoples of southwestern Nigeria (an area later known as Yorubaland) belonged to many separate states. Nevertheless, these peoples shared a common identity based on their origin in the town of Ife. The town, said to be the location of the creation of the world, was the site of an early kingdom that flourished between the 1100s and 1400s.

* **tribute**   payment made by a smaller or weaker party to a more powerful one, often under the threat of force

* **Islam**   religion based on the teachings of the prophet Muhammad; religious faith of Muslims

* **indigenous**   native to a certain place

* **jihad**   Muslim holy war

* **precolonial**   referring to the time before European powers colonized Africa

139

Nigeria

In the 1400s and 1500s, the kingdom of Benin conquered part of Yorubaland and maintained some degree of control there until the early 1800s. By the 1600s the most powerful Yoruba state was Oyo, which had an army based on cavalry forces. The plains and savannas of northern and western Yorubaland were ideal territory for mounted troops, and Oyo conquered several Yoruba states. It also took over the kingdom of Dahomey in what is now the modern nation of Bénin. Eventually Oyo became a major supplier of slaves, and by the 1700s the port city of LAGOS had become an important center of the Atlantic SLAVE TRADE.

In the 1800s Oyo collapsed as a result of civil war, and much of Yorubaland was crippled by wars among various states of the region. During that time Muslims seized control of parts of northeastern Yorubaland, while major wars continued to rage in the south. These wars resulted in the capture of many Yoruba, who were sold to European slave traders. By 1862 the state of Ibadan had emerged as the dominant power in Yorubaland. But an alliance of Yoruba states against Ibadan resulted in continued warfare until Europeans took over the region.

Precolonial Igboland and Benin. Southeastern Nigeria has been inhabited by speakers of the Edo (or Benin) language for more than 3,000 years. These peoples lived in small settlements until about 400 B.C. At that time, a growing population and the introduction of iron tools led to larger and more complex villages with forms of centralized authority and social classes of different levels. Linked to Yorubaland through trade networks, these villages eventually grew into towns and larger urban centers with rulers and elaborate royal courts.

Sometime after A.D. 1000, urban centers at Udo and Benin became the leading powers in the region. Eventually, Benin emerged as the more powerful of the two. Despite a strong government, Benin failed to expand, and about 1480 it was conquered by another state. The ruler of this new Benin state consolidated his power and then began waging war on his neighbors. Benin defeated Yoruba peoples to the west, Edo peoples to the north, and IGBO (Ibo) towns to the east. Conquered territories close to Benin came under direct rule; those farther away became provinces that paid tribute to the king of Benin. Continuing to expand, Benin reached its greatest size by about 1650.

Igboland, unlike Benin, did not develop a strong central government. Instead, the Igbo lived in independent villages that sometimes joined together to share a meeting place or market. Spread out on both sides of the Niger River, they were mostly farmers. By the 1600s the Igbo had become involved in supplying slaves to the slave traders along the coast.

Early European Influences. The Portuguese were the earliest European visitors to the region, making contact with the kingdom of Benin in 1485. Interested in gold and ivory at first, Portuguese and other European merchants eventually became involved in Africa's growing slave trade. Lagos became a principal export point for slaves bound for the Americas.

It was a desire to end the slave trade that brought Britain to Nigeria in the early 1800s. British naval vessels patrolled the coastal waters look-

* **depose**   to remove from office

ing for slave ships, and when the king of Lagos refused to sign a treaty against the trade in 1851, the British deposed* him. Ten years later they took over the slave port of Lagos.

At about the same time, Christian missionaries became active along the Nigerian coast and later penetrated inland. British merchants began to take a greater interest in regional products such as palm oil, a lubricant for early industrial machinery. These various activities led the British government to move toward setting up colonies and protectorates* in Nigeria. Fearing French competition, Britain intensified its colonization efforts in the region in the mid-1800s.

* **protectorate**   weak state under the control and protection of a strong state

Early British Rule. Britain expanded its role in Nigeria in the late 1800s, establishing the Niger Coast Protectorate in what is now southern Nigeria and forcing the states of Yorubaland to accept peace on British terms. In 1897 the British conquered the kingdom of Benin, ending organized resistance in the south. But they continued to send military expeditions on a regular basis to deal with uprisings.

While taking control in the south, Britain began to extend its authority over northern Nigeria. In 1886 it granted a monopoly* over trade along the lower Niger River area to the Royal Niger Company. Authorized to act as a political administration, this private company established local laws and administered justice. Its frequent abuse of this power led to several rebellions by local peoples. In 1900 the British government took over the lands originally granted to the Royal Niger Company and formed the Protectorate of Northern Nigeria. Three years later British forces defeated the Sokoto Caliphate*, a Muslim state that controlled much of northern Nigeria.

* **monopoly**   exclusive control or domination of a particular type of business

* **caliphate**   state in the Muslim empire

The first high commissioner of the northern protectorate, Sir Frederick LUGARD, developed a system of administration known as indirect rule. Under this policy, traditional African rulers who cooperated with the British were allowed to run local governments and courts. British officials acted as advisers rather than making policy themselves. This system of indirect rule saved the British the expense of setting up a full-scale colonial administration in the north, and they used the system later in most of their African colonies.

Indirect rule in the north did meet some opposition. Many Muslim leaders resisted the British, and armed uprisings were not uncommon. Furthermore, while indirect rule worked well in northern Nigeria, it failed in the south. Northern Nigeria had been the site of large empires for centuries and had a centralized power structure, which the British could use. By contrast, the history of southern Nigeria had been dominated by competing states, and no single political structure had developed in the region.

From Union to Independence. Northern and southern Nigeria remained separate British protectorates until 1914. At that time Britain decided to make the two into one colony ruled from the southern capital at Lagos. This merger simplified the task of ruling Nigeria, but it also planted the seeds of political division. The creation of a single colony forced long-time foes—the Hausa, Fulani, Yoruba, and Igbo—to become

A traditional fishing village stretches out along the highway in Lagos, Nigeria's main port and its most important commercial and industrial center.

part of the same nation. Britain managed to keep these ethnic rivalries in check during the colonial period, but they broke out anew after Nigeria achieved independence in 1960.

During the early years of British rule, northern Nigeria was weaker economically than the south. It also lagged behind the south in educational and political development. Christian missionaries had established many schools in the south, but Muslim rulers in the north resisted missionary activities. At first British colonial authorities excluded the north from the Legislative Council that oversaw the colony. As a result, northern Nigeria had no direct voice in colonial government.

Britain gradually introduced political changes in Nigeria. In 1939 it divided the south into eastern and western provinces. Seven years later it created a regional House of Assembly that included representatives from all parts of the country, along with a House of Chiefs for the north. Further changes over the next several years resulted in the north becoming a separate region with its own government and system of courts.

Political parties began to appear in Nigeria in the 1950s, and they played significant roles in the years leading up to independence. In the north the Northern People's Congress (NPC) and Northern Elements Progressive Union (NEPU) both drew support from the Hausa population. The NPC emerged as the stronger of the two parties, and from 1954 to 1959 it led efforts to increase the education and training of northerners in preparation for independence. The two main political parties of the south were the National Council of Nigerian Citizens and the Action Group. However, their support was not as widespread as that of the northern parties.

Independent Nigeria. Nigeria gained independence from Britain on October 1, 1960, and the NPC soon took its place as the new nation's leading political party. Nigeria's First Republic enjoyed a few years of relative quiet, but ethnic tensions were building. Once the poor neighbors of the Christians in the south, the Muslim Hausa in the north now made up a majority of the population and dominated Nigerian politics and government. Yoruba and Igbo leaders complained about Hausa control but were unable to cooperate with one another to change the situation.

A military coup* by Igbo army officers overthrew the First Republic in January 1966. Igbo control was short lived, however, as another coup in July of that year brought Hausa colonel Yakubu Gowon to power. Hausa and other northerners then launched a campaign of violence against the Igbo, killing thousands across the country. The situation turned into civil war when an Igbo colonel, Odemegwu Ojukwu, proclaimed independence for the eastern (Igbo) half of southern Nigeria—called Biafra. The Igbo fought desperately, but by 1970 their rebellion was crushed. Some two million people lost their lives in the war.

During the relatively calm period that followed the war, Gowon's government tried to smooth over ethnic differences. The challenge of rebuilding Nigeria was aided by the discovery of oil in the early 1970s. The prospect of national wealth and stability faded, though, as government officials and their friends stole much of the money produced by oil and political turmoil continued. Gowon was overthrown in 1975,

See color plate 9, vol. 2.

* **coup** sudden, often violent, overthrow of a ruler or government

and his successor was killed several months later. General Olesegun Obasanjo took control, but voluntarily stepped aside in 1979 to allow the election of a civilian government.

The new government, led by President Shehu Shagari, was marked by increasing corruption and rapidly declining oil revenues. This so-called Second Republic was even briefer than the first, lasting only four years before the military stepped in once again in 1983. The principal figure in Nigeria in the later 1980s was General Ibrahim Babangida, whose military regime* was marked by massive corruption and a complete lack of concern for public opinion. When Nigeria's economy failed to improve, and the nation's political situation remained unstable, Babangida came under increasing pressure to return Nigeria to civilian rule.

Elections in mid-1993 seemed to result in victory for Moshood Abiola, a Yoruba Muslim and friend of Babangida. However, the military overturned the election results, and General Sani Abacha took the presidency. Abacha outlawed political parties and labor strikes, seized government offices, and returned Nigeria to military rule.

When Abacha died suddenly in June 1998, he was replaced by General Abdusalam Abubakar, who promised a swift return to civilian rule. Under an arrangement with northern politicians, two southern Yoruba were named as candidates for the presidency: Olusegun Obasanjo and Olu Fulae. Obasanjo, who had given up power voluntarily in 1979, won the 1999 election. The first southerner elected to the presidency, Obasanjo quickly took steps to combat corruption in government and spent money on long neglected repairs to the country's oil refineries. He also announced a plan to privatize* some of Nigeria's state-owned corporations.

Political and human rights have improved somewhat under Obasanjo, but his government has faced unrest and turmoil. It sent military forces to put down an uprising in the oil-rich Niger Delta and to prevent a northern governor from establishing Muslim law in his state, resulting in many deaths. Economic problems as well as ethnic and regional differences continue to trouble the country.

ECONOMY

Nigeria's economy is dominated by its petroleum industry, centered in the Niger River delta. The country's enormous petroleum reserves should be the basis for a strong economy. However, corruption in the petroleum industry has shifted much of the oil revenue into the hands of government officials and their friends. Nigeria is attempting to end its dependence on oil by developing a natural gas industry.

Until the discovery of oil in the late 1960s, agriculture was the mainstay of Nigeria's economy. It still contributes nearly 40 percent of the nation's gross domestic product (GDP)*. Nigeria's major agricultural exports include cocoa, palm oil, peanuts, cotton, rubber, and timber. Although its mining industry is not well developed, Nigeria contains an abundance of mineral resources such as gold, lead, zinc, and other industrial minerals. Nigeria also contains large deposits of coal.

* **regime**   current political system or rule

* **privatize**   to transfer from government control to private ownership

See map in Minerals and Mining (vol. 3).

* **gross domestic product (GDP)**   total value of goods and services produced and consumed within a country

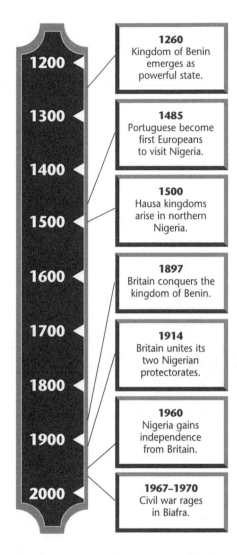

1200

1260
Kingdom of Benin emerges as powerful state.

1300

1485
Portuguese become first Europeans to visit Nigeria.

1400

1500
Hausa kingdoms arise in northern Nigeria.

1500

1600

1897
Britain conquers the kingdom of Benin.

1700

1914
Britain unites its two Nigerian protectorates.

1800

1960
Nigeria gains independence from Britain.

1900

1967–1970
Civil war rages in Biafra.

2000

* **pastoralist** someone who herds livestock

* **hierarchical** referring to a society or institution divided into groups with higher and lower levels

In the late 1940s, British colonial officials began a program of industrialization in Nigeria. However, instead of using local raw materials, the program involved importing partially processed raw materials to produce finished goods in Nigerian factories. This costly and inefficient manufacturing process continues, consuming a large portion of Nigeria's export revenues and adding to its huge foreign debt.

By the late 1980s, Nigeria's debt had forced the nation to adopt various economic reforms. These included cutting levels of government spending and employment and privatizing state-owned industries. Changes in the exchange rate led to a steep drop in the value of the nation's currency, creating severe hardship for most Nigerians. Despite these measures, the Nigerian economy remains unstable, and economic growth is still uncertain.

PEOPLES AND CULTURES

Nigeria is a highly diverse country consisting of many different ethnic groups. The most prominent are the Muslim Hausa, Kanuri, and Fulani of northern Nigeria and the largely Christian Yoruba and Igbo of the south. There are more than 450 languages spoken in the country, but the widespread use of a few major ones, such as English, Hausa, Yoruba, and Igbo, enables Nigerians from different linguistic groups to communicate.

Northern Nigeria. Northwestern Nigeria is dominated by the Hausa, who are primarily farmers and pastoralists*. During the Sokoto Caliphate in the 1800s, the Hausa absorbed many local peoples who eventually adopted Hausa culture. However, many other groups resisted the Muslim caliphate and maintained their own identities. Some of these groups, such as the Dendi, Busa, and Tienga, do not speak Hausa or Fulani languages.

Among the major groups in northeastern Nigeria are the Kanuri and Fulani. Both groups are primarily Muslim. Most of the Kanuri live by farming, although some engage in trade. Kanuri society is very hierarchical*, with a sharp division between royalty and commoners. The Fulani are both farmers and herders. Town society among the Fulani is also hierarchical, headed by a strong Islamic political leader called an emir.

Northern Nigeria is also home to a wide variety of smaller ethnic groups, many of which are organized into chiefdoms. Quite a few of these groups continue to practice traditional religions, but that number is shrinking as Christianity and Islam make further inroads in the area. Conflict between Christian and Muslim groups is common.

Southern and Central Nigeria. The Niger River divides southern Nigeria into eastern and western halves. Yoruba-speaking peoples dominate the western portion, but they have had much interaction with other ethnic groups in the region. The Yoruba had developed centralized power structures and a hierarchical social system based on descent before the arrival of Europeans. These political structures survive in local governing institutions, while ancestry is still important in determining social position and inheritance. The Yoruba are primarily farmers.

145

Nigeria

Nigeria

POPULATION:
123,337,822 (2000 estimated population)

AREA:
356,669 sq. mi. (923,774 sq. km)

LANGUAGES:
English (official); Hausa, Yoruba, Igbo

NATIONAL CURRENCY:
Naira

PRINCIPAL RELIGIONS:
Muslim 50%, Christian 40%, traditional 10%

CITIES:
Abuja (Federal Capital Territory), 378,700 (1991 est.); Lagos, Ibadan, Ogbomosho, Kano, Ilorin, Oshogbo

ANNUAL RAINFALL:
Highly variable, 70–170 in. (1,700–4,310 mm) from west to east along the coast; 20 in. (500 mm) in the extreme north

ECONOMY:
GDP per capita: $970 (1999 est.)

PRINCIPAL PRODUCTS AND EXPORTS:
Agricultural: cotton, cocoa, rubber, yams, cassava, sorghum, palm kernels, millet, corn, rice, groundnuts, plantains, maize, potatoes, fruit, livestock, fish, timber
Manufacturing: oil refining, iron and steel production, sugar refining, textiles, cement, building materials, chemicals, food processing, pharmaceuticals
Mining: petroleum, tin, columbite, iron ore, coal, limestone, lead, zinc, natural gas, gold

GOVERNMENT:
Independence from Britain, 1960. Republic, transitioning from military to civilian rule. President elected by universal suffrage. Governing bodies: National Assembly and House of Representatives (legislative bodies); Federal Executive Council.

HEADS OF STATE SINCE INDEPENDENCE:
1960–1966 Governor General Benjamin Nnamdi Azikiwe (president after 1963)
1966 Major General Johnson Aguiyi-Ironsi
1966–1975 Lieutenant Colonel (later General) Yakubu Gowon
1975–1976 Brigadier (later General) Murtala Ramat Muhammed
1976–1979 Lieutenant General (later General) Olusegun Obasanjo
1979–1983 President Shehu Shagari
1984–1985 Major General Muhammadu Buhari
1985–1993 Major General Ibrahim Badamasi Babangida
1993 Interim President Ernest Shonekan
1993–1999 General Sani Abacha
1999– President Olusegun Obasanjo

ARMED FORCES:
77,000

EDUCATION:
Compulsory for ages 6–15; literacy rate 57%

The largest group east of the Niger River is the Igbo (Ibo). Neither the Igbo nor other ethnic groups in this area ever developed centralized power structures. Christianity is the most widely practiced religion in southeastern Nigeria, but many people also follow traditional religions. Among the main sources of livelihood in the area are agriculture, fishing, and crafts such as weaving and woodcarving. Many people are also employed in the Niger Delta oil industry. As the center of crude oil production in Nigeria, southeastern Nigeria is home to some of the largest commercial centers in the country, including Onitsha, Aba, and Port Harcourt. The well-developed region is also home to numerous universities and several airports and seaports.

Central Nigeria is one of the most ethnically diverse parts of the country. It is the home of many different language and ethnic groups that have interacted extensively over time, resulting in much cultural exchange. The site of important trade routes in the precolonial era, central Nigeria was also exposed to a variety of outside influences. Most groups in the region are agricultural, while mining has attracted large numbers of people from other regions of Nigeria to the area. (*See also* **Boundaries in Africa; Colonialism in Africa; Development, Economic and Social; Energy and Energy Resources; Ethnic Groups and Identity; History of Africa; Missions and Missionaries; Sudanic Empires of Western Africa.**)

Nile River and Delta

* **tributary** river that flows into another river

The Nile, the world's longest river, begins in the heart of Africa and empties into the Mediterranean Sea. Snaking north through eastern Africa for more than 4,000 miles, the river passes through nine countries on its way to the sea. The Nile basin, the area drained by the river's tributaries*, covers 1.2 million square miles. For thousands of years, the Nile River has been the most important geographic feature of this enormous region, providing water and fertile soil for agriculture and serving as a highway for people, goods, and cultures.

Geography. The portion of the Nile that flows through EGYPT is

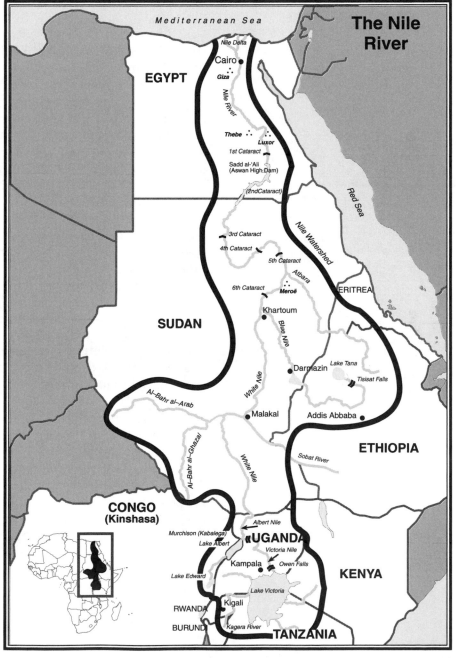

formed by the blending farther south of three main sources: the White Nile, Blue Nile, and Atbara Rivers. The White Nile, the southernmost source, originates at a spring in BURUNDI. The spring gives rise to the Kagera River, which flows into Lake Victoria, the world's second largest freshwater lake. Water runs out of the north end of the lake and through northern UGANDA to merge with the outflow from a series of smaller lakes to the west. From there the river plunges over a waterfall and proceeds northward as the White Nile. For 230 miles it wanders through a region called the *sudd,* a vast swamp in southern SUDAN. At the Sudanese city of Malakal the White Nile absorbs several tributaries flowing from the west and from the highlands of ETHIOPIA to the east. Then it heads north for 600 miles through flat, arid plains to KHARTOUM, the capital of Sudan.

At Khartoum the White Nile meets the Blue Nile, which begins at a spring in the Ethiopian highlands. The Blue Nile flows into Lake Tana, dotted with islands on which stand churches, monasteries, and the tombs of Ethiopian emperors. The river runs out of the lake, over a waterfall, and through a winding, mile-deep canyon. Descending onto the plains of Sudan, it flows northward to meet the White Nile.

North of Khartoum, the Nile travels through desert. Its only remaining tributary is the Atbara, which rushes down from the Ethiopian highlands during the wet season but is dry from January to June. Beyond the Atbara, the Nile makes a great S-shaped bend before flowing into a reservoir created by Egypt's Aswan High Dam. Released from the dam, the Nile travels another 700 miles to the sea. North of CAIRO, Egypt's capital, it separates into two branches, the Damietta and the Rosetta. Together with a network of smaller branches and canals, these river mouths form a fan-shaped delta 100 miles deep and 180 miles wide at the Mediterranean coast. About 60 percent of Egypt's population lives in the Nile Delta, benefiting from the river's gifts of water and soil.

Historical and Cultural Importance. Since ancient times the Nile has been vital to life in northeastern Africa. Not only does the river provide water in a barren region, but its annual floods, fed by the downpours of the highland rainy season, deposit moist, fertile soil along the riverbanks. The Saharan peoples who settled along those banks soon learned that although the river gave life, it could also be deadly. If the flood was too high it brought destruction, but a low flood could result in crop failure and famine.

The Nile nourished the Egyptian civilization that arose 5,000 years ago, as well as the later civilizations of NUBIA in what is now southern Egypt and northern Sudan. After Christianity became established in Egypt, the new religion spread up the Nile to Ethiopia. Then the Arab invasions of the A.D. 600s brought Islam* to North Africa, and the new faith slowly moved south along the river. The Nile could serve as a highway, but it had barriers—the swamps of the *sudd* and the warlike peoples of southern Sudan halted the southward march of Arabs and Islam into eastern Africa.

Beginning in the 1800s, Egypt and various European powers competed to control the Nile basin. As part of this effort, European explorers

* **Islam** religion based on the teachings of the prophet Muhammad; religious faith of Muslims

such as Sir Richard BURTON and John Hanning Speke searched for the source of the White Nile. By the end of the 1800s, Britain dominated the Nile from the delta to Lake Victoria. In the mid-1900s however, British colonial rule came to an end, and the African states in the region gained their independence.

During the colonial period, Britain constructed several dams to regulate the Nile for irrigation and flood control and to supply water to areas of growing population. The independent nations of the region have continued to manage and develop the river through such projects. Egypt built the Aswan High Dam to produce hydroelectric power* and to supply water for irrigation, and Sudan has also built dams. In an effort to prevent famines caused by unpredictable rainfall, Ethiopia has proposed two new dams to make use of the Blue Nile waters. In 1959 Egypt and Sudan signed an agreement that gives 20 percent of the Nile's water to Sudan. However, water needs are growing rapidly in both nations. Although the Nile is the most developed river in Africa, rivalries among the countries along its shores threaten to jeopardize regional cooperation. (*See also* **Egypt, Ancient; Fishing; Irrigation and Flood Control.**)

* **hydroelectric power** power produced by converting the energy of flowing water into electricity

Nkrumah, Kwame

1909–1972
President of Ghana

* **civil disobedience** policy of peaceful, nonviolent actions to demonstrate opposition

Francis Nwia Kofi Nkrumah, known as Kwame Nkrumah, was the prime minister and first president of GHANA. Born in the Gold Coast (present-day Ghana), Nkrumah attended Achimota College in the colony. He continued his studies in the United States, where he served as president of the African Students Association, and in England. In London he wrote a book, *Towards Colonial Freedom* (1947), that outlined his ideas on fighting colonialism in Africa.

Returning to the Gold Coast, Nkrumah became active in politics. He founded the Convention People's Party, which organized strikes and civil disobedience* against the colonial government. Jailed in 1950 for his part in a strike, he was released early in order to take a seat in the Legislative Assembly. Nkrumah became prime minister of the colony in 1952 and continued in the post five years later when Ghana won its independence from Great Britain.

In 1960 Ghana became a republic and Nkrumah was elected president. As president, he focused much of his attention on working toward African unity. Ghana's economy was initially strong due to high prices for cocoa, its leading crop. But as prices fell, so did the nation's fortunes. During the early 1960s Nkrumah escaped several assassination attempts, and each time he responded by arresting opponents and tightening his control over the country. While he was still a leader in the movement to create a unified Africa, it was clear that Nkrumah was rapidly losing power in his own nation. In 1964 he declared Ghana a single-party state under his leadership. Two years later, while Nkrumah was on a trip abroad, the military took over the government. Nkrumah returned to Africa and settled in GUINEA, where President Sékou TOURÉ named him copresident. In his later years, Nkrumah continued to write about the struggle for freedom and unity in Africa. (*See also* **Colonialism in Africa, Independence Movements.**)

NOMADS

See *Berbers.*

Nongqawuse

ca. 1840–ca. 1900
Xhosa prophet

Nongqawuse was a young woman whom the XHOSA people of SOUTH AFRICA regarded as a prophet who communicated with the spirit world. She urged them to kill their cattle—advice that proved tragic for her people and their kingdom.

An orphan, Nongqawuse was raised by her uncle, a Christian convert, in South Africa's Transkei region. In 1856 she claimed that she could see and talk with the spirits of the dead. The communications she relayed from the ancestors made no sense, so her uncle interpreted them for the Xhosa. The spirits ordered the Xhosa to kill all their cattle, destroy their corn, and throw away their magical devices. Soon the dead would rise, bringing a perfect new world. Cattle and corn would be plentiful, the blind would see, the old would grow young, and no one would suffer again. These prophecies offered hope to the Xhosa, who were suffering from a long epidemic of cattle sickness and from conflict with white settlers over their land.

After 15 months of cattle killing, about 40,000 Xhosa had starved to death, including Nongqawuse's uncle. Another 150,000 had abandoned their homes to search for food. For 80 years the Xhosa kingdom had blocked the advance of the British Cape Colony. However, the disastrous cattle-killing movement devastated the kingdom, and white settlers snatched up much of the Xhosa territory. Colonial authorities held Nongqawuse for a time in Cape Town. Details of her release and later life are not known, but she is thought to have spent the rest of her life with relatives on a white-owned farm. (*See also* **Prophetic Movements, Religion and Ritual, Southern Africa, History.**)

North Africa: Geography and Population

* **sub-Saharan** referring to Africa south of the Sahara desert

North Africa consists of five countries that border the Mediterranean Sea—EGYPT, LIBYA, TUNISIA, ALGERIA, and MOROCCO. The SAHARA DESERT, the dominant feature of the North African landscape, sweeps across the southern part of the region. The Sahara serves as a geographical boundary between North Africa and sub-Saharan* Africa, except in Egypt. It also marks a transition zone from the largely Arab population of North Africa to black Africa of the south.

The Land. North Africa has three main geographic features: the Sahara, the ATLAS MOUNTAINS in the west, and the NILE RIVER AND DELTA in the east. The Atlas Mountains—a complex cluster of ranges, ridges, plateaus, and basins—stretch for 1,200 miles along the North African coast from southwestern Morocco across Algeria to northeastern Tunisia. The tallest peaks are in the High Atlas range in south-central Morocco, which has many snowcapped peaks.

African Apes in Europe

North Africa's native monkey is a tailless, ground-dwelling member of the macaque family that lives in Algeria and Morocco. It is called the Barbary ape—although it is a monkey, not a true ape— because North Africa was formerly known as the Barbary coast. Barbary apes also live in Gibraltar, a British-controlled peninsula in southern Spain. They are Europe's only wild monkeys, possibly carried to the continent by the Moors, Arabs from North Africa who invaded Spain in the Middle Ages.

* **pastoralist**   someone who herds live-stock

South of the Atlas Mountains is the dry and largely barren expanse of the Sahara. In places the desert is cut by irregular watercourses called wadis—streams that flow only after rainfalls but are usually dry. The Sahara's major landforms include *ergs,* large seas of sand that sometimes form into huge dunes; the *hammada,* a level rocky plateau without soil or sand; and the *reg,* a level plain of gravel or small stones. The Sahara covers the southern part of Morocco, Algeria, and Tunisia, and most of Libya. Only two regions of Libya are outside the desert: Tripolitania in the northwest and Cyrenaica in the northeast.

Most of Egypt is also desert, except for the Nile River and the irrigated land along its banks. The Nile Valley is a narrow green and fertile thread that runs the length of the country. The Egyptian desert also contains oases, fertile areas around natural water sources. Oases are scattered through other parts of the desert as well.

Climate, Water, and Resources. Coastal North Africa has a Mediterranean climate, with hot summers and mild, damp winters. Along the Atlas chain, the mountains trap moisture-laden clouds blowing south from the Mediterranean Sea. The moisture falls as rain on the mountains' northern slopes. As a result, these slopes and the coastal area between them and the sea are well-watered and fertile, compared with the more arid conditions on the southern side of the mountains. Similar conditions exist in Libya, where cliffs and low mountains separate Tripolitania and Cyrenaica from the desert interior.

Throughout North Africa, the availability of water has always been the chief factor in determining where and how people live. In Egypt, 95 percent of the people live within a short distance of the Nile River or in the delta at its mouth on the Mediterranean Sea. Water from the river is used to irrigate fields of cereal grains, vegetables, cotton, and other crops.

In the other North African countries, about 90 percent of the people live within 200 miles of the coast, generally in valleys that have streams and rivers. These areas are suitable for agriculture, especially with the aid of irrigation. Citrus fruits, olives, and grapes are major crops. Farther south, drier hills and grasslands bordering the desert have long been the home of pastoralists* who raise herds of sheep, goats, cattle, and camels. The only farming in the desert takes place in oases, where the main crops raised are date palms, fruit, and cereal grains.

North Africa possesses valuable mineral resources. Libya and Algeria have extensive deposits of petroleum and natural gas. Industrial development of these resources has been underway since the 1950s, and fuel exports are a major source of revenue for these countries. Egypt and Tunisia have oil industries as well, though on a smaller scale. The region also contains small quantities of other minerals, such as copper, zinc, and manganese. Morocco and Tunisia have fairly significant deposits of phosphates, while iron ore is found in Algeria, Libya, and Tunisia.

The People. North Africa's geographical setting has determined its population and its place in world affairs. In some ways, North Africa is

151

North Africa: Geography and Population

closer to Europe and the Middle East than to the rest of Africa. The northernmost point in Morocco lies only eight miles from Europe across the Strait of Gibraltar. The Tunisian coast is just 85 miles from the Italian island of Sicily. North Africa has had extensive contact with Europe over the centuries, and in ancient times it was part of the Roman Empire. Moreover, the Sinai Peninsula, the northeastern part of Egypt, borders the Middle East. Contacts between the Middle East and North Africa also go back many centuries.

The population of North Africa is mainly white, like the peoples of Europe and the Middle East. But racial mixing has occurred over the years between the people of North Africa and the black population of sub-Saharan Africa. North Africa shares the Middle East's dominant ethnic group (Arab), language (Arabic), and religion (Islam*). For this reason North Africa is sometimes considered part of the Middle East, at least culturally. Arabs have long used the term MAGHREB (or Maghrib), meaning "west," to refer to Libya, Tunisia, Algeria, and Morocco, which they consider the westernmost part of the Arab world.

The most significant feature of North Africa's population is that it is more uniform than the population of any other African region.

* **Islam** religion based on the teachings of the Prophet Muhammad; religious faith of Muslims

Arab culture and the Islamic religion have dominated much of North African life since the invasion of Muslim Arabs in the 600s. Most of the women shown in this picture of Tunis, the capital of Tunisia, wear traditional Muslim garb.

Although minority populations exist in all five nations, most North Africans are either Arabs, BERBERS, or a mixture of the two groups. The Berbers were the original inhabitants of North Africa. Between the A.D. 600s and 1000s, Muslim Arabs from Arabia swept across the region in a wave of conquest. The two peoples, physically quite similar, formed a single population in many areas as Berbers merged into Arab society.

The Arabs brought with them to North Africa the Arabic language and the Islamic religion. Both the language and the faith, along with many other features of Arab culture, became dominant across North Africa. Some Berber groups, however, have maintained their separate identity. These groups generally live in the more isolated or remote mountain and desert areas of Tunisia, Algeria, and Morocco.

Although Muslims, the Berbers often continue to speak their own languages and follow their traditional pastoralist, and sometimes nomadic* or seminomadic, way of life. One Berber-speaking group—the TUAREG—live primarily in the desert regions of North Africa and cling strongly to their traditional lifestyle. Despite such differences, however, centuries of interaction between the Berbers and Arabs has created a strong sense of cultural unity.

The people of North Africa are overwhelmingly Muslim. Egypt has a small but significant group of Coptic Christians, followers of an early form of Christianity. Jewish communities have existed in North Africa since ancient times. In recent years, however, they have almost disappeared as North Africa's Jews have emigrated to Israel or Europe.

North Africa's population numbered approximately 144 million in 2000. The country with the largest population was Egypt, with more than 68 million inhabitants. Algeria had 31 million people, Morocco 30 million, and Tunisia nearly 10 million. Libya's population numbered only 5 million. Arabic is the official language of all five countries, but many North Africans also speak other languages. French is often used in business in the former French colonies of Morocco, Algeria, and Tunisia. Many Libyans, especially in the cities, understand English and Italian, and many urban Egyptians speak English. Berber is most often heard in Morocco and Algeria, which have large Berber populations.

North Africa has had cities since ancient times, when ALEXANDRIA in Egypt and CARTHAGE in Tunisia were major Mediterranean ports. CAIRO in Egypt and Fez in Morocco flourished as centers of the caravan trade during the Middle Ages. More recently, trade and industrial development have stimulated the growth of several port cities in North Africa. Major urban centers now include Alexandria, Cairo, Tripoli in Libya, Tunis, ALGIERS in Algeria, and Casablanca in Morocco. (*See also* **Arabs in Africa, Climate, North Africa: History and Cultures, Roman Africa.**)

* **nomadic** referring to people who travel from place to place to find food and pasture

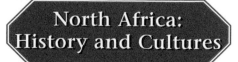

North Africa: History and Cultures

Separated from the rest of Africa by the SAHARA DESERT, the peoples of North Africa share a language and many cultural, political, and economic traditions. The term *North Africa* refers to the modern states of EGYPT, LIBYA, TUNISIA, ALGERIA, and MOROCCO, as well as the territory of WESTERN SAHARA. In ancient times the lands north of the Sahara and west

153

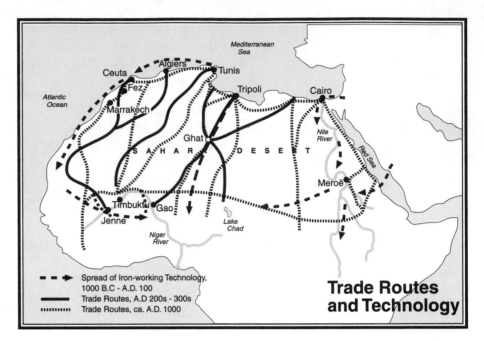

Map legend:
- - - → Spread of Iron-working Technology, 1000 B.C - A.D. 100
——— Trade Routes, A.D 200s - 300s
·········· Trade Routes, ca. A.D. 1000

Trade Routes and Technology

of Egypt were treated as a single unit. The Greeks called the region "Libya," and the Arabs referred to it as "Jazirat al-Maghreb," meaning "island of the west." Although the geography and history of North Africa might suggest that the region developed separately from the rest of the continent, in fact its peoples have always had close contact with their neighbors south of the Sahara.

EARLY HISTORY

By about 40,000 years ago, North Africa's first human inhabitants had developed complex stoneworking techniques. This achievement led to the spread of human settlement across the region. After these Stone Age people began to form communities, a series of long droughts occurred in the Sahara. The change in climate drove the human inhabitants north, east, and south in search of better lands. Over the next 30,000 years, the Sahara had several wet and dry cycles. During each wet phase people would form settlements, only to move on as drought made the lands barren.

Migration and Settlement. Some people migrated east until they reached the NILE RIVER. By about 6000 B.C. they had developed a culture based on fishing, which eventually grew into the great civilization of Egypt. Others traveled north to the Mediterranean coast, where they found fertile lands and learned to grow grains. Those who traveled south settled around oases in the desert or found their way to the lands beyond the desert. These southern migrations provided the foundation for what would later become the great Saharan trade routes.

By about 1000 B.C. the domestication* of crops and animals had spread throughout North Africa and ironworking technology had developed. The peoples who had settled along the Nile learned to control the river's flooding and improved their farming techniques. The population

* **domestication** adapting or training plants or animals for human use

154

Instead of going straight across the desert, early Saharan trade routes wandered from one Berber settlement to the next. These settlements were located near natural wells that provided water for the desert-dwelling peoples and their animals. In the 600s B.C., Berbers from the Atlas Mountains and the northern Sahara traveled from one oasis to another, exchanging salt for food, copper, gold, and other items. At the end of their journey the Berbers headed for the wealthy Phoenician city of Carthage, where there was a ready market for goods from tropical Africa.

* **monopoly** exclusive control or domination of a particular type of business

* **sub-Saharan** referring to Africa south of the Sahara desert

* **indigenous** native to a certain place

of the region increased rapidly and new forms of social organization developed. Small states arose along the Nile's fertile valley and delta. In about 3000 B.C. King Menes united the entire region—from the southernmost settlements to the Nile Delta in the north—and became Egypt's first pharaoh.

Egypt. Over the next several hundred years, Egypt expanded northward into Palestine and became the most powerful nation in the region. Farther north in what is now Turkey arose the Hittite Empire, and to the east in Mesopotamia emerged the empire of Babylon. By 2000 B.C. the southern border of Egypt had extended beyond Aswan to include the region known as NUBIA. For the next 1,000 years, Egypt was the gateway for new inventions and trade goods entering Africa from the Middle East.

Centuries of Invasions. By the 600s B.C. the Assyrian Empire (in modern Iraq) had conquered the Hittites, the Babylonians, and Egypt. Later, the Persians, who came from what is now Iran, overthrew the Assyrians. At about the same time, traders from Phoenicia in the eastern Mediterranean began sailing along the North African coast. They established settlements where they could repair and provision their ships on the way to Spain. The most important of their settlements, CARTHAGE in present-day Tunisia, grew into a major city—and eventually an empire. The Phoenicians also founded three cities in what is now Libya, around which developed the region known as Tripolitania.

The city of Carthage formed trade relationships with the nomads of North Africa's interior, such as the Sanhaja BERBERS. These nomads had a monopoly* on trade across the Sahara, exchanging salt from North Africa for food, gold, ivory, and slaves. By 600 B.C. Carthage had achieved great wealth and become an independent state.

As the demand for trade goods increased, Carthage's commercial network expanded south to the NIGER RIVER and west to settlements in what is now MAURITANIA. These trading contacts provided for the exchange of more than goods: along with salt and cloth the visitors from the north brought skills, such as ironworking, to their trade partners in the sub-Saharan* lands.

The Phoenicians, however, were not the only people to claim land on the North African coast. The Greeks had reached northeastern Libya in about 1100 B.C. They had formed alliances with indigenous* tribes and launched an unsuccessful attempt to invade Egypt. When the Greeks returned to North Africa about 500 years later, Phoenicia had already gained control of most of the coast. The only territory left unclaimed was the stretch of shore on which the Greeks had originally landed. Here they founded the town of Cyrene (in modern Libya) in about 630 B.C.

At first the Greek colonists settled into friendly relations with the local peoples, but as their numbers increased relations turned hostile. The greatest threat to peace, however, came from outside. Egypt tried, and failed, to invade the Greek territory in 570 B.C. Less than 50 years later, the Persians conquered the region. Persia held it for about 200 years, until Alexander the Great defeated Persia and claimed its North

155

The fortified complex of Chella, near Rabat, Morocco, includes an Islamic burial site from the 1300s.

African colonies. After Alexander's death in 323, his general, Ptolemy, became pharaoh of Egypt and ruled the region from the newly created capital city of ALEXANDRIA.

ROMAN RULE

The arrival of Romans in North Africa deeply influenced the region's development. As Rome grew it sought to gain land, resources, and commercial opportunities in Africa.

Relations with Local Kingdoms. Rome began by challenging Carthage for control of the North African coast. The Phoenician army rose in defense, assisted by leaders of some of the indigenous peoples ruled by Carthage, including the Numidian commander Masinissa. In 204 B.C. the Romans promised to recognize Masinissa as king of Numidia (now part of Tunisia and eastern Algeria) if he would abandon Carthage. Not a strong supporter of Carthage, he quickly switched sides. Soon afterward, a Berber leader named Bocchus struck a similar deal with the Romans and was recognized as king of Mauretania (present-day Morocco and western Algeria).

Rome destroyed Carthage in 146 B.C. and sent its own colonists to North Africa. Settling on the coast, the Romans built great plantations that were worked by slaves from nomadic groups in the Sahara. Over time resentment of the Romans grew among some of the peoples of the interior. Mauretania remained loyal, but the Numidians began raiding Roman settlements.

In 46 B.C. the Romans overthrew the Numidian monarchy and made the kingdom into a Roman province. They spent the next several decades consolidating their holdings in North Africa. Having already gained control of Egypt's Libyan province, Cyrenaica, they took over Egypt in 30 B.C.

As Roman control spread across North Africa, opposition stirred among the indigenous peoples. Even in Mauretania, where the kings continued to support Rome, independent Berber groups mounted raids against Roman estates. Over time, however, these conflicts lessened. Rome had powerful reasons for maintaining peace and order in North Africa. The farms in the region produced an abundance of grain, and the Saharan trade routes were a source of great wealth.

Trade. Trade flourished in North Africa under Roman rule. The Romans built garrisons* to protect their colonies and the trade routes. Caravans increased in size and number and trading centers—such as Leptis in Libya and Djemila in Algeria—grew rapidly. Berber groups dominated commerce across the region.

Trade brought the ivory and gold merchants of the western Sudan into contact with the Mediterranean region and with new development from the world outside of Africa. The rise of the early SUDANIC EMPIRES along the Niger River occurred in large part as a response to the rich trade in ivory, gold, slaves, and other goods. The wealth generated by this trade was so great that merchants from other regions were attracted to North Africa. Arabs from Yemen on the Arabian Peninsula established commercial centers in Africa, extending the Saharan trading network as far east and south as ZANZIBAR.

The peace and prosperity of North Africa under Roman rule allowed Christianity to spread across the region. Christian communities began to appear in the A.D. 100s, and by the 300s the new religion had reached ETHIOPIA. The movement spread down the Nile River into Nubia and provided a common faith for many of the independent peoples of the region.

In the 400s the Roman Empire came under attack from the north. The Goths and Vandals of northern Europe stormed the city of Rome and, in a series of invasions, broke the strength of the empire. What remained of Roman territory was an area that came to be known as the Byzantine Empire, based around Constantinople (modern Istanbul in Turkey). The Vandals took over Rome's colonies in North Africa, and the Romans lost their share of the Saharan trade. However, within 150 years the Byzantine Empire had regained control of Rome's former territories in Tunisia.

* **garrison**   military post

Cyrene

Stately Greek columns and crumbling houses and temples mark the site of the ancient city of Cyrene in modern Libya. Founded by Greek immigrants in about 631 B.C., Cyrene grew into a prosperous colony with a port on the Mediterranean Sea and several outlying towns. Taken over by Egypt in 323, Cyrene became a great center of scholarship that boasted a medical school and renowned philosophers and geographers. In 96 B.C. the Romans conquered the region, known as Cyrenaica. After the fall of Rome in the A.D. 400s, Cyrene fell into decline, but the province of Cyrenaica became part of the modern state of Libya.

MUSLIM RULE

* **Islam** religion based on the teachings of the prophet Muhammad; religious faith of Muslims

Soon after the collapse of Roman rule, the religion of Islam* was founded. This new faith quickly gained followers and became a major cultural and political force in North Africa and the Mediterranean region.

The Rise of Islam. In 622 the prophet Muhammad rose to power in the Arabian city of Medina and founded Islam. The Muslim leaders, or caliphs, who followed him used the religion to solidify and expand their rule throughout the Middle East and into North Africa. By the mid-600s they had invaded Egypt and the territories of Cyrenaica and Tripolitania in Libya. Then they expanded their North African holdings as far west as Tunis, spreading the new faith as they went.

Arab Trade and Culture. By the early 700s the Arabs had extended their empire across North Africa and up into Spain. Waves of settlers from Arabia came to live in North Africa, strengthening Arab control of the coast and trading with the Berber merchants of the region. Once again, trade provided a means of spreading new ideas. Through Arab merchants Islam quickly expanded beyond the Sahara, as far south as the Niger River and as far west as present-day SENEGAL.

Gradually, Arabic became the language used in everyday conversation and in literature and scholarship. Many people came to know Arabic through the Qur'an, the Islamic holy scripture. The spread of Islam also brought Islamic customs and religious practices to a wide area. The Arab rulers used Islamic law, called Shari'a, to settle disputes.

Under Arab rule, trading caravans ran more frequently and commercial networks expanded, accelerating the spread of Islam to distant regions. The Arabs relied on camels in their Saharan caravans and passed their skill in handling the animals on to the Sanhaja Berbers. The camels, superbly adapted to the desert, allowed merchants to travel more quickly and cover greater distances. New Berber groups became involved in trade and new routes opened up from Algeria south into Songhai and Mali.

* **dynasty** succession of rulers from the same family or group

Ruling Dynasties. By the late 900s the Arabs were well established in North Africa and had achieved independence from Baghdad (in modern Iraq), the political center of the Islamic world. In North Africa various powerful families worked to establish themselves as hereditary monarchs. A dynasty* called the Tulunids took over in Egypt, and the Ahglabids rose to power in Algeria. The Idrisids gained influence in northern Morocco. These dynasties controlled the coastal strip of North Africa. However, in the south, the Berbers—particularly the Sanhaja and the TUAREG—remained independent.

For the next 400 years, different forms of Islam competed for dominance in North Africa. A version of the religion called Shia Islam was practiced by the Fatimid dynasty, which claimed descent from Muhammad's daughter Fatima. Gaining influence in Egypt and Tunisia, the Fatimids attempted to spread Shia Islam to the rest of North Africa.

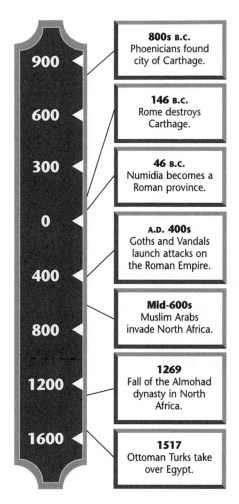

900	**800s B.C.** Phoenicians found city of Carthage.
600	**146 B.C.** Rome destroys Carthage.
300	**46 B.C.** Numidia becomes a Roman province.
0	
400	**A.D. 400s** Goths and Vandals launch attacks on the Roman Empire.
800	**Mid-600s** Muslim Arabs invade North Africa.
1200	**1269** Fall of the Almohad dynasty in North Africa.
1600	**1517** Ottoman Turks take over Egypt.

* **sect** religious group

* **doctrine** set of principles or beliefs accepted by a religious or political group

The followers of Sunni Islam, the more widespread version of the religion, opposed the Fatimids.

The conflict among these different forms of Islam kept the peoples of North Africa divided until a few great dynasties consolidated them. The Almoravids, Sanhaja Berbers who practiced Sunni Islam, rose to power in the west. By the 1100s, they had united the area from Morocco to Algeria and south into Senegal, Ghana, and Songhai. They also conquered much of Muslim Spain. Even after the Almoravid movement had passed on, it left a strong legacy in northern Africa. In its wake, it left behind the Maliki school of Islamic law, which became the dominant form of Islam in the region. It remains a powerful presence in parts of Africa. The Ziriids, also Sunni, came to power in western Algeria and Tunisia. The Fatimids remained in Egypt. Two Arab, rather than Berber, dynasties also gained some influence: the Hilali in western Algeria and Tunisia, and the Sulaym in Libya.

The Almoravids were the most powerful of these North African dynasties. However, in the 1100s the Soninke of Ghana challenged the Almoravids from the south. At the same time, the Almohads, a dynasty led by Berbers from the Atlas Mountains, began to challenge the Almoravids. The Almohads took the Almoravids' Spanish provinces and their lands along the North African coast. They held the region until 1269, when three new Berber states arose, ruled by the Marinid, Hafsid, and Zayyanid dynasties.

The Berber States. The Marinid dynasty held power in the territory now called Morocco, the Hafsids ruled from western Libya (Tripolitania) to eastern Algeria and Tunisia, and the Zayyanids controlled most of western Algeria. These rulers decided not to identify their states with any single religious sect*, and they encouraged cooperation among followers of different doctrines*. In this atmosphere, Islam thrived and the major cities of North Africa became important centers for scholarship and culture.

Relations among the three Berber states were frequently strained. In the mid-1300s the Marinid sultans, Abu al-Hasan Ali and Abu Inan, launched attacks on their eastern neighbors but were forced back. Such conflicts continued throughout the 1300s and 1400s, and territory in the region traded hands several times. The Marinids tried to take advantage of this instability and gain control of the entire region. But before they could do so, armies from Europe began to invade North Africa.

Toward the end of the 1400s, the conflict between Christian Europe and Muslim North Africa intensified. The Spanish and Portuguese captured several towns, leading the peoples of the North African states to join forces to defend the coast. To defeat the Portuguese, the Sa'di family of southern Morocco organized a movement that succeeded in occupying Marrakech in 1525. Within 30 years the Sa'dis had gained control of Morocco. Meanwhile, the Ottoman Turks had taken over Egypt in 1517. Since the Ottomans were Muslim, the other North African states turned to them for support in their fight against Christian conquest. Algeria was the first to seek help from the Turks. However, Turkish assistance came at a price—Algeria had to submit to Ottoman rule.

Ottoman Takeover. Once the Ottomans had a foothold in the region, they attempted to take over the port city of Tunis, then occupied by Spanish troops. The Ottomans expelled the Spanish in 1534 but held Tunis for only a year before Spain recaptured it. Forty years later the Turks finally won the city. In 1551 Ottoman forces seized Tripoli from its Christian rulers and took Libya. Morocco remained outside the Ottoman Empire because the Sa'dis had succeeded in repelling the Christian invaders without assistance from the Turks.

North Africa's membership in the Ottoman Empire marks the beginning of the formation of its modern nation-states. Morocco remained independent of Turkish rule. Algeria, Tunisia, Libya, and Egypt became provinces in the Ottoman Empire, ruled by military governors. Eventually the provinces became autonomous* states under the Ottoman sultan. These states did not become independent nations for a long time, partly because of the arrival of European powers in the region. Beginning in the 1800s, England, France, Germany, and Italy all attempted to claim territory in North Africa. The status of Western Sahara was disputed for decades and still has not been clearly determined. (*See also* **Animals, Domestic; Arabs in Africa; Christianity in Africa; Egypt, Ancient; History of Africa; Islam in Africa; North Africa: Geography and Population; Roman Africa; Trade.**)

* **autonomous**   self-governing

Nubia

Nubia, a region along the NILE RIVER, is now divided between southern EGYPT and northern SUDAN. The region takes its name from the Nubians, a distinctive ethnic group who speak languages of the Nubian family. Although there has never been a nation called Nubia, the region has been home to a number of empires and states.

Around 2,000 years ago, Nubian-speaking people began migrating from western Sudan into the Nile Valley. They settled in the Sudanese empire of Kush, a state that maintained a capital in the city of MEROË and that had a long history of interaction with ancient Egypt. Gradually the Nubian languages replaced the old languages of Kush. By the time the empire broke up in the A.D. 300s, the people of the region spoke Nubian languages.

When Christian missionaries entered Nubia in the 500s, they found three well-established kingdoms. Nobadia was in the north on the Egyptian border; farther south was Makuria; and the southernmost kingdom was Alodia (also known as Alwa). All three Nubian kingdoms rapidly accepted Christianity, and the Nubian church became part of the Coptic Orthodox Church of Egypt.

Less than a century after Christianity came to Nubia, Arabs conquered Egypt and introduced the Islamic* faith. After Arab forces tried and failed to conquer Nubia, the Arabs made a treaty that guaranteed peace to Nobadia and Makuria for 600 years in exchange for regular shipments of slaves. As a result of this treaty, medieval* Nubia was peaceful and prosperous. Art, architecture, and literature all reflected the strong influence of Christianity. Brightly colored paintings on

* **Islamic**   relating to Islam, the religion based on the teachings of the prophet Muhammad

* **medieval**   referring to the Middle Ages in western Europe, generally considered to be from the A.D. 500s to the 1500s

church walls and elaborately decorated pottery were the outstanding artistic achievements of Nubian civilization.

In time, the kingdoms of Nobadia and Makuria were combined under a single ruler, but they had separate administrations. Nobadia used Egyptian money and allowed Arab traders to travel and settle down. The king ruled Makuria more directly and controlled all commerce. The united kingdoms flourished for several centuries, sending gold, ivory, slaves, ebony, and ostrich feathers to Egypt in exchange for cloth, glassware, and wine.

When a different group of Islamic rulers seized power in Egypt in 1250, Nubia began to decline. Egypt's new rulers broke the ancient treaty and launched attacks on Nubia. In the long run, mass migrations of Arab nomads proved more destructive to Nubian civilization than military attacks. Arabs from Egypt and the Arabian peninsula overran Makuria and Alwa, where Arabic gradually replaced the Nubian languages. Although Christianity survived for a while in a small kingdom called Dotawo, it had disappeared by the late 1600s. After the end of the fifteenth century, information about Dotawo is primarily based on archaeological evidence, as the historical record for the region vanishes for several centuries. Archaeologists have determined that after lower Nubia was taken over by the Ottoman Empire near the end of the seventeenth century, all traces of Christianity and the Nubian church disappeared. The people of the region converted to Islam, though they continued to speak Nubian rather than Arabic.

Today there are about 1.2 million speakers of Nubian living in Egypt and Sudan. The name Nubia now applies only to the region they traditionally occupied, from Aswan south to Ed Debba in Sudan. The building of the Aswan High Dam in the 1960s flooded much of Nubia, requiring some inhabitants to be resettled in distant parts of Egypt and Sudan. (*See also* **Egypt, Ancient; Copts.**)

Nujoma, Samuel Shafiishuna

1929–
President of Namibia

* **League of Nations** organization founded to promote international peace and security; it functioned from 1920 to 1946

Sam Nujoma was a political organizer in colonial NAMIBIA (then known as South West Africa), who became the country's first president. As a young man, Nujoma worked for the railway but was fired from his job for attempting to organize a union. In 1958 he founded and became president of the Ovamboland People's Organization. His goal was to end an arrangement of the League of Nations* that placed Namibia under the control of South Africa. Forced to flee the country in 1960 because of his political activities, he formed the South West African Peoples Organization (SWAPO).

Nujoma returned to Namibia but was deported. He then established SWAPO headquarters in TANZANIA. Under his leadership, SWAPO waged an armed struggle against South African rule. After nearly 30 years of fighting, his country won its freedom and took the name Namibia. In 1990, Nujoma was elected president of Namibia and was reelected again in 1994 and 1998. World leaders have praised Nujoma for his steady rule and commitment to democracy. (*See also* **Colonialism in Africa, Independence Movements.**)

Nujoma, Samuel Shafiishuna

The first president of Namibia, Sam Nujoma has won respect abroad for his commitment to democratic rule.

Number Systems

The peoples of Africa employ a wide variety of systems for counting objects or representing numbers. Many of these are verbal systems, others involve gestures, and some use pictures or other counting devices.

Verbal number systems use words to express quantities. Most are founded on the numerical bases of 5, 10, and 20. For example, the Makhwa of MOZAMBIQUE use five *(thanu)* and ten *(nloko)* as bases. Their expression for six is *"thanu na moza,"* or "five plus one." To describe 20, they say *"miloko mili,"* or "ten times two." Some verbal number systems also use subtraction to form number expressions.

Many African groups traditionally use gestures to count and describe numbers. The Yao of Malawi and Mozambique represent the numbers one through four by pointing with the thumb of the right hand at extended fingers on the left hand. Making a fist with the left hand indicates the number five. Raising the fingers of both hands and joining the hands together is the signal for ten.

Visual number systems employ devices such as knotted strings or sticks. For example, Makonde women of Tanzania and Mozambique tie a knot in a string at each full moon to keep track of how many months it will be until they give birth. The Fulani herders of Nigeria place sticks in front of their houses to indicate how many cattle they own. A "V" indicates 100 animals, an "X" symbolizes 50, and an "I" indicates single animals. In front of one particularly wealthy household the following arrangement of sticks was found—VVVVVVXII, indicating that the owner of the house had 652 cows.

Nwapa, Flora

1931–1993
Nigerian writer

* **secede**   to withdraw formally from an organization or country

One of Africa's leading female authors, Flora Nwapa used her work to promote the role of women in society. She was the first black African woman to have a novel published, and she founded Tana Press in 1977 to bring the works of African women to the public.

Born at Oguta in eastern Nigeria, Nwapa was educated in the cities of Lagos and Ibadan and at the University of Edinburgh in Scotland. She later worked as a teacher and college administrator in Nigeria. After the war in which the southeastern region of Nigeria tried to secede* from the rest of the country, she served on the East Central State Executive Council. One of her works, *Never Again,* was a memoir of the war.

Nwapa's first novel, *Efuru,* tells the story of an Igbo woman who rises to prominence in her society as a trader and priestess. The novel reflects the author's view that African women can only achieve social independence through financial independence. The author of four novels, several collections of short stories, and many books for children, Nwapa was honored with many awards during her lifetime. (*See also* **Literature, Publishing.**)

Nyerere, Julius Kambarage

1922–1999
President of Tanzania

Julius Nyerere led the fight to end British rule in Tanganyika (now Tanzania) and served as the country's president from 1962 to 1979. He also played a key role in Africa's struggle for freedom and social justice, and African independence movements found refuge in his country.

The son of a chief, Nyerere was educated in Uganda and worked as a teacher before attending Edinburgh University in Scotland. Graduating in 1952 with a master's degree in history and economics, he returned to Tanganyika to teach. Nyerere soon became active in politics, and in 1954 he founded the Tanganyika African National Union (TANU). Calling for social equality and racial harmony, he became a leading figure in Tanganyikan politics.

* **socialism** economic or political system based on the idea that the government or groups of workers should own and run the means of production and distribution of goods

* **apartheid** policy of racial segregation enforced by the white government of South Africa to maintain political, economic, and social control over the country's blacks, Asians, and people of mixed ancestry

Tanganyika gained its independence in 1961 with Nyerere as prime minister. When the country became the United Republic of Tanzania three years later, Nyerere was elected its president. Establishing one-party rule, he followed a policy of socialism* and self-reliance called *ujamaa*. However, his program failed to develop agriculture and industry, and Tanzania's dependence on outside aid increased. Within Africa, Nyerere was a founder of the ORGANIZATION OF AFRICAN UNITY and a supporter of the fight against apartheid* in South Africa. After resigning as president of Tanzania in 1979, he worked as a political writer and commentator. (*See also* **Colonialism in Africa, Independence Movements.**)

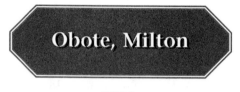

Obote, Milton

1924–
President of Uganda

* **nationalize** to bring land, industries, or public works under state control or ownership

* **coup** sudden, often violent, overthrow of a ruler or government

* **regime** current political system or rule

Milton Obote sought to end British colonial rule in East Africa and twice served as president of UGANDA. Expelled from Makerere University in Uganda for political activity, he moved to KENYA where he joined a number of African political groups. When he returned to Uganda several years later, he was elected to the newly formed Legislative Council. In that position he frequently criticized British colonial policy.

In 1959 Obote formed his own political party, the Uganda People's Congress. Three years later he was elected prime minister of the colony. When Uganda won its independence later that year, Obote continued as prime minister with King MUTESA II of Buganda as the country's president.

In 1966 Obote seized control of Uganda and forced Mutesa into exile. Obote suspended the constitution, declared himself executive president, and nationalized* many foreign businesses. During this time, he worked closely with army officer Idi AMIN DADA, who helped him to expand the government's power. Within a few years, however, Obote began to distrust Amin and placed him under house arrest.

In 1971 Amin led a military coup* that overthrew Obote. Amin took over the presidency and established a ruthless regime*, killing his enemies and opponents in the government. Seven years later forces from TANZANIA defeated the Ugandan army, toppling Amin's government. Obote, who was living in Tanzania, returned to Uganda and was elected president the following year.

Obote had no more success in his second term as president. After Amin's terror-filled reign, Uganda's economy was in ruins and law and order had broken down. Obote faced a restless population, a disgruntled army, and a rebellion led by his 1980 political opponent Yoweri MUSEVENI. In 1985 another military coup toppled Obote, who fled to ZAMBIA. (*See also* **Colonialism in Africa.**)

OLDUVAI GORGE

See *Humans, Early; Leakey Family.*

Olympio, Sylvanus Epiphanio

1902–1963
President of Togo

* **coup**   sudden, often violent, overthrow of a ruler or government

* **authoritarian**   relating to strong leadership with unrestricted powers

The first president of TOGO, Sylvanus Olympio was also the first leader of an independent African country to be overthrown by a military coup*. Olympio was born into a wealthy family and studied in Europe before embarking on a career with a multinational company operating in Togo. He rose high in the company but was exiled from Togo for political activity prior to World War II. He returned after the war, when France allowed elections in its African colonies.

Togo achieved independence in 1960, and Olympio was elected president the following year. However, his authoritarian* style of rule, strict budget-cutting measures, and continued ties with France made him unpopular. Furthermore, the northern Togolese held few posts in his government and resented the exclusion. His refusal to expand the army and increase its pay finally led to the coup that toppled and killed him in 1963.

Oral Tradition

* **epic**   long poem or story about legendary or historical heroes, written in a grand style

* **medieval**   relating to the Middle Ages in western Europe, generally considered to be from the A.D. 500s to the 1500s

Every society passes information about its history, myths, and customs along to new generations. In many African societies such material has been transmitted orally, through the spoken word. This method of passing along literature and history is oral tradition.

African oral tradition involves both the material that is spoken—the oral art—and the setting in which it is spoken. Although very old, oral tradition remains alive and meaningful for many Africans. Performers and audiences have adapted oral tradition, adding new content and making use of new communications tools.

Oral Art and Its Uses.   Among the many varieties of oral art are songs, chanted recitations, poems, and PROVERBS AND RIDDLES. Dramas, epics*, and other stories about the real or imaginary past are also important.

Oral art is more than simply telling or repeating something—it is a carefully crafted performance. Artists use a variety of stylistic devices to highlight certain aspects of the stories they tell and the songs they sing. These stylistic devices are also memory aids. One device of this sort is the repetition of key phrases or sentences, such as a hero's features or virtues. Another is onomatopoeia, the use of words that sound like what they represent, such as the noises made by animals or by the wind.

Songs and dramas may be accompanied by musical instruments. The music is more than a background and can add to the meaning of the spoken text. For example, a performer reciting the epic of SUNDJATA, a legendary medieval* warrior king of the Mali Empire, might play a harp. At key points in the story the performer may suddenly change rhythm and play a pattern associated with Sundjata. This honors the hero and flatters those people in the audience who consider themselves his descendants.

Skilled oral artists appeal to the audience's eyes as well as its ears, using body movements, gestures, and objects to illustrate or emphasize important points in the story. Performers also incorporate DANCE to add visual and dramatic impact to their recitals.

165

Oral art forms serve many purposes. Performances can amuse or educate an audience, either at formal gatherings, such as official celebrations, or at informal gatherings of family and friends. Some take place during religious ceremonies. Songs and recitations are often used to increase the reputation of particular individuals or groups.

Performers and Patrons. Men and women with extraordinary memories and public-speaking talents are well suited to become oral artists. Their skills earn them great respect, especially if they also possess musical abilities. While many are known only within their local communities, a few individuals acquire far-reaching fame as artists.

See color plate 4, vol. 1.

Some societies do not regard oral artistry as a distinct profession, and artists in these communities do not earn a living by performing. In other groups, however, oral artists are recognized as professionals who specialize in communication. Whether or not they are members of a professional group, oral artists need a long period of training. They must memorize vast amounts of material, learn to use appropriate performance techniques, and perhaps practice playing an instrument. A young artist may learn these skills from a recognized master, working for the master in return.

In the past, many oral historians and artists were supported by royal, noble, or wealthy patrons. In exchange for food, housing, and protection, the artists defended their patrons' interests and promoted their honor and fame. At important public events in the royal court of RWANDA, oral performers would praise their patron families' legendary pasts or current achievements. Retelling a ruling family's history in public could help a king maintain his leadership. Griots, as storytellers are called in the SAHEL of western Africa, performed this function in the royal courts of the SUDANIC EMPIRES OF WESTERN AFRICA. Among the XHOSA and ZULU of southern Africa, a performer called an *imbongi* specialized in glorifying the ruler.

Some oral artists still perform on behalf of families or individuals. However, social and political changes have altered the old relationships, and artists can no longer count on support from patrons. Print publications, radio, television, and other media now compete with storytellers as shapers of public opinion. Yet oral artists can change with the times. In the cities of GUINEA, SENEGAL, GAMBIA, and MALI, some griots now broadcast their songs on television and radio. Cassette tapes of their performances reach even remote rural areas. By blending new technology with ancient oral tradition, some of these artists have gained an international reputation. (*See also* **Literature, Music and Song, Mythology, Popular Culture, Writing Systems.**)

ORANGE FREE STATE See *South Africa.*

Organization of African Unity

The Organization of African Unity (OAU) is an organization founded to promote harmony between African governments. It seeks to coordinate and increase cooperation among African nations, to defend their independence, and to eliminate all forms of colonialism from Africa. The OAU also promotes international cooperation in keeping with the charter of the UNITED NATIONS and the Universal Declaration of Human Rights.

The OAU grew out of the Pan-African movements of the early to mid-1900s, such as those led by Marcus GARVEY and Kwame NKRUMAH. These groups promoted African unity in the struggle against domination by European colonial powers. In 1963 the leaders of the 32 independent African nations that existed at that time met in ADDIS ABABA, Ethiopia, for the Conference of Independent African States. On May 25 they signed the charter that created the OAU.

In articles II and III of the charter, the members agree to promote unity and solidarity, cooperate to create better lives for African people, defend their borders and independence, wipe out all forms of colonialism in Africa, and promote international cooperation, especially with regards to the United Nations and the Universal Declaration of Human Rights. In addition, OAU member states also agreed to coordinate their policies in a number of fields. These included politics and diplomacy; economics, including transportation and communications; education and cultural affairs; health, sanitation, and nutrition; and defense and security. The states also pledged to recognize the equality of member states, to avoid interfering in members' internal affairs, and to seek a peaceful settlement to disputes. They stated that they would condemn assassination or other subversive activities, strive for the independence of all African states, and stay free from other political associations.

* **mediator**   go-between

The OAU has had several notable successes. Serving as a mediator*, it helped resolve disputes in the 1960s between ALGERIA and MOROCCO and between SOMALIA and its neighbors ETHIOPIA and KENYA. The OAU sparked the creation of the African Development Bank, which finds investors and financing from around the world to help pay for African development projects. It has established several helpful commissions, including one that works to place and educate refugees within Africa and another that promotes HUMAN RIGHTS throughout the continent. In 1991 the OAU created the African Economic Community to coordinate economic policies between member states.

* **coup**   sudden, often violent, overthrow of a ruler or government

Despite its achievements, the OAU has had little impact on some of the greatest problems facing Africa. It has failed to prevent or end most of the continent's wars and has rarely condemned military coups*, unconstitutional rule, or conflict between ethnic groups within member states. In a speech marking the OAU's 35th anniversary in 1998, Secretary General Salim Ahmed Salim acknowledged the organization's shortcomings. He called on member nations to rededicate themselves "to the elimination of poverty, misery and blood-shed" and challenged them to turn "declarations and blueprints into concrete programs and activities." In 2000, the OAU adopted a resolution banning from the organization leaders who came to power by corrupt and undemocratic means. (*See also* **Global Politics and Africa**, **Nationalism**.)

167

Osei Tutu

ca. 1636–1717
Asante king

Osei Tutu, the first king of the ASANTE people of western Africa, united the people in campaigns of military conquest and expansion. In about 1685 Osei Tutu succeeded his uncle as ruler of Kumasi, one of many Asante states. He continued the wars of expansion that his uncle had begun and brought the various Asante territories together against common foes (1699–1701). This military union provided the framework of Asante unity. Osei Tutu made Kumasi the capital of a growing Asante kingdom, which under his successors included most of present-day GHANA and eastern IVORY COAST.

As *asantehene,* or king, Osei Tutu introduced several institutions that endure today. One is the Golden Stool, the supreme shrine of the Asante people and a symbol of their spiritual and political identity. Another is *odwira,* an annual festival that brings together all Asante. Osei Tutu also established a set of laws that the Asante regard as the basis of their nation. (*See also* **Festivals and Carnivals, Kings and Kingship, Laws and Legal Systems.**)

OUSMANE, SEMBÈNE

See *Sembène Ousmane.*

Paton, Alan

1903–1988
South African writer

* **apartheid** policy of racial segregation enforced by the white government of South Africa to maintain political, economic, and social control over the country's blacks, Asians, and people of mixed ancestry

Alan Paton was a white South African novelist and a dedicated political activist. Through his writing and his political efforts, he protested against racial injustice and apartheid*.

Born and educated in Pietermaritzburg in the Natal province of South Africa, Paton worked as a schoolteacher. Then he served as the head of a reform school for African boys, where he tried to improve conditions for the students. In 1948 he published his first book, *Cry, the Beloved Country,* a novel about a black minister whose son is convicted of killing a white man. It enjoyed international acclaim and made readers around the world aware of South Africa's struggle with race relations.

Encouraged by his success, Paton left the reform school and devoted himself full-time to writing and fighting racism. In 1953, he helped found the anti-apartheid Liberal Party of South Africa and served as its national president. From 1960 to 1970, the government took away his passport to punish him for expressing his opposition to apartheid. His works of fiction include *Too Late the Phalarope* (1953), *Tales from a Troubled Land* (1961), and *Ah, But Your Land Is Beautiful* (1981). Paton also wrote essays, biographies, and a two-volume autobiography.

Peasantry and Land Settlement

* **urbanization** referring to the growth of towns and cities

In Africa, despite increasing urbanization* a majority of the population can still be classified as peasants. Peasants are people such as farmers and livestock herders who make their living off the land, generally using only manual labor and nonmechanized technology. Africa's climate and the poor quality of much of its soil have long presented challenges to peasants. These factors have shaped the livelihoods of peasants and the ways in which they interact with each other. Along with Africa's colonial history, they have also profoundly affected land settlement and land use patterns on the continent.

PEASANT FARMERS AND HERDERS

Most African peasants fall into two broad groups: agriculturalists who make their living from farming and pastoralists who herd livestock. In many areas of Africa these two groups have traditionally lived in close contact with one another, sometimes sharing the same land during parts of the year. The groups also share common values and traditions. Agriculturalists generally have a strong sense of membership in a community, often with deep roots in a particular geographic location.

Peasant Livelihoods. In Africa, peasant farming communities traditionally have been concentrated in regions that have fertile soil and ample rainfall. Households in these communities produce a variety of crops for their own use, and perhaps grow a surplus for market. They often raise a few animals as well, particularly sheep, goats, and chickens.

Although peasant farmers use manual labor and only simple technology, they have devised various agricultural practices—such as rotating

Peasant farmers in Tanzania prepare the soil before planting crops.

crops and cultivating several crops in the same field—that have enabled them to take advantage of climatic conditions, variations in soil quality, landscape, and water availability. Men, women, and children all play important roles in farming activities, often with different responsibilities based on gender.

Bordering the more fertile areas of Africa are marginal lands that are drier and have less vegetation. Few crops can grow in such regions, but the shrubs and grasses can support the livestock grazing of pastoralists for much of the year. As grazing exhausts vegetation in one area, pastoralists move their herds to new pastures. When they reach areas cultivated by peasant farmers, the pastoralists often graze their herds on crop stubble left in the fields after harvesting. At the same time, the manure from the animals helps to fertilize the fields in which they graze.

Sometimes the timing of the herders' migrations brings animals to areas where crops have not yet been harvested from fields. This can cause conflict between the peasant farmers, who must protect their crops from the animals, and the pastoralists, who need pasture for their livestock. In general, however, the interaction between the two groups benefits both of them.

Peasant Economics. While peasants are defined by their livelihood and their relationship to the land, relatively few earn a living solely from farming and herding. Many can provide for their basic needs, but they have to acquire certain goods—such as tools, utensils, shoes, and salt—from other sources. In addition, they need cash to pay tribute* to local rulers or taxes to government officials. For this reason, African peasants have always been tied into economic systems beyond the village or pastoral group and have engaged in such activities as TRADE and CRAFTS to supplement their earnings.

In the past, the need to find alternate sources of income led to extensive migration among African peasants. When farming or herding failed to provide for a family's needs, male members often traveled long distances to find other work. Much of the migration for all Africans is seasonal. The peasants work their farms during the growing season, and then leave to look for other work after the crops have been harvested. This process accelerated during the colonial era as white settlers forced many Africans off the land. Landless peasants had little choice but to seek employment in towns or on white-owned farms, plantations, and mines. Labor migration continues to be an important part of the economy in Africa, and many peasant families rely heavily on money sent by relatives working far from home.

LAND SETTLEMENT AND USE

Traditional patterns of land settlement in Africa were based on the understanding that different groups needed to share lands. However, the Europeans who colonized Africa came from societies with very different ideas about land ownership and use. The introduction of European notions about land to Africa disrupted rural economies and peasant societies, and it has had a major impact on the continent's development.

* **tribute** payment made by a smaller or weaker party to a more powerful one, often under the threat of force

Impact of Colonial Policies. During the colonial period, white settlers and colonial governments rejected African traditions of land use. They relied on their own ideas of private land ownership to justify taking land from Africans. The seizure of land produced a crisis for Africa's peasant farmers and pastoralists. Driven off the land, they were often forced to work as wage laborers on land they had once farmed. Others moved to towns to seek employment, finding only low-paying jobs. This led to the creation of large slums that remain a feature of urban life throughout Africa. Those who continued to farm on their own usually had to make do with the worst lands. Those farmers who were forcibly resettled by colonial governments often did not receive the money they were promised in exchange for their land, or, if the cash was received, it was never enough to provide a long-term living for the farmer who had lost his land.

European landowners and colonial governments also denied African pastoralists access to the seasonal pastures they needed. Many herders lost their livelihoods in this manner. Like peasant farmers, they had to work as wage laborers in rural or urban areas. Because of the devastating impact that Europeans had on their way of life, peasant farmers and pastoralists were often strong opponents of colonial rule.

Modern Land Settlement. After independence, African countries had to deal with the problems created by colonial land policies that drove so many Africans off the land. Different countries took different approaches. UGANDA gave small plots of land to thousands of landless peasants. KENYA consolidated many small plots of land into larger holdings. By doing this, the government hoped to make mechanized farming possible. Larger landholdings were also easier to tax.

Neither of these land reform policies proved very successful. In Uganda the division of land was unequal, with influential people receiving larger or better quality plots. Many farmers in Kenya resisted land consolidation because they could farm smaller plots more efficiently. Moreover, those who received larger holdings often did not report the transactions in order to avoid paying fees or taxes.

Some countries that adopted socialist* land reforms, such as TANZANIA, outlawed private landholding altogether. They resettled peasants into cooperative farms* and villages and promised to provide basic services such as water, health care, and schools. However, the villagers soon exhausted the surrounding land as well as nearby supplies of firewood and water. As a result, either they had to travel farther each day to tend crops and get supplies, or they had to split up their families to establish distant homesteads.

While some type of land reform could help African peasants, reform alone will not solve the problems they face today. For better or worse, African peasants are part of a global economy. To compete successfully they need modern tools and machinery, better roads to transport goods to market, and greater access to social services such as schooling and health care. Because governments provide many of these services, the future of African peasants is tied closely to the condition of their nation's economy. (*See also* **Animals, Domestic; Colonialism in Africa; Land Ownership; Livestock Grazing; Plantation Systems.**)

* **socialist** relating to an economic or political system based on the idea that the government or groups of workers should own and run the means of production and distribution of goods

* **cooperative farm** large plot of land worked by many farmers

171

Pereira, Aristides Maria

**1924–
President of Cape Verde**

* **guerrilla** type of warfare involving sudden raids by small groups of warriors

Aristides Maria Pereira helped transform CAPE VERDE from an island colony into a modern nation. He fought for independence and then, as president, guided the new country through its first 15 years.

Pereira was born in Boa Vista in the Cape Verde Islands off the coast of West Africa. The islands were then a colony of Portugal, and after he finished school, Pereira went to work for a Portuguese trading company. In 1956 Pereira and several others, led by Amílcar CABRAL, founded a secret movement aimed at freeing Cape Verde and the mainland colony of Guinea from Portuguese rule. Pereira played a leading role in the guerrilla* war that led to independence for GUINEA-BISSAU in 1974 and for Cape Verde in 1975.

After independence, Pereira became Cape Verde's first president. He worked to modernize the country and to create democratic institutions, including a multiparty political system introduced in 1990. The following year, the people of Cape Verde voted Pereira and his party out of office. He accepted the defeat as an expression of the democratic principles for which he and his fellow party members had fought. (*See also* **Colonialism in Africa**.)

Pests and Pest Control

African farmers generally face a tougher battle with pests than do farmers in temperate regions. The warm temperatures and abundant rainfall of the continent's tropical regions create an environment in which pests flourish. To make matters worse, chemical pesticides developed in Western nations are of limited use in Africa.

Insects and rodents do the most damage to African crops. Insects of all sizes consume up to 15 percent of African crops in the field, and they destroy between 10 and 50 percent more during storage, processing, and marketing. Swarms of locusts periodically descend on huge areas of land to devour the green parts of every type of plant. Termites and rats damage many stored foods. In addition, weeds and other parasitic plants harm crops as they grow by competing for food, water, and light.

The chemical pesticides used in western nations have many drawbacks in Africa. These pesticides often are not effective against species found primarily in Africa. Also, the continent's high temperatures and heavy rains reduce the long-term strength of chemical pesticides. In any event, few African farmers can afford them.

For these reasons, African farmers rely heavily on a variety of physical, biological, and cultural pest control methods. Physical pest control methods include dragging brushes or tarred paper over crops to remove or crush insects and creating metal barriers to keep termites out of storage bins. Biological methods involve the use of living organisms to fight pests. For example, a type of American wasp has been imported to combat a pest that destroys cassava, an important staple crop in Africa. Cultural pest control includes practices such as rotating crops and planting different types of crops on the same land to control the spread of insect pests and weeds. Farmers also select crop varieties that show the greatest natural resistance to pests.

Several recent technological advances in pest control may help African farmers. Farmers may use packages that combine seeds with weed killers and fertilizers, or they may plant crops that are genetically engineered to be resistant to certain pests. However, since these technologies can be expensive, experts are also working to develop new practices that take advantage of indigenous* farmers' knowledge and locally available tools and materials. (*See also* **Agriculture, Plants: Varieties and Uses.**)

* **indigenous**   native to a certain place

Pharaohs

* **dynasty**   succession of rulers from the same family or group

* **deity**   god or goddess

* **cosmic**   large or universal in scale; having to do with the universe

* **ritual**   religious ceremony that follows a set pattern

Although today the kings of ancient Egypt are referred to as pharaohs, that term was never part of their official titles. The word *pharaoh* developed from an Egyptian phrase meaning "great house" and was first used to describe the royal palace. Around 1500 B.C. Egyptians began using the word to refer to their king, and by 730 B.C. *pharaoh* was a term of respect.

Between about 3000 and 30 B.C., Egypt was ruled by a long string of pharaohs—including one queen, Hatshepsut—from 32 different dynasties*. The basic Egyptian idea of kingship changed very little during this period. The pharaoh was not only the ruler of the Egyptian people; he was also a link between the human and the divine worlds.

The Egyptians identified their kings with the gods, especially the sun and sky gods. In their eyes, the pharaoh was a deity* who embodied sacred or magical powers. He was the source of all justice. People believed that the pharaoh maintained order in Egypt as well as a cosmic* order or balance that they called *ma'at*. On a more basic level, the pharaoh owned much of the land and property in Egypt and determined both how it would be used and who would use it. He had the last word over every aspect of life in Egypt, including the lives and deaths of each of his subjects. No one person, however, could attend to every decision involved in administering a kingdom. Pharaohs shared their authority with high-ranking assistants at court and with officials in the provinces.

The combination of divine and royal status set the pharaoh apart from all other people. Pharaohs lived out of public view. Often they married their sisters or daughters, who were also thought to be divine. Court ceremonies and religious rituals* emphasized the pharaoh's role as a god. Pictures and statues of pharaohs, especially those that showed the kings as warriors defending Egypt, often portrayed the rulers as much larger than everyone else. When a pharaoh died, priests carefully preserved the ruler's body so that he could live on as a god in the afterlife. Some pharaohs were buried in elaborate tombs that they had built for themselves in caves or PYRAMIDS.

Although the Egyptian people spoke of their pharaohs as divine, they clearly recognized the human shortcomings of their rulers. They rebelled against some pharaohs and even assassinated a few of them. Like monarchs in many times and places, the pharaohs of Egypt faced ambitious rivals, palace plots, discontented populations, and enemies they could not overcome on the battlefield. (*See also* **Egypt, Ancient; Kings and Kingship.**)

Photography

People have been taking photographs in Africa almost since the invention of photography. Early images taken by foreign travelers reflect European views of Africa, while photos taken by Africans shed light on African ideas of beauty, identity, and art.

History. In the mid-1800s, Europeans who had mastered the complex technique of early photography documented their journeys to Africa. A member of explorer David LIVINGSTONE's 1858 expedition on the Zambezi River took some of the first photos of the African interior. Fascination with the exotic monuments of ancient Egypt drew other European photographers to the Nile River valley.

By the 1880s, photographic equipment had become more widely available and easier to use. Missionaries, colonial officials, and scientists working in Africa took photos for personal mementos, research projects, and exhibits. Some Europeans specialized in anthropological* photography designed to sort the African population into racial and cultural types or categories. Sets of these pictures entered the collections of many museums.

From the late 1800s to the mid-1960s, European colonial governments in Africa used photography to advertise the success of their administrations. The rapid growth of photojournalism and documentary photography produced a flood of images from Africa after the 1920s. European and American photographers—as well as some Africans—recorded current events and social conditions around the continent. Although some photographers worked for colonial governments, many others worked for independent publications.

Some of the first non-European photographers in Africa were Indians, who operated photo studios in eastern Africa as early as the 1860s. Africans soon entered the business, opening studios or working as traveling photographers. At first, they specialized in portraits or group pictures of members of the upper class, such as teachers, priests, and clerks.

By the 1940s photographers also were covering social and political events. At the same time, magazines in South Africa and Nigeria began publishing the work of African photojournalists. Some work from this period has gained recognition as fine art as well as a valuable record of African culture. In 1997, photos by Seydou Keïta of Mali were published and exhibited in the United States and Europe.

Cultural Role. Local beliefs and values affected the practice of photography in Africa. At first, some Africans resisted having their pictures taken. They believed their souls and shadows could be stolen through magic, and photography appeared to be a magical art. This fear quickly

* **anthropological** relating to anthropology, the study of human beings, especially their social and cultural characteristics

faded, however. In some cases photography replaced earlier art forms. In Ghana, for example, people began taking photographs of the dead instead of making traditional pottery images in their honor. Elsewhere, people adopted photographs for use in ancestor worship, medicine, and magic. Some traditional healers use photos to diagnose illness, and the "love magic" practiced to bring back a lost lover often features the use of photos.

Photography also gained a place in social customs. In many areas, Africans welcome visitors to their home by presenting the family photo album. As elsewhere in the world, photography in Africa has become an important part of wedding feasts and other major celebrations. In some African cultures, the quantity and quality of photographs given to guests at a wedding demonstrates the host's standing in society. Africans also enjoy exchanging photos as reminders of events and as signs of friendship.

* **sub-Saharan** referring to Africa south of the Sahara desert

Style. Much of the photography in sub-Saharan* Africa shares a common style. Nearly all photographs are images of people, rather than of landscapes and other subjects. They are usually formal pictures, with the subject in the center, facing forward. A person's entire body is usually included in the picture. Whereas Western photographers generally use techniques that emphasize depth and make the subject stand out from the background, most African photographers favor images that appear flat, with the subject blending smoothly into the background.

Studio photography is highly popular in many African countries. Studio owners provide backdrops, such as paintings of urban scenes or rooms filled with modern appliances. They also offer a wide range of props, such as royal ornaments, and items of Western and traditional clothing. African studio images are not intended to reproduce reality; they are ways of making a statement about one's standing in the world. (*See also* **Art**.)

Plaatje, Sol

1876–1923
South African writer

An accomplished writer and a founder of the African National Congress, Sol Plaatje worked for political and cultural causes in SOUTH AFRICA. He was born in Boshof in what was then the Orange Free State of South Africa, one of the AFRIKANER REPUBLICS founded by Dutch colonists. He spoke the Setswana (or Tswana) language and worked for the government as an interpreter. When the South African (Boer) War broke out between the Dutch colonists and the British in 1899, Plaatje kept a record of it in a journal. Having discovered that he could write, he founded a newpaper in 1901, the first Setswana newspaper.

Plaatje's career in journalism led to an interest in politics. In 1912 he helped organize the South African Native National Congress (SANNC), which eventually became the African National Congress (ANC). As the group's first general secretary, he led an effort to oppose land laws that prevented Africans from owning or living in territories that the British had chosen as their own. He went to London to protest the land laws to the British government, but his protests were not successful.

Plaatje remained abroad, spreading the news about South Africa's racial troubles. He stayed in England for three years, lecturing on race issues and working as a language assistant at the University of London. He spent a year in Paris, where he attended several international conferences, including the Pan-African Congress. Plaatje also traveled to the United States to meet with American publishers. He returned to South Africa in 1923.

Plaatje was passionately devoted to the preservation of the Setswana language and culture. He wrote several books on Setswana life and culture, and he translated two of William Shakespeare's plays, *Comedy of Errors* and *Romeo and Juliet,* into Setswana. His final book, a novel called *Mhudi: An Epic of South African Native Life a Hundred Years Ago,* was published in 1930.

Plantation Systems

In Africa, plantations are large farms that specialize in one or two crops grown for export. They produce many of the continent's most important export crops such as coffee, cocoa, tea, sugarcane, tobacco, rubber, and bananas. Plantations also handle at least some processing of the crops, and typically maintain a large unskilled labor force. Nevertheless, the plantation system does not dominate African agriculture as it does in some parts of the world.

History of African Plantations. The first plantations in Africa were founded between 1500 and 1800 on islands such as CAPE VERDE, SÃO TOMÉ AND PRÍNCIPE, ZANZIBAR, MAURITIUS, and RÉUNION. Early Portuguese sugar plantations based on slave labor eventually failed because of slave rebellions and difficult farming conditions. French and Dutch plantations in SOUTH AFRICA and the Indian Ocean were more successful. They employed better technology and planted improved varieties of sugarcane. Also, after the SLAVE TRADE was abolished in the 1800s, these plantations had access to indentured labor* from Asia.

Until the early 1900s, many West African plantations were established and run by indigenous* rulers using local slave labor. They produced sugar and groundnuts as well as palm oil, which was used for making soap and lubricating machinery. As Europeans began to colonize large parts of Africa, they shut down many indigenous plantations and set up their own.

Plantation owners soon found that the cost of housing and feeding large numbers of unskilled laborers made plantations less profitable than small farms producing the same crops. To help planters stay in business, colonial governments gave them low-cost land grants and forced the local population to work on the plantations. They also gave planters a monopoly* by preventing the sale of crops grown by other farmers. These state-supported plantations often produced most of a colony's exports.

* **indentured labor** form of labor in which a worker is bound into service for a set time to repay a debt

* **indigenous** native to a certain place

* **monopoly** exclusive control or domination of a particular type of business

As African nations gained independence in the mid-1900s, many plantations were broken up and the land was given to small farmers. However, some countries continued to rely on plantations to grow many of their export crops. Governments profited from successful independent plantations by taxing their profits. Some countries placed plantations under state ownership and allowed the workers to participate in their management.

Plantations in Modern Africa. Today, the major part of Africa's crops comes from small farms rather than from plantations. Even coffee and cocoa, once grown almost exclusively on plantations, are now primarily small-farm crops. Large international firms run most of the successful plantations in Africa, including rubber plantations in LIBERIA and tobacco plantations in MALAWI, ZIMBABWE, and South Africa. Modern research and development have made these operations somewhat more efficient than earlier efforts. However, labor is still a problem. Most Africans avoid plantation work, and organizing and managing a large labor force remains costly.

The traditional plantation system is gradually being replaced by a system in which plantation owners contract with small farmers to produce crops. The farmers bring their crops to a central location for processing, marketing, and distribution. In this way, planters profit from the efficiency of processing large amounts of crops at one time, and farmers benefit from the ability to bring their crops to a wider market. In addition, advances in agricultural technologies, management methods, and communications are making it easier to produce and export crops without the use of plantations. (*See also* **Agriculture, Colonialism in Africa, Development, Economic and Social, Economic History, Plants: Varieties and Uses.**)

Plants: Varieties and Uses

* **domesticated** raised by humans as farm animals or pets; plants adapted for use as crops

* **savanna** tropical or subtropical grassland with scattered trees and drought-resistant undergrowth

The enormous array of plants native to Africa have always been a valuable resource for the continent's inhabitants. Africans use plants for food, medicine, fuel, paper, construction materials, and many other purposes. Some plants have been domesticated* for agriculture; others are gathered in the wild. Africans have also adopted plants from other parts of the world, and a number of African plants are now grown on other continents.

Varieties of Vegetation. The vegetation that grows in any given area is determined by natural factors such as climate, elevation, and soil type, as well as by human activities such as clearing land, gathering firewood, and grazing livestock. There are three broad categories of African plant life: forest, desert and semidesert, and a group that includes open woodlands and grasslands such as the savanna*.

Africa's forests cover about 20 percent of its land area. They are concentrated in the lowlands of coastal West Africa, the Congo basin of central Africa, and the mountains of East Africa. The tropical rain forests

Plants: Varieties and Uses

* **mangrove**   tree found in coastal areas that grows in dense clusters

Lentils

*Lentils are the flat seeds of a plant that produces a leafy stalk. In Ethiopia, they are cooked with onions, garlic, and spices to make a pungent stew. To prepare Ethiopian Red Lentils, soak **1/2 pound red lentils** in cold water for 30 minutes. Rinse and drain. Peel and finely chop **1 onion**. Sauté the onion in **1/4 cup oil** until golden. Add **11/2 tablespoons tomato paste** and **1/4 teaspoon paprika** and stir. Add **2 cloves mashed garlic, 1/4 teaspoon ground ginger, 1/4 teaspoon pepper, 1/2 teaspoon salt, and 11/2 cups water**. Stir the mixture well, cover, and heat until boiling. Then add the lentils and cook on low for 20–30 minutes, until the lentils become soft.*

contain an astonishing variety of plant species, including many large trees up to 150 feet high. The rain forest on the island nation of MADAGASCAR is somewhat drier, with smaller trees, while the continent's Indian Ocean coast has a belt of similar lowland forest, mixed with evergreen trees. Africa also has dense mangrove* forests along its tropical coastlines.

About 40 percent of Africa's land area is desert or semidesert. This includes the enormous SAHARA of North Africa and the Namib and KALAHARI Deserts in southern Africa. Vegetation in these zones consists mostly of tough, hardy bushes and grasses that require little water. These and other desert plants generally grow more readily in rocky areas than in areas of shifting sands. The Sahara has fewer plant species than most parts of the world. Some Saharan plants exist mostly beneath the surface, with wide-spreading root systems and only small parts exposed above ground.

Africa's semidesert zones gradually merge into grassy savanna or bushland, an area with mixed shrubs and thorny bushes. Some 40 percent of Africa is covered by grasslands, bushlands, and dry open woodlands, which have a thin covering of drought-resistant trees. The coastal areas of North Africa and South Africa—which have a Mediterranean climate with dry summers and mild rainy winters—contain woodland vegetation. Although these areas do not have dense forests, they contain some palm trees and hardy, low-growing species of oak, cedar, and juniper trees. A special type of grassland occurs along the NILE, NIGER, and ZAMBEZI RIVERS. Called *sudd*, which means "barrier," along the Nile, it contains a thick growth of reeds and water plants that can interfere with river traffic.

Food Plants. People who live in Africa's tropical forests and woodlands gather and eat various wild fruits, though these are not major items in their diets except in times of food shortage. Instead, Africans cultivate a wide range of domesticated food plants. Food plants native to Africa fall into four main groups, each associated with a particular climate or environment.

The most widespread of these is the savanna food group, which consists of plants adapted to grassland and woodland environments. The key savanna crops are cereal grains, including sorghum, pearl millet, and rice. Sorghum, the most important of these, covers more ground than any other African food plant. Also in the savanna food group are watermelons, earth peas, black benne seeds (sesame seeds), and African tomatoes.

The forest margin group of plants includes the oil palm, the yam, a grain called Guinea millet, the kola nut, beans, potatoes, and peas. The third main group, the Ethiopian group, consists of plants native to Ethiopia in the eastern highlands of Africa. Among the plants in this group are coffee; *teff,* a cereal grain; *noog,* an edible oil plant; and a banana-like plant called *enset.* The last food plant group, the Mediterranean, includes date palms, grain barley, lentils, and olive and fig trees.

Deforestation, caused by fires or by cutting down stands of trees, changes the growing environment for plants. It increases the amount of heat and light reaching the ground and can lead to soil erosion.

* **deforestation**   removal of a forest as a result of human activities

Other Plant Uses. Africa's plants have many other uses in addition to providing food. Thousands of years ago the ancient Egyptians perfected the art of making paper from the stems of papyrus, a plant that forms part of the *sudd* vegetation. Esparto grass, which grows on North African grasslands, is used in papermaking today and is exported by Tunisia and Algeria.

Wood is Africa's primary source of energy, either as firewood or as charcoal, a fuel made of partially charred wood. City dwellers generally buy fuelwood or charcoal at markets, but rural people gather their own. Women are the main collectors and users of fuelwood for household purposes, favoring small pieces of dry, fallen wood that are easy to gather and carry. Men generally collect larger quantities and bigger pieces of wood needed for projects such as smoking fish and firing bricks. Fuelwood also provides energy for industries, such as tobacco curing in Malawi. The demand for fuelwood is a leading cause of deforestation* in parts of Africa.

179

Africans have traditionally built houses and other structures from plant materials. Construction usually requires many wooden poles of different sizes, bark-fiber ropes for tying them together, and grass for covering the roofs and sides of structures. Woodlands and forests are an important source of timber for construction. However, in places where forest resources have been overused, the large posts of durable wood needed as major support pieces in buildings have become scarce or even unavailable.

Wood is also the principal material for homemade or locally produced household items such as plates and bowls; for tools such as ax handles, bows, and arrows; and for CRAFTS such as wood carving. Certain trees are favored for particular uses—light, flexible woods for making bows and strong, split-resistant woods for ax and hoe handles. Other tree products include dyes, gums, oils, and chemicals useful in tanning leather. New leaves on trees and bushes are a welcome source of food for both domestic livestock and wild grazing animals during the dry season, and farmers and gardeners gather fallen leaves to use as fertilizer.

In addition to their practical uses, plants play a role in many African spiritual and cultural traditions. Groves of trees used as burial sites, for example, are often the settings for traditional religious ceremonies. The roots, leaves, and bark of many species of plants are key elements in traditional medicines, and many of the plants used are thought to have magical or religious properties. People in rural areas without formal health care facilities are especially dependent on plant medicines.

Many Africans know how to select and prepare plant remedies for common ailments such as coughs, headaches, sores, and diarrhea. For more serious complaints they may consult traditional healers or herbalists—specialists in the use of plant medicines. Although the disappearance of woodlands is making medicinal plants harder to find, an informal trade in these plants exists among collectors and herbalists in different African countries. (*See also* **Deserts and Drought, Ecosystems, Food and Drink, Forests and Forestry, Healing and Medicine, Hunting and Gathering.**)

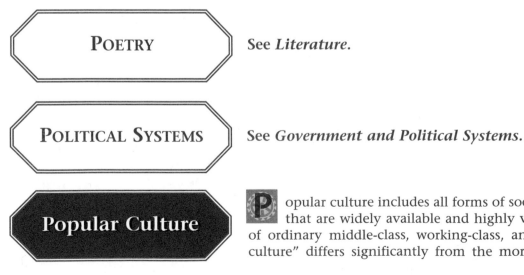

POETRY

See *Literature.*

POLITICAL SYSTEMS

See *Government and Political Systems.*

Popular Culture

Popular culture includes all forms of social and personal expression that are widely available and highly visible. Related to the world of ordinary middle-class, working-class, and poor people, this "mass culture" differs significantly from the more formal "high" culture of privileged and well-educated people. Often mass produced and current, popular culture includes forms of music, theater, and the other arts. It incorporates elements of everyday life such as hair and clothing styles, jokes, advertising images and slogans. Even "sidewalk radio"—an African practice of passing along rumors, gossip, and news in conversation, usually after reading the pages spread out on sidewalks by newspaper vendors—belongs to popular culture.

* **indigenous**   native to a certain place

African popular culture is an ever-shifting mix of indigenous* and foreign elements. Some Western influences, such as European languages and clothing styles, stem from the colonial period. Other international elements, such as kung fu movies, reflect the development of a global popular culture communicated through magazines, television shows, films, CDs, and videos from abroad.

African popular culture reflects local or regional traditions as well. It may carry meanings related to current events, politics, or the sense of identity of those who produce and consume it. An example is the *chiluba,* a jacket made from secondhand imported Western clothing that was worn in Zambia in the 1990s. The name of the garment came from Frederick Chiluba, Zambia's first democratically elected president, who wore such jackets. The name and the jacket together symbolize a new freedom, a new style of government, and Zambia's entry into the international marketplace.

South Africa. The history of popular culture in SOUTH AFRICA reveals the creative energy of black peoples who continually found new ways to respond to apartheid*, poverty, and oppressive* social conditions. Between the 1920s and the 1950s, urban black popular culture in the region produced local jazz clubs, dance competitions, and gospel churches. That culture was nearly destroyed in the 1960s, when government apartheid policies forced blacks to move from cities and suburbs to distant townships consisting of rows of cheap, similar brick houses. Despite limited resources, residents of the black townships created new forms of popular culture that helped their homes and communities bloom amid the barren surroundings.

* **apartheid**   policy of racial segregation enforced by the white government of South Africa to maintain political, economic, and social control over the country's blacks, Asians, and people of mixed ancestry

* **oppressive**   referring to unjust or cruel exercise of authority

Drawing upon African American popular music and culture for inspiration, black South Africans asserted their identity in their popular culture. During the 1950s, a handful of magazines published political articles. By 1963 the government had banned these magazines. Some writers fled the country; others fell silent. During the 1970s, however, writers found a new outlet—poetry that encouraged black pride and identity. After a time, the government outlawed the publication of new collections of black poetry, but in the 1980s artists turned to oral poetry and drama to express themselves. Performed without written texts and presented in a mixture of English and African languages, these works challenged apartheid and supported the struggles of workers and the poor. Out of this tradition came South African musicals such as *Sarafina!,* which addressed serious social problems yet offered song, dance, and the appeal of popular entertainment.

By the 1990s, black South Africans had achieved some of their political goals, and the energy of their struggle for liberation found a new

Popular Culture

Effects of "Sidewalk Radio"

The gossip of the rumor mill known as sidewalk radio can have serious effects. For example, in 1990 in what is now Congo (Kinshasa), "sidewalk radio" spread rumors that a new currency note featuring the image of a gorilla incorporated satanic symbols. These symbols supposedly linked the forces of evil to the nation's president and other prominent individuals. Many people refused even to touch the currency for fear of being contaminated. The picture of the gorilla also led to anger. The Congolese word for monkey was a common racial insult in colonial times, and many people thought that the image of the gorilla was a way of calling the people uncivilized savages.

* **genre**   type of literary or artistic work

focus in a youth popular culture oriented toward performance and the media. "Culture clubs" and youth clubs sprang up in black urban communities throughout the country, offering entertainment as well as educational programs and job training to the young people of the townships.

Central and Eastern Africa. In eastern and central Africa, popular music reflects the ability of African popular culture to blend and reshape elements borrowed from many sources. Pop music in the region includes an Arab style of singing called *taarab,* reggae sounds from the Caribbean, rhythms called *benga* from rural KENYA, and other influences. Many songwriters focus on love, marriage, betrayal, life, and death, but their words often incorporate political and social commentary as well.

The blend of foreign sources in the region's popular culture can be seen in the American, Indian, British, and Chinese movies, videos, CDs, books, and television shows available in all major cities. The influence of Western culture is particularly strong, especially in film. This has led to an interest in developing a local film industry. Images from Western popular culture also appear almost everywhere within the region.

African authorities have recognized that popular culture can be an effective means of communicating a message. In TANZANIA, UGANDA, Kenya, and ZIMBABWE, the ruling parties have used popular theater performances as a way to promote economic and social policies. Private groups in Uganda have also turned to popular culture to spread health information. However, authorities have sometimes interfered. In 1977 the government of Kenya disbanded a theater group that had been working with laborers and peasants to revive an adult education center. The government saw this project as a threat to established authority, which led to the arrest and exile of one of the group's members, NGUGI WA THIONG'O.

Throughout eastern and central Africa, popular novels offer stories that are easy to read, emotional rather than intellectual, and intended primarily to entertain rather than to educate. Published in English and a variety of African languages, this popular fiction draws on two influences: the Western novel and traditional storytelling. Many of the novels deal with the difficulties of human relationships and the struggle to survive and succeed in a modern urban society. Some African writers have adapted Western fiction genres*, such as romance and mystery novels, to African settings and culture. For example, Aubrey Kalitera of MALAWI has written stories of dramatic and often ill-fated romances in Malawian settings, using local names and landscapes rather than exotic foreign ones. Also popular are crime novels dealing with African concerns, such as ivory smuggling. Kenyan popular novelist Meja Mwangi has explored issues such as crime and punishment and ethnic and racial tensions in urban areas.

Western Africa. Some aspects of popular culture draw on traditional forms of expression that have not been greatly affected by Western influence. The masquerade—masked ceremonies or drama—has long

* **ritual** religious ceremony that follows a set pattern

been associated with social and religious rituals* in western Africa. However, masquerades can also provide entertainment and offer ordinary citizens a way to express their views. At events such as the *okumpka* masquerades of southern Nigeria, people can make fun of or criticize chiefs, elders, and local politicians through masks, costumes, dancing, and songs.

During the colonial period, new forms of popular culture emerged in the urban areas of western Africa. Some of the most distinctive of these forms were musical. Highlife, a style of music born in Ghana in the 1920s, became popular and spread across much of the region in the decades that followed. Using a wide range of instruments, highlife musicians drew upon Western styles such as jazz and swing music as well as traditional African rhythms and songs. With the introduction of electric amplification in the 1940s, highlife became the dominant form of popular music in the region. Highlife songs often offered the male view of the changing customs and social patterns in the region's fast-growing cities, especially of the changes in GENDER ROLES of urban men and women.

By the 1970s new regional forms of popular music, such as the *juju* music of the YORUBA peoples of southwestern Nigeria, began replacing highlife music. Another important development in the 1970s was the introduction of the cassette recorder, which allowed musicians to record and sell their own music and brought them greater recognition. At the same time, many musicians in the region began returning to their African musical roots. Most did not abandon Western instruments and equipment—instead, they combined African and Western traditions. Singers began performing and recording in local languages and dialects. As in other parts of Africa, popular music in western Africa sometimes carried a political message and could get the singer in trouble. In 1984 Nigerian musician Fela Anikulapo-Kuti was jailed for 20 months because his Afro-beat songs repeatedly criticized the government.

Local traditions are often incorporated into African popular music and performance. Here the group Heshoo Beshoo performs in Cape Town, South Africa.

The 1990s brought a surge of interest in griot artists, who belong to a centuries-old tradition of storytelling and singing. In MALI and SENEGAL, griot music is now strongly associated with national identity. Some of the most successful singers have been women called *djely mousso*—praise singers who recount the origins and achievements of noble families. In recent years some of these artists have recorded with orchestras and achieved great success, inspiring other women to become musicians.

North Africa. While influenced by Western culture to some extent, popular culture in North Africa is largely shaped by the customs and laws of Islam, the region's dominant religion. For example, Islamic law bans the creation of images of people or animals, and this has affected the development of painting, poster-making, and other art. North Africa's popular culture is also deeply influenced by Arab traditions. Pop music in North Africa is generally sung in Arabic and incorporates many elements of traditional Arabic songs. Islam and Arab culture are also strongly reflected in much of the region's popular literature, filmmaking, and theater.

North Africa has produced its own styles of pop music. One of the best known is Algerian *rai,* a style of music that uses Western equipment such as drum machines and synthesizers. Portable cassette players helped spread *rai,* which is associated with urban youth, the celebration of pleasure (including drinking alcohol, which is forbidden to Muslims), and a rebellious attitude toward authority. That rebelliousness is not just a pose. Several music producers and singers have been killed for violating traditional Islamic customs. In North Africa and elsewhere on the continent, popular culture is intended to entertain, but it often makes a powerful personal or social statement as well. (*See also* **Art, Body Adornment and Clothing, Cinema, Dance, Festivals and Carnivals, Islam in Africa, Literature, Masks and Masquerades, Music and Song, Oral Tradition, Photography, Proverbs and Riddles, Publishing, Radio and Television, Sports and Recreation, Theater.**)

Population

Africa's population is growing at a faster rate than that of any other region of the world. According to the International Data Base of the U.S. Bureau of the Census, the estimated population of the continent in 2001 was 823.2 million people. The same organization projects that by the year 2050 Africa will have 1.8 billion people—perhaps 20 percent of the world's population.

Information about population figures and trends is of vital importance in determining how to use resources and plan for the future. Demographers, the researchers who study population data, are interested in more than just the number of people living in a particular country or region. They also want information about the age and gender of the population, the number of children born to each woman, and the number of deaths each year. These factors help them predict how the

* **sub-Saharan**   referring to Africa south
of the Sahara desert

See color
plate 14,
vol. 3.

population will change in the coming years. For a number of reasons,
population data is less certain for Africa, especially sub-Saharan* Africa,
than for any other major world region. Demographers know, however,
that sub-Saharan Africa has the world's highest birth, death, and population growth rates.

Gathering Population Data. No reliable information about Africa's
overall population existed before the 1900s. Colonial officials in British-
administered colonies such as EGYPT and SIERRA LEONE did begin taking
censuses—systematic counts of the population—in the late 1800s, and
by the mid-1900s other colonial administrations were carrying out censuses as well. The concept of counting people and keeping records was
new to Africans, and census takers had to devise methods that people
could easily use. Some of the early solutions were creative, such as having villages send gourds containing a bean for each man, a nut for each
woman, and a stone for each child who lived in the village.

Beginning in the 1950s, censuses took on new importance for development planning. They also had a role in the independence movement
because officials often used census data to prepare lists of voters. The
new censuses were more reliable than earlier ones, partly because of the
greater number of educated Africans, especially schoolteachers, who
could serve as census takers. The UNITED NATIONS became involved in
1971 with the establishment of the African Census Program, which has
held at least one census in every African nation.

Despite improvements in census taking, problems remain. Many
Africans have been reluctant to provide information, generally because
they fear being identified for tax purposes. Counters have sometimes
inflated the numbers for some groups because of ethnic or political rivalries or because the distribution of promised resources is based on population counts.

Recording people's ages is another problem. In many African cultures,
people do not reckon their age in years. Instead, they consider themselves part of an age-set, a group of individuals who are about the same
age. Demographers cannot obtain more precise information from official records because no African nation has a completely effective system
for recording the births and deaths of all citizens.

Current Information and Trends. The rapid rate of Africa's population growth is due to two main factors. One is mortality—the number
of deaths in a given time or place. Africa's mortality rate has fallen for
the past 100 years. In general, this means that more people are living
longer, although mortality rates are uneven across the continent. A person born in sub-Saharan Africa today can expect to live an average of 49
years, while in North Africa the life expectancy is 68 years. Infant mortality—the number of infants who die in the first year of life—is also
higher in sub-Saharan Africa than in North Africa.

The second factor is the birth or fertility rate, based on the average
number of children a woman bears in her lifetime. Like the mortality
rate, the fertility rate varies across Africa. North Africa's fertility rate has
fallen somewhat to an average of four children per woman, while in sub-

Saharan Africa the fertility rate has remained fairly steady at nearly six-children per woman, the highest in the world. Reasons for North Africa's birthrate decline include greater ease of divorce, marriage at later ages, and increased educational and job opportunities for women. Demographers expect that as such trends become stronger in sub-Saharan Africa, the birthrate will fall there also.

Overall, Africa's is an extremely young population. In most of the continent, more than 40 percent of the population is under 15 years of age. This high percentage of children and young adolescents means that even if each young woman bears fewer children than her mother or grandmother did, Africa's population will keep growing at a high rate for some time. (*See also* **Age and Aging, AIDS, Diseases, Health Care, Hunger and Famine, Warfare.**)

PORTS

See *Transportation.*

PORTUGUESE COLONIES

See *Colonialism in Africa.*

PREHISTORIC AFRICA

See *Archaeology and Prehistory.*

Prempeh, Agyeman

ca. 1871–1931
Asante king

* **confederacy** alliance or league of peoples or states

* **Anglican** of the Church of England

Agyeman Prempeh was king of the ASANTE (Ashanti), a people who once controlled much of present-day GHANA and IVORY COAST. Prempeh took power in 1888 after defeating rivals for the Asante throne. As king of a confederacy* of Asante chiefdoms, he tried to unite his people by ending fighting in the central region and conquering rebels in the north.

In addition to internal problems, Prempeh faced outside threats. For some years the British had been trying to weaken the Asante by supporting their enemies and interfering with their laws. In 1896 a British force invaded Kumasi, the Asante's capital city. The invaders banished Prempeh to SIERRA LEONE and then to the SEYCHELLES Islands.

During his years in exile, Prempeh learned English and joined the Anglican* Church. Meanwhile, the Asante confederacy had become a British colony. In 1924 the British allowed Prempeh to return to his homeland as a citizen. Taking advantage of the former king's influence with his people, they made him ruler of Kumasi state. Between 1926 and his death, Prempeh reorganized the laws and politics of Kumasi. He also helped pave the way for the return of the Asante confederacy, which was reestablished in 1935. (*See also* **Akan Region, Colonialism in Africa.**)

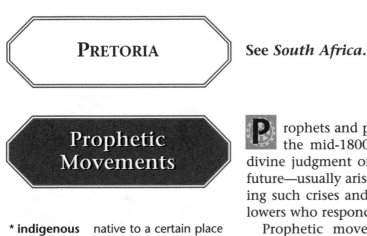

PRETORIA

See *South Africa.*

Prophetic Movements

* **indigenous** native to a certain place

* **Islamic** relating to Islam, the religion based on the teachings of the prophet Muhammad

* **sect** religious group

Prophets and prophetic movements have flourished in Africa since the mid-1800s. Prophets—religious leaders with messages about divine judgment or moral law who often make predictions about the future—usually arise in groups facing major social upheaval. By addressing such crises and offering radical solutions, they tend to inspire followers who respond with fervor to their message.

Prophetic movements in Africa have drawn from indigenous*, Christian, and Islamic* traditions. Many emerged in response to the dramatic changes that followed European colonization of the continent. Most of these movements were short-lived, lasting only until the resolution of the particular crisis at hand. Others, however, took root and continued to thrive long after the situations that inspired them had ended. Some have even grown into mainstream religious sects* with many thousands of followers.

ROOTS OF AFRICAN PROPHECY

African societies have long included individuals who claimed to have the ability to communicate with sources responsible for good and bad fortune. Seers*, diviners*, spirit mediums*, or dream interpreters have played a role in virtually every indigenous belief system in Africa. However, there are significant differences between such religious figures and prophets. These differences relate both to the nature of the person's vision and the sources of his or her ideas and symbols.

* **seer** one who can predict the future

* **diviner** person who predicts the future or explains the causes of misfortune

* **medium** person called upon to communicate with the spirit world

Magicians, Healers, and Prophets. The KONGO people of west-central Africa make a useful distinction between the *nganga* (magician or healer) and the *ngunza* (prophet). Both employ mystical power from the dead to benefit the living. However, the *nganga* does so for private or personal ends, while the *ngunza* does so for the public good.

The *nganga* are traditional religious figures who establish contact with the spirit world through dreams, trances, or possession. Called on for help in dealing with sickness, crop failure, or everyday problems, the *nganga* serve mainly to identify the source of a problem and recommend an action to overcome it. The *nganga* rarely offer new remedies. Instead, they explain how to use old, traditional remedies more effectively.

The *ngunza,* on the other hand, deals with extraordinary crises that affect the group as a whole. Sometimes a traditional African society

Prophetic Movements

reaches a point at which social ills or other problems seem overwhelming. The members of the community interpret the crisis to mean that the charms or fetishes* that protected them from evil powers have lost their power. This is usually the moment when a prophet arises to destroy old fetishes and reveal new ones, to establish new shrines and rituals*, or to bring about a new religious order.

The *ngunza* promotes new solutions to problems, rather than relying

Many African prophets have been inspired by Christian beliefs. Here, a prophet visits a village in Ivory Coast to teach the local people about Christianity.

188

on old ones. Such solutions typically involve reforming society, as old ideas are rejected and replaced by new ones. At some point, however, the new order will also lose its effectiveness and a new prophet will arise to overturn society once again.

Before the colonial period, the process of social reformation led by African prophets usually occurred within limits set by the existing culture. However, the unique circumstances and profound changes brought by European colonization led African prophets to promote much more radical changes in society.

The Influence of World Religions. While based on indigenous religious beliefs and practices, most African prophetic movements have drawn heavily on ideas and symbols from Islam and Christianity. One idea found in both of these religion is millennialism—the belief that the world will be destroyed and re-created anew, bringing about a thousand-year period of peace and justice.

Millennialism blended well with the African prophetic tradition of reforming society through the elimination of witchcraft or evil. Its impact was greatest when applied to the "evils" of colonialism. Millennialist ideas inspired prophets such as UTHMAN DAN FODIO, who led a Muslim jihad, or holy war, against French forces in West Africa.

Christianity has been an important source of inspiration for many African prophets. The Bible offers numerous examples of prophets who predicted the fall of the old, corrupt social order and told people what to do to bring in a new one. Many of the missionary groups that came to Africa also incorporated millennialist ideas in their teaching. Christian practices such as mass baptisms and the rejection of traditional charms and idols echoed prophets' calls for social purification and a new beginning, and African prophets adopted many of these ideas.

PROPHETS AND PROPHETIC CHURCHES

The European conquest of Africa was a sign to many Africans that the old fetishes and gods had lost their power. Throughout the continent, prophets preached the need to abandon the old sources of spiritual power and seek renewal through new means.

Major Prophets and Movements. A number of well-known African prophets and prophetic movements emerged during the years of European colonialism. Among the earliest prophets were William Wadé Harris of LIBERIA and Garrick Sokari BRAIDE of NIGERIA. Both men joined and then broke away from missionary churches to preach against witchcraft and old fetishes.

In the Belgian Congo (present-day CONGO, KINSHASA), Simon KIMBANGU also spoke out against the evils of witchcraft and called on his followers to destroy ritual objects. Although Kimbangu's message was not political, Belgian authorities considered him a threat and imprisoned him in 1921. Although his movement—Kimbanguism—was banned, it took root and led to the establishment of a church that later played a major role in the country's religious life. It also inspired Congolese nationalism* and the movement for independence.

* **nationalism** devotion to the interests and culture of one's country

189

Prophetic Movements

Eastern Africa saw a wave of politically inspired prophetic movements in the early 1900s. Leaders of the MAJI MAJI rebellion in Tanganyika (present-day TANZANIA) and the Yakan movement of UGANDA both claimed to receive prophetic gifts and power from magical water. Drinking the water supposedly brought back dead ancestors, made the drinker immune to bullets, and would cause invading foreigners to vanish. Both movements ended in brief and bloody uprisings that were crushed by colonial troops.

Another East African prophetic movement with political ties was the Watu wa Mungu ("People of God"), which rejected European culture and clothing. The group apparently had links to the MAU MAU uprising, an anticolonial guerrilla* movement in Kenya in the 1950s. Jomo KENYATTA, the first president of independent KENYA, was associated with the Watu wa Mungu.

Alice LENSHINA, a female prophet in ZAMBIA, spoke out against colonialism and instructed her followers to withdraw from all secular* activities. Lenshina established the Lumpa Church, a movement that swept through much of Zambia in the 1950s. In the months before Zambia gained its independence in 1964, Lumpa followers engaged in fierce battles with colonial forces. When the fighting ended, many Lumpa fled Zambia or were imprisoned, including Lenshina herself.

A more recent example of a prophetic movement with political goals is the Holy Spirit Movement in Uganda. Alice Auma, the movement's leader, claimed to be a medium passing along the commands of a prophet called Lakwena. In the mid-1980s she built up a military force dedicated to cleansing the world of evil and building a society in which humans, the spirit world, and the environment would coexist in peace. Auma directed military operations against the Ugandan army until her troops were defeated in 1987. Remnants of her army continue to fight in Uganda under the name the Lord's Resistance Army.

New Christian Churches. Many prophetic movements were founded by African followers of Christian mission churches. They left mission churches because European clergy* failed to treat blacks equally or to entrust them with responsible positions. The new African-led churches retained much of the structure and teachings of the mission churches.

Most of these prophetic movements split from Protestant churches; very few developed in areas dominated by Catholics or Muslims. Because Protestant churches preached that few people would be chosen for salvation, a steady stream of converts left the church to begin their own sects. The approach of Catholicism was different. It baptized all who entered the church and attempted to work out problems with individuals, rather than rejecting them as unworthy. Catholic Africans thus had less compelling reasons to leave the church than Protestant Africans.

Prophetic and Charismatic Churches. Another independent church movement in Africa led to the formation of prophetic churches based on prayer, healing, and prophecy. African men and women who felt the call to prophecy established a number of such churches in West

* **guerrilla** type of warfare involving sudden raids by small groups of warriors

* **secular** nonreligious; connected with everyday life

* **clergy** ministers, priests, or other religious officials

Africa during the early 1900s. These are often called spirit churches or Aladura, a Nigerian word meaning "people of prayer." The earliest were the Church of the Lord, the Christ Apostolic church, and the Cherubim and Seraphim church. Fast-growing prophetic churches of recent times include the Celestial Church of Christ and the Brotherhood of the Cross and Star.

Though vastly different in many ways, prophetic churches generally have little formal structure or dogma*. Authority lies entirely with their founders, whose preaching and instruction are considered divinely inspired. Worship tends to be inventive and often includes preaching based on ORAL TRADITION and the use of African music and dance. Although the churches recognize traditional Christian holy days and sacraments such as marriage, they often have their own special practices and taboos*.

The churches known as Pentacostal-Charismatic are evangelical* groups that emphasize the conversion of their members from traditional to "born again" Christianity. Services feature speaking in tongues, healing, and miracle working. The church emphasizes the role of God in providing material success and prosperity for members. Widespread throughout West Africa in particular, Pentacostal-Charismatic churches have a global outlook, with leaders maintaining contact with similar religious groups around the world.

Both charismatic and prophetic churches focus on the primary concerns of all African religious communities: healing, well-being, material success, and long life. Although both have condemned indigenous religion as "pagan," they recognize the endurance of beliefs such as WITCHCRAFT AND SORCERY. They have waged a continuing battle against indigenous religious institutions and ritual practices by burning shrines, destroying charms and fetishes, and casting out "demons" from people's bodies.

African Independent and Zionist Churches. Frustrated by unequal treatment in white churches, a group of black Protestants in southern Africa founded several African Independent Churches (AICs). These churches followed the doctrines and organization of the white Protestant churches but were controlled entirely by blacks. AICs have grown rapidly since the early 1900s, especially in urban areas of SOUTH AFRICA. Once closely allied with nationalist movements, most have become more traditional since independence.

The prophetic movement in southern Africa also led to the establishment of Zionist churches, which arose among farm workers exploited* by white landlords. These churches have no central organization and are characterized by a wide variety of beliefs and practices. However, most of the churches seek to ease the suffering of the poor by urging them to work hard, avoid alcohol, save money, and support each other. Zionist churches also believe in prayers to the Holy Spirit to accumulate spiritual power for healing the sick.

Zionist churches are popular among women. For one thing, they admit women to the clergy and even have female bishops. Furthermore, the churches promote a hardworking, disciplined, family-oriented

* **dogma** system of established principles

* **taboo** religious prohibition against doing something that is believed to cause harm

* **evangelical** referring to Protestant groups that stress the importance of personal religious experience and the authority of the Scriptures

* **exploit** to take advantage of; to make productive use of

Worldwide Appeal

Africa's major Pentacostal-Charismatic churches operate in very similar ways to charismatic churches throughout the world. Many hold large revival meetings and open-air services. They use electronic media, such as recorded music, videos, and electronic keyboards to enliven religious meetings. Between services, the churches publish weekly and monthly literature, including prayers, selections from the Bible, and Bible reading guides. These materials are usually printed both in English and in local African languages, helping the churches attract a wide variety of followers.

lifestyle that is often lacking in modern urban Africa and is especially appealing to women.

The Watchtower. The movement known as "Watchtower" or "Kitawala" offers an example of the entire range of beliefs, methods, and ideologies* of African prophetic movements and independent churches. It is based on the ideas of the American Watch Tower Bible and Tract Society (now known as the Jehovah's Witnesses), which an English preacher named Joseph Booth brought to Africa in the early 1900s.

* **ideology**   set of concepts or opinions of a person or group

Kitawala, the African form of the movement, claimed that Christian missions deliberately withheld biblical truth and baptism from blacks. It also denounced British rule and said that the end of the world would be marked by the defeat of the British and the recapture of Africa from European control. One characteristic of the movement was its rejection of politics or allegiance to any government. During World War II, Kitawala followers were persecuted for their refusal to participate in the military.

Like other prophetic movements, Kitawala imported foreign ideas and then adapted them to the conditions in Africa. It called for a rejection of both traditional fetishes and mission-based Christianity. It replaced white male religious leaders with black African men and women. It also gave rise to many related groups, each practicing its own form of the religion with different focus and rituals. Like most of Africa's prophetic movements and churches, the defining features of Kitawala are constant change, fresh division into new sects, and a commitment to spread its message across the continent. (*See also* **Chilembwe, John; Christianity in Africa; Divination and Oracles; Healing and Medicine; Independence Movements; Islam in Africa; Kimpa Vita; Missions and Missionaries; Nongqawuse; Religion and Ritual; Shembe, Isaiah; Spirit Possession; Taboo and Sin.**)

PROTESTANT CHURCHES

See *Christianity in Africa.*

Proverbs and Riddles

In most African societies, proverbs and riddles are forms of art. They are simple and elegant ways to communicate a lot of meaning in few words. Proverbs and riddles play an important role in the traditions of African speech and conversation.

African proverbs are sayings that express the shared wisdom of a culture. Based on close observation of life and nature, colored by thoughtful reflection, they are believed to express truths that no one can dispute. Many collectors and scholars of African art study proverbs, which are found in nearly all African cultures.

Proverbs are often used as a tactful and delicate way for people in close-knit African communities to comment on and correct each other's behavior. Some sayings express how people in a society are supposed to behave. The Jabo people of Liberia say that "a grown-up who [imitates] children is a fool." Other proverbs sum up an event in life. When a person is laid low by misfortune, the Zulu of southern Africa say, "The beast has fallen on its horns."

Like proverbs, African riddles are brief and based on observations of nature. However, with riddles, the listener is expected to guess the answer to a question or the meaning of a statement. Sometimes a riddle is nothing more than a sound. "Seh!" is a riddle of the Kamba people of Kenya. Its answer is "a needle stabbed the sand," because "seh" is the sound of the needle entering the sand. In Africa, riddles are often used as the introduction to storytelling. They catch the audience's interest and prepare people for the meaning of the story that is to come. (*See also* **Oral Tradition**.)

Publishing

* **Islam** religion based on the teachings of the prophet Muhammad; religious faith of Muslims

* **indigenous** native to a certain place

Writing and LITERATURE have a long history in Africa, beginning in ancient EGYPT with the picture-writing called hieroglyphics. Publishing traces its roots to the rise of Islam* on the continent, and printed works in Arabic appeared in major cities and trading centers by the 1600s. However, it was through the work of European missionaries and colonial governments in the 1800s and 1900s that publishing became established and spread throughout Africa. Today small publishing industries exist in every African country.

Early Book Publishing in Africa. Missionaries brought printing presses to Africa as early as the mid-1700s and produced Bibles, prayer books, and hymn books in many indigenous* LANGUAGES. Because these languages lacked written forms, missionaries first had to compile vocabulary lists and grammars. Within 100 years, presses were running in NIGERIA, KENYA, and SOUTH AFRICA, and some of them still exist today. By the early 1930s, many colonial governments had set up Vernacular (in the local language) Literature Bureaus to publish reading materials for an African audience. In 1931, Algerian reformers founded the Association of Algerian Muslim Ulama to encourage Islamic culture and Arabic language in the face of French colonialism. The association ran a press that nurtured the growth of Algerian Arabic literature by publishing local poetry and fiction.

The rapid expansion of EDUCATION in Africa after World War II—especially as countries won their independence—led to a great need for textbooks. Most of these books were published abroad and did not serve the needs of African readers. Many contained material that was racist. Books written in Africa by Africans did not become widely available until the 1960s.

By the 1970s, indigenous publishers were expanding their businesses and began to challenge the dominance of foreign publishing corporations. However, economic crises in the 1980s took a severe toll as governments cut funds that supported publishing and libraries. Even where governments remained involved, publishing suffered from government bureaucracy, inefficiency, and censorship.

* literacy   ability to read and write

Book Publishing Today. African book publishers today face a variety of special problems involving the size of the market. The continent's literacy* rate of less than 50 percent limits the number of people who can read or buy books. Publishers can rarely market a book widely because Africans speak a great variety of languages, none of which is common throughout the continent. One option is to write and publish in European languages that more people speak but few people favor. In addition, distributing the books is difficult because economic declines of recent years have led to unreliable electricity, poor roads, and few vehicles.

African publishers have responded to these challenges in many ways. Some have promoted inexpensive paperback novels designed to appeal to a popular audience. Some critics have attacked these books for questionable morals, but such novels have attracted many new readers who previously had little enthusiasm for books.

African publishers have also joined together in groups such as the African Publishers Network, which trains people who work in publishing. The African Books Collective works to win an international audience for African literature and to promote writing and scholarship in Africa. A major prize called the Noma Award has also encouraged the growth of the industry.

Newspapers and Periodicals. Colonial governments supported many newspapers, magazines, and journals for the benefit of European settlers. Colonial newspapers typically backed government policies and the interests of the settlers against the rights of indigenous peoples. Among the first was *Al-Mubashir*, printed in 1847 in Algeria. In other colonies, an opposition press developed to give voice to African ideas, to challenge official policies, and to promote independence. Examples of such early publications were *Muiguithania* in Kenya and *Drum* in South Africa.

After independence, many African rulers took control over the main newspapers to reduce the ability of the press to criticize their governments. However, by the 1980s pressure for more open government led to greater freedom for the African press. When MALAWI's president agreed to allow opposition political parties in 1993, the country had only two newspapers. Three years later, more than 15 publications covered Malawi's politics, economics, and social issues.

However, many states still exercise control over the media, and publishers that challenge government policies or officials often face harassment and imprisonment. So many attacks have been made against journalists and publishers in TUNISIA that the country's president, Zine el-Abidine Ben Ali, has been declared one of the world's top ten enemies of the press. Nigeria and Kenya boast vigorous local presses, but the governments of those nations often shut down newspapers and magazines that criticize too harshly. Yet the publications least like-

Nigerian Bestsellers

In the mid-1940s, local writers in Onitsha, Nigeria, began producing small, inexpensive booklets called chapbooks. Some of them offered practical instruction, such as How to Succeed in Life *and* How to Avoid Enemies and Bad Company. *Others were emotional dramas about troubled relationships—*Agnes the Faithful Lover *or* "Innocent Grace" and Her 23 Husbands. *Some Onitsha chapbooks sold hundreds of thousands of copies. Although desktop publishing and slick paperbacks have replaced the old chapbooks, many Nigerian towns still have vigorous publishing industries.*

The development of a free and independent press is a continuing issue in much of Africa. Fred M'membe, editor of a Zambian newspaper, was accused by the government of publishing secret information about plans to change the nation's constitution.

ly to support government policies are often the most popular. In 1996 the circulation of Kenya's independent daily paper, *The Nation,* reached about 190,000, while that of the government-owned *Kenya Times* remained at about 6,000.

As Africa moves into the twenty-first century, illiteracy, financial difficulties, and undemocratic governments present the main challenges to developing a free and financially sound press. However, African publishers have so far shown remarkable durability and resourcefulness under difficult conditions. Those that survive could play a major role in addressing the continent's political and social problems. (*See also* **Christianity in Africa, Colonialism in Africa, Missions and Missionaries.**)

Pygmies

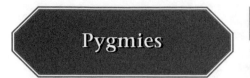

* **anthropologist** scientist who studies human beings, especially in relation to social and cultural characteristics

The term *Pygmies* refers to a number of peoples in central Africa who share two characteristics. Most of them are quite short, and they live by HUNTING AND GATHERING in forests. Since ancient times, both Africans and outsiders have recognized Pygmies as distinct from other people on the continent. Anthropologists* do not know whether the peoples called Pygmies are a true racial group or whether they are racially the same as their non-Pygmy neighbors. They may simply be shorter than neighboring peoples because they have lived in the forest for generations. Unlike ethnic groups, the Pygmies do not share a common language or use languages of their own. Each Pygmy group uses the languages of its non-Pygmy neighbors. The four main Pygmy groups are the Aka or BaBinga of Congo (Brazzaville), Gabon, and the Central African Republic; the Mbuti of the Ituri forest in Congo (Kinshasa); the Twa of Rwanda and Burundi; and the Gesere, who live near Lake Kivu, between Rwanda and Congo (Kinshasa).

There is no single Pygmy society or culture. These people live in small bands that do not have chiefs or other political heads. Most bands are isolated from other Pygmies and are linked to local farming peoples, with whom they trade. The Pygmies exchange forest products such as game or honey for grain, iron, and salt, and sometimes they provide hunters and soldiers to neighboring chiefs. Traditionally Pygmies have been nomads. However, in some regions, the destruction of their environment by mining, logging, and farm expansion now threatens their ability to live off the forest. In addition, some governments have policies to encourage Pygmies to settle down and become farmers.

Pyramids

Although many cultures have constructed pyramids, those of Egypt are among the most famous structures in the world. The ancient Egyptians erected huge pyramids as burial monuments for their kings, the PHARAOHS.

Around 2650 B.C. an Egyptian architect named Imhotep built the oldest known pyramid for his king, Djoser. It was the first royal tomb in Egypt to be made entirely of stone, instead of mud-brick. It consists of six layers, each smaller than the one below it, and is known as the Step Pyramid. Beneath the pyramid is a network of underground rooms and tunnels, including the king's burial chamber.

The next 500 years were the golden age of pyramid construction in Egypt, as kings and nobles ordered ever more massive or elaborate structures. Surrounding each pyramid, which contained or stood on top of the tomb, the Egyptians erected many other buildings, such as temples and smaller pyramids for family members. In some cases, a wall enclosed the entire complex, and passages and shafts ran underneath the structures. The pyramids were built of mud-brick or limestone blocks and were covered on the outside with a layer of the whitest limestone.

Of the 80 or so pyramids found in Egypt, many fell into ruin long ago. The best-preserved structures are found at Giza, Dahshur, and

Saqqarah, sites south of CAIRO that were close to the ancient Egyptian city of Memphis. The three large pyramids at Giza have been a major Egyptian tourist attraction since the 400s B.C., when the Greek historian Herodotus marveled at them. They were built between 2575 and 2465 B.C. for the kings Khufu, Khafre, and Menkaure. The largest, the Great Pyramid of Khufu, has been called the largest building ever constructed. It measures 756 feet on each side and was 481 feet high when it was new. It is shorter today because people stripped its outer limestone blocks for use in other structures. The Great Pyramid contains about 2.3 million blocks of stone weighing almost 6 million tons. Nearby is the Great Sphinx.

The pyramids were designed to proclaim the might and power of the kings who lay buried beneath them. Unfortunately, they called too much attention to the royal burial sites. Beginning in ancient times, robbers looted nearly all the tombs, carrying off the goods and treasures that were buried with the royal and noble dead. Eventually, the kings of Egypt stopped erecting pyramids and instead built secret royal tombs in the remote caves of the Valley of the Kings. (*See also* **Egypt, Ancient**.)

Qaddafi, Muammar al-

1942–
Libyan military and political leader

* **nationalist** devoted to the interests and culture of one's country

* **coup** sudden, often violent, overthrow of a ruler or government

* **Islamic** relating to Islam, the religion based on the teachings of the prophet Muhammad

* **guerrilla** type of warfare involving sudden raids by small groups of warriors

Muammar al-Qaddafi (also spelled Khadafy or Gadhafi) has been the head of the government of LIBYA since 1969. He was born in northern Libya into a family of Bedouin, nomadic desert-dwelling Arabs. After attending a local Muslim school, he entered the Libyan Military Academy and began rising through the ranks of the Libyan army. Qaddafi became a committed nationalist*, determined to reform his country. In 1969 he and several other officers led a coup* that overthrew King Idris I. Qaddafi became commander in chief of Libya's military forces and chairman of the Revolutionary Command Council, which he established as the nation's governing body.

Qaddafi took immediate steps to transform Libya and purge it of European influences. He enforced Islamic* law and outlawed alcohol, nightclubs, and non-Muslim churches. He closed U.S. and British military bases, forced most Italian and Jewish citizens to leave the country, and seized control of foreign-owned petroleum plants. During the 1970s, income from petroleum sales supported the Libyan economy while Qaddafi experimented with economic reforms, such as abolishing retail stores and giving landlords' property to tenants.

Qaddafi tried to forge unions between Libya and other Arab nations in the Middle East, but he was unsuccessful. He bitterly criticized EGYPT for entering peace talks with Israel, and he involved Libyan forces in civil conflicts and coup attempts in Egypt, SUDAN, and CHAD. Many countries criticized Qaddafi for his support of guerrilla* movements such as the Palestine Liberation Organization (PLO), the Black Panthers, and the Irish Republican Army. The United States viewed him as an enemy and a sponsor of international terrorism.

In 1986, in response to the bombing of a German nightclub thought to have been carried out by Libyan agents, U.S. forces bombed Qaddafi's

* **Soviet Union** nation that existed from 1922 to 1991, made up of Russia and 14 other republics

residence in Tripoli. He escaped but began to make fewer public appearances. During the 1990s, Qaddafi's program of reform suffered setbacks after the Soviet Union*, which had supported his government, collapsed.

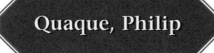

Quaque, Philip

1741–1816
Ghanaian missionary and educator

* **Anglican** of the Church of England

Philip Quaque was a missionary, an educator, and the first African to become a priest in the Church of England. Although he failed in his efforts to spread Christianity and education in the Gold Coast (present-day Ghana), his writings are a valuable source of information about the struggle for control of western Africa in the early 1800s.

As a young man, Quaque left his home at Cape Coast and went to England to study. His training was sponsored by the Society for the Propagation of the Gospel in Foreign Parts (known as the SPG). He became a deacon of the Anglican* Church, then a priest. When he returned to Cape Coast as a Missionary School Master in 1766, he worked for the SPG and the Company of Merchants Trading to Africa, an association of British merchants involved in the SLAVE TRADE.

Quaque had mixed results in achieving his goals in Cape Coast. As a minister he practiced "fortress Christianity," focusing on converting chiefs and other rulers rather than ordinary people. His efforts failed because the chiefs feared that their authority would be weakened by becoming Christian. Quaque had little more success as a teacher. He attracted few students and was unable to build a new school. Still, he did train some students who became teachers themselves and helped to spread education throughout the Cape Coast area.

While Quaque was trying to convert chiefs and other rulers, he watched how these leaders governed and how they responded to Europeans. His writings on what he observed have given scholars a better understanding of political relations in western Africa in the late 1700s and early 1800s and of the role Europeans played in the region. (*See also* **Christianity in Africa, Education, Ghana, Missions and Missionaries.**)

Queens and Queen Mothers

African monarchies have always been dominated by men. Their authority over kingdoms is patterned on the role of male heads of households and families. However, royal women have held and still hold considerable power. A few have reigned as queens in their own right, but more often the power, influence, and responsibility of royal women lies in their relationship to kings, as mothers, sisters, or wives.

Only a few cases of ruling queens are known. The Lovedu kingdom of SOUTH AFRICA switched from a king to a queen in about 1800, and all Lovedu rulers since that time have been female. Known as Rain-Queens, they have little political authority but are believed to have mystical power over rain. The Rain-Queen is symbolically both male and female. She has no husband and is not supposed to bear children. In return for rain, chiefs and nobles present her with "wives," and she in turn gives

Queen Regent Ntombi ruled Swaziland until 1986, when her son the crown prince came of age and was crowned King Mswati III.

these wives to other nobles. The children of these unions regard the Rain-Queen as their father.

In the 1800s women took over the monarchies of the Merina and Sakalava peoples of MADAGASCAR. Europeans were gaining influence in the area, and the people of these kingdoms may have put queens rather than kings on the throne in an attempt to avoid conflict with Europeans. Among both groups, queens are referred to in language that conceals the fact that they are women. The Merina queen is called "the person who rules," while the Sakalava queen is addressed as a male.

Although reigning queens are rare, in most African kingdoms certain female relatives of the king have important roles. They may act as

Queens and Queen Mothers

* **regent** person appointed to rule on behalf of another

* **clan** group of people descended from a common ancestor

* **matrilineal** tracing ancestry or descent through the mother's side of the family

regents* for kings who are too young to rule, or they may maintain courts of their own and exercise powers similar to those of senior chiefs. These women are generally the sisters or mothers of kings. Most African kings have many wives, and although the wives play significant roles, they seldom have influence over the entire kingdom. Instead, they serve as representatives at court for their various clans*.

A king's sister, on the other hand, may be regarded as a partner in rule. The Lozi people of ZAMBIA divide their kingdom into northern and southern parts, with identical capitals 25 miles apart. The southern one is ruled by a sister of the king, who has her own chiefs, advisers, and army. Her realm serves as a refuge from the king's anger.

The queen mother, who may be the king's mother or another female relative, can have similar powers. Among the Shi people of eastern CONGO (KINSHASA), the queen mother controls about half the land in the kingdom and rules until her son is old enough to take power. Among the ASANTE and other matrilineal* peoples of GHANA, queen mothers do not rule the kingdom, but they have the authority of royal men to judge issues. They are not just female chiefs—in fact, they have the same royal status as a man does, and they even dress as men and have more freedom in marriage than other women.

The Ganda kingdom of UGANDA illustrates how complex the roles of royal African women can be. Kingship is divided between the living king and the most recently deceased king. Both are addressed by the title *kabaka,* and so are the mother of the living king, his oldest sister or half sister, known as the queen sister, and his chief wife. Together, these individuals form a total kingship. (*See also* **Cleopatra; Gender Roles and Sexuality; Kings and Kingship; Kinship; Marriage Systems; Ranavalona, Mada; Women in Africa.**)

Radama I

**ca. 1793–1828
King of Merina**

Radama I became king of the Merina kingdom in MADAGASCAR in 1810. He succeeded his father, who had founded the kingdom. In 1816 Radama negotiated an agreement with the British government that provided military and administrative support to Merina. Radama went on to conquer most of Madagascar.

Under the terms of the agreement, the British supplied Radama's army with weapons and training. They also trained Merina's government officials in schools run by the London Missionary Society. In exchange, Radama banned the export of slaves from his kingdom. The ban increased his power by weakening his rivals, who had benefited from the SLAVE TRADE.

Radama's military campaigns cost the lives of many of his soldiers. As a result of the loss of large numbers of men, Merina's households were increasingly headed by women. The king's most vocal opponents were women who objected to the growing influence of European culture. In 1822 a group of women staged a revolt when the king cut his hair in a European fashion. Radama's wife, Mada RANAVALONA, who succeeded him, attempted to eliminate European influence from Madagascar.

Radio and Television

Radio and television can communicate information, arouse strong emotions, and inspire action. African governments, both the European-run colonial administrations and the independent nations that followed them, have been sharply aware of the power of these broadcast media. Governments have generally owned and controlled most national broadcast stations and have used them to promote their views, often censoring programs that opposed those views. Under pressure from both inside and outside Africa, however, governments began allowing a few private stations to operate in the late 1980s. Gradually radio and television broadcasts in some areas are beginning to reflect a broader diversity of opinions.

Role of Radio and TV. Radio got an early start in Africa. The first regularly scheduled broadcasts began in SOUTH AFRICA in 1924, just four years after programming started in the United States. By 1932 EGYPT had several stations broadcasting news, music, and readings from the Qur'an, the Islamic* holy book. As colonies gained their independence as nations in the 1950s and 1960s, many established new national stations. Radio became an important way for governments to communicate with their citizens and with people beyond their borders. In Egypt, Gamal Abdel NASSER used radio as a propaganda tool, launching a powerful station called Voice of the Arabs that broadcast to other countries in the Middle East. Radio also became a teaching aid, as in the literacy* programs broadcast on many national radio stations.

Today radio remains the most influential electronic medium in Africa because radio receivers are relatively inexpensive, widely distributed, and portable. In addition, radio programming is cheaper to produce than television broadcasts. In rural areas where there are few television sets and in places with limited television service, radio is the main source of information, education, and entertainment. Television, however, is popular in urban centers, as are videotapes. People buy or rent videos of movies from the United States, Europe, India, Japan, and China. Some are legal copies; others are pirate editions made in violation of international copyright laws.

Programming. African radio and television stations broadcast dramas, news, music, talk shows, and documentaries about health, the environment, agriculture, and other topics. Many countries have used fictional but realistic dramas to educate people about social issues such as the status of women. African stations also broadcast international programming, including material from CNN, the Voice of America, and the British Broadcasting Corporation. These radio and television shows include international news as well as programs developed especially for African audiences and delivered in various indigenous* LANGUAGES. The Voice of America, for example, produces a daily 30-minute segment focusing on African news as well as events around the world that affect Africa.

* **Islamic** relating to Islam, the religion based on the teachings of the prophet Muhammad

* **literacy** ability to read and write

* **Indigenous** native to a certain place

A South African family watches an evening television program. Television is popular in urban areas of Africa, but radio reaches a much broader audience.

Imported entertainment shows, such as television soap operas from the United States, Mexico, and Australia, have loyal audiences, although some critics argue that these programs' violence, sexuality, and emphasis on Western lifestyles make them inappropriate for African viewers. Ideas about how radio and television should operate in Africa often generate debate. Media critics generally agree about calling for an end to government control of the airwaves, but they may have different opinions about what audiences ought to see and hear. Some feel that the flow of programs from industrialized nations to less-developed African countries promotes Western views that are harmful to Africa.

African nations have taken steps to develop their own media industries and services. The Union of National Radio and Television Organizations of Africa (URTNA) was established in 1962. Funded in part by the UNITED NATIONS and international agencies, it promotes the exchange of television and radio programs within Africa, the training of personnel, the media coverage of African cultural and sports events, and the international marketing of African television programs. It also conducts research on the technical aspects of broadcasting and organizes seminars to improve the use of the media in national and regional development. The Television News Coordinating Centre, opened in ALGIERS in 1991, organizes television news broadcasts transmitted by satellite. (*See also* **Cinema, Oral Tradition, Popular Culture, Publishing, Theater.**)

RAIN FORESTS

See *Ecosystems; Forests and Forestry.*

Ranavalona, Mada

1788–1861
Queen of Madagascar

* **clan** group of people descended from a common ancestor

* **Malagasy** referring to the people of Madagascar

Mada Ranavalona was the wife of MADAGASCAR's King RADAMA I, who unified most of the island under the rule of the Merina clan*. When Radama died in 1828 without naming an heir, Ranavalona assumed power. She secured her position by negotiating with Merina nobles and military leaders, and by executing all potential rivals.

A fierce defender of Malagasy* traditions, Ranavalona reversed her husband's pro-Western policies. Radama had negotiated with the British to protect Madagascar from interference by other nations. He also welcomed European traders and adopted many European customs. Ranavalona terminated the agreement with Britain. She would allow foreign traders to do business only at ports controlled by Malagasy governors, where the foreigners were sometimes subjected to forced labor and ordeal by poison.

Ranavalona suppressed CHRISTIANITY because it undermined support for traditional religious practices and because it opposed slavery, an important feature of Malagasy society. In 1835 she declared it illegal for a Malagasy person to convert to Christianity. Throughout her reign, she tortured and killed many Christians and exiled missionaries.

While she added no new territory to the Merina kingdom, Ranavalona strengthened royal control over the lands conquered by Radama. She ruthlessly defended the kingdom against attacks by the British and French navies, displaying the heads of those who died in battle. In the late 1850s when she uncovered a plot to bring Madagascar under French rule, she imprisoned and killed over 1,000 of her subjects and banished all Europeans from the island. Upon her death in 1861, Ranavalona's son Prince Rakoto succeeded her, becoming Radama II.

Rawlings, Jerry

1947–
President of Ghana

* **coup** sudden, often violent, overthrow of a ruler or government

* **regime** current political system or rule

Jerry Rawlings, an air force officer, ruled the nation of Ghana from 1981 to 2000. Originally named Jerry Rawlings John, he was the child of a Ghanaian mother and a Scottish father. After attending the respected Achimota Secondary School, he joined the Ghanaian air force in 1967. During his years as a fighter pilot, he became increasingly frustrated with Ghana's government, which he believed was both corrupt and ineffective.

In 1979 Rawlings led a coup* against the military regime* of I.K. Acheampong and F.W.K. Akuffo. As leader of the Armed Forces Revolutionary Council (AFRC), he took over the government, promising to introduce civilian rule. However, the AFRC tried and executed Acheampong, Akuffo, and other former leaders before holding elections for a civilian government. After Hilla Limann won the presidency, the AFRC stepped down from power. Rawlings soon lost faith in Limann's administration, and in 1981 he led another military coup. Rawlings and several others formed a new one-party government, the Provisional National Defense Council (PNDC). To revive Ghana's struggling economy, Rawlings launched an economic program created by the World Bank and International Monetary Fund. The program, which reformed tax and trade policies and privatized* many state-owned industries, is considered one of the most successful of its kind in Africa.

* **privatize** to transfer from government control to private ownership

In 1992, in response to growing political opposition and accusations of human rights abuses, Rawlings and the PNDC again transformed Ghana's government. They adopted a new constitution that was approved by a national vote and held multiparty elections for a parliamentary government. Running as the National Democratic Congress candidate, Rawlings won the presidency and was re-elected in 1996. After serving a second four-year term, Rawlings left office as called for in the constitution. John Kufuor succeeded him as president.

Refugees

Refugees are forced migrants, people driven from their homelands by violence, fear, or other conditions that make it impossible for them to remain. Throughout the history of Africa, famine, disease, war, environmental disasters, and competition for resources have created refugees by causing people to flee from troubled areas. In the past, most refugees eventually settled in the regions to which they fled. Since the 1980s, however, African nations and international aid agencies have viewed refugees as people who will eventually be repatriated, or returned to their native countries. As a result, some displaced Africans have spent years in refugee camps originally meant to provide temporary shelter.

* **precolonial** referring to the time before European powers colonized Africa

Causes of Forced Migration. In precolonial* Africa, warfare caused much migration and population resettlement. Chain reactions occurred, in which the people displaced by a conflict went on to displace other groups. For example, conflicts with the ZULU drove the NDEBELE people from southern Africa into what is now western ZIMBABWE. As they fled, the Ndebele displaced the SHONA. Tensions still exist between the Ndebele and other groups who consider themselves the original inhabitants of the land. Similar situations have occurred across Africa.

From as early as the A.D. 800s, the SLAVE TRADE was another major cause of involuntary population movements. Over the next thousand years, the trade took millions of Africans away from the continent and made others flee the operations of slave raiders and traders. Even after slavery had officially ended, competition among European powers for trade, influence, and territory in Africa continued to disrupt African communities. White colonists drove Africans off their land. They also required tax payments that forced Africans to seek wage labor, sometimes traveling great distances to work in agriculture or mining.

Beginning in the mid-1900s, Africa's European colonies became independent states. Many won their independence through wars that produced refugees. The new national boundaries corresponded to the old colonial borders that Europeans had drawn with little regard for the identities or relations of the various ETHNIC GROUPS within them. In the modern era, a number of wars have been fought over national borders. In addition, civil wars have erupted as various groups within nations have tried to secede*. All of these conflicts have produced refugees.

Racial, religious, and ethnic differences have also created refugees. Apartheid* forcibly uprooted millions of people within SOUTH AFRICA and forced thousands of others to seek safety outside the country. After the Jewish state of Israel declared its independence in 1948, EGYPT became involved in hostilities between Arab states and Israel, and thousands of Jews fled Egypt for Israel, Europe, or the Americas. Thousands of other Jews left the former French colonies of MOROCCO, TUNISIA, and ALGERIA for Israel or France.

Many of the newly independent African states forcibly drove out minority groups. UGANDA, for example, expelled 40,000 Asians in 1972 and more than 500,000 members of African minority groups in the 1980s. SIERRA LEONE expelled Ghanaians; GHANA expelled migrant workers who came from NIGERIA, NIGER, and Upper Volta (present-day BURKINA FASO); and in 1989 MAURITANIA began violently expelling its black population. During the 1990s hundreds of thousands of people belonging to the Hutu and Tutsi groups fled bloody ethnic warfare in RWANDA and BURUNDI. In SOMALIA several factors combined to drive people from their homes: a series of droughts in the 1970s and 1980s, conflicts over the border with Ethiopia, and the Somali civil war, which began in 1991.

* **secede** to withdraw formally from an organization or country

* **apartheid** policy of racial segregation enforced by the white government of South Africa to maintain political, economic, and social control over the country's blacks, Asians, and people of mixed ancestry

People forced from their homes often have to leave most of their possessions behind and live in crowded, makeshift shelters. These refugees in Congo (Kinshasa) wait at a camp near the border with Rwanda.

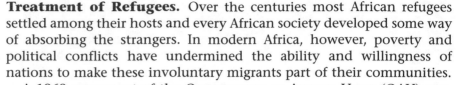

See color plate 12, vol. 1.

Treatment of Refugees. Over the centuries most African refugees settled among their hosts and every African society developed some way of absorbing the strangers. In modern Africa, however, poverty and political conflicts have undermined the ability and willingness of nations to make these involuntary migrants part of their communities.

A 1969 agreement of the ORGANIZATION OF AFRICAN UNITY (OAU) governs the status of refugees in Africa. The agreement, which defines a refugee as someone forced to seek safety outside his or her country of origin, reflects the concerns of states seeking to control their borders and their populations. The OAU agreement forbids states to forcibly repatriate refugees, but it includes provision for voluntary repatriation. This wording has encouraged the African nations to regard refugee status as temporary.

African countries rely on international aid to feed and supply their refugee populations, which are often quite large. The office of the United Nations High Commissioner for Refugees (UNHCR) oversees many aid programs. Its policy is to settle refugees in camps where they can easily be counted and where food and other aid can be most conveniently distributed. To receive UNHCR aid, African states have had to discourage refugees from settling in local communities. In some cases they have used army troops to force refugees into camps.

The UNHCR's encampment policy was intended to make refugees self-sufficient. But it has not achieved this goal, and since the early 1980s the organization has increasingly promoted repatriation. A few countries, however, have rejected the policies of encampment and repatriation in favor of more traditional ways of dealing with refugees. Both Sierra Leone and GUINEA have turned down offers of international aid administered by the UNHCR. Instead, both nations have absorbed large numbers of refugees from wars in neighboring countries, incorporating the newcomers into their national economies. With millions of people on the continent coping with forced displacement, African nations and the international aid community face the challenge of finding ways to solve the problem that meet the needs of states and also respect the rights of refugees. (*See also* **Diaspora, African; Genocide and Violence; Human Rights; United Nations in Africa; Warfare.**)

Religion and Ritual

* **ritual** religious ceremony that follows a set pattern

* **Islam** religion based on the teachings of the prophet Muhammad; religious faith of Muslims

Religious beliefs and rituals* play a central role in the everyday lives of most Africans. Few African societies make a rigid distinction between religious behavior and other forms of social conduct. In fact, most African languages lack a word that could be translated as "religion," and many of the words associated with the idea have a meaning closer to "custom" or "proper behavior" than to "religion."

The arrival in Africa of CHRISTIANITY and Islam* had a major impact on the development of African religions. Hundreds of millions of Africans now claim one of these faiths as their chosen religion, and Africa is currently the site of a dramatic growth in Christian converts. However, relatively few Africans—even those who identify themselves as Muslims or Christians—have completely abandoned traditional religious beliefs and practices. Most still turn to local gods for help with traditional problems or situations.

ELEMENTS OF AFRICAN RELIGIONS

* **indigenous**   native to a certain place

Although there are as many indigenous* religions in Africa as there are different societies, these religions share many common features and beliefs. Their beliefs deal with the relation of humans to the divine and with communication between the human world and the spirit world. African religions also share many ideas with world religions such as Judaism and Buddhism. Yet certain aspects of African faiths differ from those of most world religions.

* **deity**   god or goddess

Gods and Spirits. Most African religions acknowledge the existence of a supreme deity* who created the world and then, in most cases, retired from dealing with earthly affairs. This deity is usually male and often rules with a female earth goddess or mother goddess. As in the Christian and Muslim faiths, the supreme being of African religions possesses attributes* that define him as the opposite of humans—immortal, all powerful, all knowing, and incapable of error. However, while the God of Christians and Muslims is concerned about all humans, the supreme deity of African religions generally cares only for the people of a particular society.

* **attribute**   quality, property or power of a being or thing

See color plate 7, vol. 4.

In some African religions, the supreme deity continues to have dealings with humans after creating the world. More often this duty falls to a host of lesser spirits or mystical beings. Generally considered living aspects of the supreme deity, these spirits may hold power over humans, who are usually unaware of them. The spirits have no shape or form and cannot be detected unless they wish to be. They are often associated with a sacred site, which may serve as their dwelling place or shrine. A major distinction from one African religion to another is that each has its own unique set of spirits.

* **rite**   ceremony or formal procedure

Ancestors are considered a special type of spirit in many African religions, and ancestor worship plays an important role in various rituals. Not all deceased individuals become ancestors. Individuals must be selected for the honor and then receive proper funeral rites*. The individuals chosen vary from one society to another but may include men who have fathered children and women who were the firstborn in their families. Meanwhile, Africans offer prayer and sacrifices to ancestors to protect the living and punish those who harm or are disloyal to the family groups or clans* of descendants.

* **clan**   group of people descended from a common ancestor

Myths. All African religions feature myths, which are stories that are used to explain the nature of society and of the universe. Myths tell about the creation of the world, ancestral origins, historical events, and heroes. Many Africans regard myths as representing basic truths, though they may be clothed in fanciful narratives. What matters is that myths help explain the past and present, resolve moral and social issues, and provide a cosmology—an account of the structure and purpose of the universe.

Entry into many traditional African religious cults involves a ritual of initiation. The ceremony of a Bwiti cult in Cameroon, pictured here, represents a journey to the land of the dead.

Creation myths are an essential part of African religions. All share a basic pattern: a supreme deity creates the world from nothing, sacred figures appear and use magic or divine power to form society, and then humans appear and create the earthly history of a group. The creation story emphasizes the separation between humans and the divine, which is often represented by the division between the earth and the sky. This separation occurs because of the wickedness of humans, which causes them to break up into many cultures and languages and lose their divine nature.

Other common African myths deal with the relationship between humans and animals and the differences in the natures of men and women. Many of these myths serve to explain and justify the distribution of power and authority among humans and other living things.

Like the myths of other cultures, African myths help to explain the world and human society, making the world more predictable and controllable. However, the deeper meaning of the myths may be available only to individuals who have the special training or insight needed to communicate with the world of the spirits.

Evil and Witchcraft. All African religions contain notions of evil, which may take the form of sudden illness or death, unexpected failure, or bad dreams or visions. Believed to originate outside the individual, these forms of evil may affect the body and eventually cause it to break down and disintegrate. The occurrence of evil may be unexpected, may spring from a sense of guilt, or may be punishment for antisocial actions.

* **divination**   practice that looks into the future, usually by supernatural means

Africans use divination* to explain and combat forms of evil and to identify its source—either spirits or other humans. The spirit world is usually considered the source of "predictable" misfortune, that is, punishment for misdeeds or the result of personal actions. In such cases, the evil is removed through sacrifice. Unjust or unexplained misfortune is typically blamed on humans known as witches and sorcerers*.

* **sorcerer**   magician or wizard

In all African societies, WITCHCRAFT AND SORCERY usually express jealousy and hatred between rivals, and it is assumed that the victim and evildoer know one another. Remedies for the problem are based on this rivalry and may include forcing the accused person to withdraw the evil or misfortune. The evildoer may be punished or even killed, especially if accused of witchcraft or sorcery on many occasions. Frequent accusations against an individual are usually a sign of a long-standing unpopularity in the group. Belief in witchcraft and sorcery occurs among urban Africans as well as among rural folk.

RELIGIOUS PRACTICES AND PROHIBITIONS

Contact and communication between the living and the nonliving are at the heart of almost all African religions. Communication between humans and the spirit world can be led by human intermediaries*—such as priests, diviners, or prophets—in the form of prayer, visions, prophecies, and sacrifice. It can also be initiated by spirits through possession of humans.

* **intermediary**   go-between

Sacrifice and Rituals. Sacrifice is a way to purify the community or an individual through ritual. Often performed on a regular basis, sacrifices are usually conducted to remove contamination caused by existing conditions. The most common regular sacrifices are rites of passage, which are rituals performed at important moments of transition in a person's life.

African rites of passage usually occur at birth, marriage, and death; on initiation into SECRET SOCIETIES (often associated with reaching a certain age); and on achieving an important position such as that of king or priest. In rites of passage, the person being initiated is typically separated from the everyday world both physically and symbolically. This period of seclusion, which may be long or short, is marked by symbolic reversal of the normal order—such as wearing forbidden clothes or eating forbidden foods. It may also involve performing actions such as wild dancing or working oneself up into an ecstatic state to show closeness to the source of divine and spiritual power.

In addition to regular sacrifices, special purification sacrifices can be performed at any time to heal individuals struck down by sickness, physical or psychological harm, or moral impurity. Such sacrifices often include killing and feasting on an animal that is blessed and identified

Religion and Ritual

* **medium** person called upon to communicate with the spirit world

with the person for whom the sacrifice is being performed. Slaughtering and cooking the animal carries away the person's sin or sickness. By eating the animal's flesh together, the community symbolically renews the communal bond that was disrupted by the pollution of the affected individual.

Possession and Divination. Communication between the living and nonliving may also occur through possession, a condition in which a spirit or ancestor takes control of a living person. Possession is seen as a mystical link between the person being possessed and the spiritual agent that takes control. When a person with no special religious status is possessed, it is seen as a sign that he or she has been chosen by the spirits and linked to their world. Individuals with professional skill or knowledge may be able to convince a spirit to possess them through dancing, hyperventilation (becoming dizzy by rapid breathing), or the use of drugs. Although either men or women may be possessed, the majority who reach this state are women. Well-known examples include the *bori* cult of northern Nigeria and the *zar* cult of northeastern Africa, in which women possessed by spirits form cult groups around the particular possessing spirits. The possessed person often does not recall the experience. As with sacrifice, one effect of possession is the purification of the victim and a change of status, such as being removed from certain family or social obligations.

Another form of communication with the spirit world is the practice of divination. Diviners, the men and women who perform divination, are believed to speak for spiritual forces. They may explain past misfortunes or foretell likely future events. Many diviners act as mediums*, communicating with spirits through possession or trance. The mediums often wear clothing or eat foods that symbolize the "wilderness" that is the source of their special knowledge. Other diviners interpret physical signs, such as animal tracks or the arrangement of items in a basket, as spiritual messages. A type of divination called oracle consultation is sometimes used to determine guilt. In consulting an oracle—usually a material object or a place thought to contain spirits—the diviner asks it to respond to a series of yes-or-no questions to reveal a person's guilt or innocence.

Religious Reform. African history is filled with the appearance of prophets who have come from outside the community to reform or reshape a society and its religion. The upheaval caused by European colonization of Africa inspired many prophets who promoted political as well as religious change, including some who led their followers into battle for independence. In recent times, prophets have drawn heavily on ideas and symbols from Islam and Christianity. Many prophets have founded new Christian churches that focus on African concerns, including healing, well-being, material success, and long life. Others have merged ideas from indigenous and foreign faiths into religious groups that are unique to Africa. (*See also* **Death, Mourning, and Ancestors; Divination and Oracles; Healing and Medicine; Initiation Rites; Islam in Africa; Masks and Masquerades; Mythology; Prophetic Movements; Spirit Possession; Taboo and Sin.**)

Réunion

Réunion, a small island lying about 500 miles east of MADAGASCAR, is ruled as an overseas territory of France. Along with the islands of MAURITIUS and Rodrigues, it forms a region of great natural beauty known as the Mascarene Archipelago.

Land and Peoples. Despite its small size, Réunion has a diverse geography. Three peaks of over 9,000 feet form wide valleys drained by several rivers. The southern and eastern portions of the island receive up to 300 inches of rain per year, while the north and west receive only about 25 inches. The climate is tropical in low-lying regions and much cooler and drier in the mountains. Forests cover one-third of the country.

Arriving in the early 1600s, the French were the first people to live on Réunion. Dutch, Italian, English, and African settlers soon joined them. The Europeans imported slaves from India and Africa until the practice was outlawed in the mid-1800s. Later, they brought indentured laborers* from Asia and Africa. The island's current population is mostly descended from African slaves who intermarried with other groups. Most citizens are Catholics and speak both creole* and French, the nation's official language.

History, Government, and Economy. In the 1700s the French used the island, then called Île de Bourbon, as a naval base from which to attack India. After the French Revolution, the island's name was changed to Réunion and a colonial assembly was created. However, French emperor Napoleon Bonaparte soon restored royal control of the island's government. Britain seized the island during the Anglo-French War of the early 1800s but returned it to France after Napoleon was defeated in 1814. In 1848 France abolished slavery and gave colonial subjects the right to elect deputies to the National Assembly.

Since 1946, Réunion has been an overseas territory of France with its own elected assembly. France provides welfare payments and other forms of social relief to many islanders. However, these benefits are less than those paid to French citizens in France, and islanders have sometimes protested this unequal treatment with demonstrations, strikes, and riots.

Sugarcane dominates Réunion's economy, with almost 70 percent of the arable* land dedicated to sugar cultivation. This is still true even though old laws regarding land use, aging plants, droughts, and tropical storms have greatly reduced the sugarcane output on the island. The sugarcane trade is dominated by 10 sugar estates that are controlled by roughly five large sugar companies. Smaller sugar planters used to play an active role in the economy, but the high cost of buying mechanized equipment and the rising prices charged for imported fertilizers drove out all but the largest companies. Other important crops include vanilla and various plants used in making perfumes. Declining sugar prices and high unemployment have led to widespread poverty. The government has taken steps to diversify the economy, with limited success. The tourism industry also brings revenue to Réunion, which is a popular vacation spot. (*See also* **Colonialism in Africa**.)

* **indentured labor** form of labor in which a worker is bound into service for a set time to repay a debt

* **creole** language developed from a mixture of two or more languages

* **arable** suitable for producing crops

Rhodes, Cecil John

**1853–1902
British colonial leader**

ecil John Rhodes rose to a position of great wealth and power in Britain's Cape Colony in southern Africa. He developed the region's diamond mines and was responsible for British expansion northward into the land that is now ZAMBIA and ZIMBABWE.

The son of a clergyman in Bishop's Stortford, England, Rhodes left home at 17 to seek his fortune in southern Africa. After a period of farming cotton in Natal, he headed for the diamond fields of Kimberley in the Cape Colony. So successful was he that by age 36 he controlled South Africa's diamond mines through his company, De Beers Consolidated Mines. He also owned many of the region's gold mines. Although Rhodes had received a limited education in his youth, he obtained a degree from Britain's prestigious Oxford University in 1881.

That same year Rhodes was elected to the Cape Colony's parliament, and from 1890 to 1896 he served as the colony's prime minister. With ambition to match his wealth, he promoted the conquest of African lands north of Cape Colony. That conquest took most of the 1890s and resulted in new British colonies called Southern Rhodesia (now Zimbabwe) and Northern Rhodesia (now Zambia) in Rhodes's honor. Rhodes's political power was brought to a sudden end in 1895 by the Jameson Raid. An official appointed by Rhodes staged the disastrous attack on Transvaal, a colony ruled by Afrikaners, white settlers of Dutch origin. The embarrassing failure forced Rhodes to resign as prime minister.

Among Rhodes's many legacies were the racist legislation that took voting rights away from blacks in the Cape Colony, the introduction of scientific citrus farming to South Africa, and the Rhodes scholarship, which enables students from abroad to study at Oxford. (*See also* **Colonialism in Africa; Southern Africa, History.**)

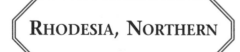

See *Zambia.*

See *Zimbabwe.*

Rock Art

any thousands of years ago, the ancestors of modern Africans created rock art—pictures on boulders, cliffs, and the walls of rock shelters. Carved rock art images are known as petroglyphs, while painted ones are pictographs. These rock pictures offer haunting glimpses of the lives of people long vanished. Some images also show an ancient environment very different from that of modern Africa.

Southern Africa. Some of the oldest rock art—often made on small, portable stones—comes from southern Africa. In a rock shelter in

212

NAMIBIA, six portable painted stones were found in a layer of deposits estimated to date from around 26,000 years ago. Stones with petroglyphs created between 4,000 and 10,000 years ago were discovered in SOUTH AFRICA. People have found similar examples of portable rock art in caves along the South African coast. Most pieces are about 2,000 years old. After that time people appear to have stopped making portable rock art, working instead on fixed rock surfaces.

The ancient people who created most of the rock art in southern Africa probably had beliefs and rituals* similar to those of the people who inhabit the KALAHARI DESERT today. Their artwork shows people performing a dance with the same postures and gestures used in the trance dance, a central ritual of Kalahari people. Rock art also features many images of eland, a kind of antelope that the people of the Kalahari believe to be magical. These pictures establish a link between past and present cultures. They also indicate that the rock art of southern Africa was more than a pastime or even a historical record. It was an expression of religious and magical beliefs.

Eastern Africa. Most of the rock art in eastern Africa is found in central TANZANIA. The most common images are pictographs related to hunting, including realistic illustrations of wild animals such as giraffe, eland, and elephants. Painted in shades of red, the animals are sometimes running away, lying on the ground, or shown with lines drawn from their mouths, which may indicate bleeding. Human figures are also shown, sometimes dancing or holding bows. The age of this work is unknown, but it may be 20,000 years old.

More recent rock art from Tanzania consists of human and animal forms, especially giraffes and lizards, drawn in thick white paint. Some works also feature handprints, spirals, circles and rays, and other symbols. This art may have been associated with ancient rituals. Even today, certain rock art sites are used for magical or spiritual ceremonies.

Rock art in ERITREA, ETHIOPIA, and SOMALIA shows more cattle than wild animals, suggesting that the artists who created it were herders. Circles, spirals, and other geometric patterns found with these images and in western Kenya resemble designs that people of the region today use as cattle brands. The oldest cattle images may date from several thousand years ago, but some rock art around Lake Victoria and other eastern lakes is much more recent. One image shows a canoe with a type of sail that was unknown in the area until the 1800s.

Northern Africa. Northern Africa is especially rich in rock art, with more than 30,000 paintings and carvings discovered in the SAHARA DESERT alone. These pictures reveal dramatic changes in the environment and culture of the area over the past 10,000 years.

The oldest images are petroglyphs made after about 8000 B.C. Like the rock art of central Tanzania, they represent the world of the hunter. Hippopotamus, giraffe, buffalo, ostrich, elephant, and antelope are portrayed realistically—sometimes life-sized—on the rock walls of valleys. Human figures are much smaller and less realistic. They may hold axes, clubs, or bows, and they sometimes carry animal masks. All of these

* **ritual** religious ceremony that follows a set pattern

See color plate 2, vol. 2.

See color plate 3, vol. 3.

213

* **savanna** tropical or subtropical grassland with scattered trees and drought-resistant undergrowth

* **pastoralist** related to or dependent on livestock herding

* **abstract** in art, referring to designs or shapes that do not represent a recognizable object or person

images reflect the Sahara when it was an immense savanna* dotted with lakes, not the desert it is today.

The first Saharan pictographs date from around 6000 B.C. and are found at Tassili n'Ajjer, a site in ALGERIA. Most of the paintings show groups of human figures with round heads that may represent ceremonial masks. They were drawn with ochre (a reddish or yellowish clay) mixed with a protein-filled liquid, such as milk or blood.

Later pictographs at Tassili n'Ajjer show the cultural changes that occurred as the Sahara region gradually became drier. As game grew scarce, pastoralist* groups replaced hunters. They painted images of humans and cattle, showing people in everyday activities, such as tending herds and talking. Details such as hairstyles and clothing are clear, and the use of different colors suggests that both light-skinned and dark-skinned people lived in this herding culture. The rock art made after 1200 B.C. contains many images of horses and chariots, introduced by newcomers to the region. More recent images from the past 2,000 years show the desert environment and feature pictures of camels.

Rock carvings have also been found in North Africa, high in the Atlas Mountains of Morocco. These petroglyphs feature abstract* and geometric designs and pictures of weapons. They appear to be the work of a Mediterranean culture that left no traces elsewhere in Africa. (*See also* **Archaeology and Prehistory, Art, History of Africa.**)

Roman Africa

* **archaeological** referring to the study of past human cultures and societies, usually by excavating ruins

See color plate 4, vol. 2.

For centuries North Africa was part of the ancient Roman Empire, linked to Rome by conquest, colonization, and trade. Remains of Roman glory can still be seen at numerous archaeological* sites from MAURITANIA in the west to EGYPT in the east.

Rome gained a foothold in Africa in 146 B.C., when it conquered the Phoenician colony of CARTHAGE in what is now TUNISIA. Eventually Carthage became the capital of the Roman province of Africa. West and south of Carthage lay Numidia, located in parts of present-day Algeria and Tunisia. Masinissa, a Numidian chieftain, had joined forces with Rome against Carthage in return for Roman recognition of his kingship. In 46 B.C. eastern Numidia became a Roman province called Africa Nova ("New Africa"). A separate province called Numidia was created later.

After Rome had acquired Carthage, Julius Caesar and his successor, Augustus, founded new settlements in Africa and extended Roman territory eastward to Cyrenaica (northeastern LIBYA). Roman forces also pushed south to the edge of the Sahara. In the A.D. 100s they constructed walls and ditches to mark the boundaries between Roman settlements and the nomadic peoples who roamed the desert and mountain regions to the south. By that time Egypt had also become Roman. Augustus once boasted that "[he had] added Egypt to the empire of the Roman people." In 31 B.C. his forces triumphed over those of his Roman rival Marc Antony and the Egyptian queen Cleopatra. Their defeat at the Battle of Actium paved the way for Augustus to claim Egypt as a Roman province. About 70 years later, Mauretania, west of Numidia, was divid-

* **annex** to take over or add a territory to an existing area

* **imperial** relating to an empire or emperor

ed into two Roman provinces. By that time, all of North Africa had been annexed* by Rome.

Roman Africa played a significant role in the affairs of the Roman Empire. Egypt served as the launching point for military expeditions into Arabia. Many men born in the African provinces served in high positions in the imperial* administration or in the Roman Senate. Septimius Severus, who became emperor of Rome in A.D. 193, came from a wealthy African family.

Africa's primary contribution to the empire, however, was food. Although Roman Africa engaged in trade and small-scale industries such as pottery-making, agriculture was the backbone of its economy. The region's principal exports were cereal grains and olive oil. As early as the first century A.D., Africa was supplying two-thirds of all grain consumed in the city of Rome. Much of the region's agricultural production came from farms owned by the thousands of retired Roman soldiers who had received land in the African provinces for their service to the empire.

A key feature of Roman Africa was the development of urban life. A few major cities, such as Carthage and ALEXANDRIA, existed before the Roman annexations. Rome established new cities and towns throughout the provinces, introducing urban culture to present-day ALGERIA and Tunisia. Wealthy citizens erected temples, theaters, and public baths in their African towns, just as wealthy people had done in Rome and in northern Roman provinces. Built of local marble and adorned with statues and colorful mosaic tiles, these structures are an enduring reminder of the time when North Africa belonged to Rome.

After the mid-400s, Roman control over the region weakened. When Arabs invaded the Roman provinces in the 600s, the struggling Byzantine Empire—all that remained of the former Roman Empire—offered little resistance. (*See also* **Archaeology and Prehistory; Egypt, Ancient; North Africa: History and Cultures.**)

ROMAN CATHOLIC CHURCH

See *Christianity in Africa.*

Rwanda

Rwanda is a small landlocked country in East Africa whose scenic alpine landscape led early European observers to call it the "African Switzerland." In recent years Rwanda's natural beauty has been marred by a civil war that killed nearly a million people. During the conflict millions of refugees fled to the neighboring countries of BURUNDI, UGANDA, TANZANIA, and CONGO (KINSHASA).

GEOGRAPHY

Nestled in the heart of the Great Lakes region of East Africa, Rwanda consists mainly of high plateaus dominated by rolling hills and towering volcanic peaks. Many small lakes and marshy plains break up the hilly

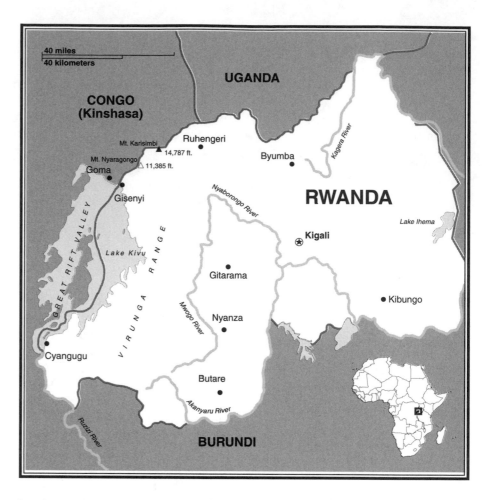

landscape. Because of the country's geography, local people have long referred to Rwanda as the "land of a thousand hills."

Beautiful Lake Kivu forms Rwanda's western border with Congo. Just east of the lake lie the Virunga Mountains, with peaks rising to nearly 15,000 feet. Although the country is located near the equator, it has a fairly temperate climate because of its high elevation. At the same time, sharp differences in climate and vegetation from one part of Rwanda to another have contributed to the development of distinctive subcultures.

Rwanda suffers from an acute shortage of land, a factor that contributed to the civil war that ravaged the nation in 1994. At that time, tiny Rwanda was the most densely populated country in Africa. The shortage of arable* land led to social tension. As large numbers of rural people migrated to urban centers, the competition for jobs increased and ethnic differences grew.

* **arable**   suitable for producing crops

HISTORY

The history of Rwanda has been shaped largely by the interaction between its two main ETHNIC GROUPS, the Hutu and the Tutsi. During the civil war, leaders on both sides used ethnic differences to stir up hatred between these groups. However, in many ways the causes of the war were more political and cultural than ethnic in nature.

Early History. Rwanda's original inhabitants were a hunting and gathering people known as the Twa, a PYGMY group. The Twa were eventually displaced by the Hutu, a BANTU farming people from West-Central Africa who migrated to the region several hundred years ago. In the 1500s or 1600s, the Tutsi, a warrior people who herded livestock, invaded Rwanda from the north.

Partly by assimilating* the Hutu and Twa, the Tutsi conquered Rwanda and established a highly centralized and hierarchical* kingdom. Tutsi overlords forced the Hutu to become serfs—peasant workers bound to the land in a state of semibondage. Each Hutu had to choose a Tutsi lord as a protector. The protector allowed his Hutu serfs to use, but not own, cattle, which were the Tutsi's highest status symbol and source of wealth. The Tutsi dominance of Rwandan society created great resentment among the Hutu, who were far more numerous than their masters.

The Colonial Era. In 1899 Rwanda became part of the colony of German East Africa. Realizing that the country had an efficient administration run by Tutsi rulers, the Germans decided to leave the existing political structure in place. German officials ruled the colony, but they allowed Tutsi lords to control local affairs.

After Germany's defeat in World War I, the League of Nations* appointed Belgium to administer Rwanda and neighboring Burundi, which together became known as Ruanda-Urundi. Like the Germans, the Belgians made use of Tutsi lords as local administrators to reduce the expense of running the colony. However, the society changed somewhat during this time. The Belgian colonial government encouraged the Hutu to grow coffee as a cash crop*, which increased Hutu economic power.

By the late 1950s, increasing land shortages, combined with longstanding tensions between the Hutu and the Tutsi, laid the groundwork for ethnic warfare. In 1959 the Hutu finally revolted and killed tens of thousands of Tutsi. In this atmosphere of exploding violence, Belgium decided to grant Rwanda its independence. Elections held in 1961 resulted in a landslide victory for the Hutu presidential candidate, Grégoire Kayibanda. For the first time ever, the Hutu majority ruled over their former Tutsi masters. Rwanda gained full independence the following year.

Rwanda Under the Hutu. The Hutu revolution of 1959 to 1960 forced hundreds of thousands of Tutsi into exile in neighboring countries. These REFUGEES formed the nucleus of a force that would engage in a 30-year struggle against the Hutu government of Rwanda. Meanwhile, President Kayibanda and his Hutu political allies from southern and western Rwanda worked to consolidate their power. Northern Hutu, who had been incorporated into the Tutsi monarchy during the colonial era, held little power in the Kayibanda government.

In 1972 ethnic tensions in Rwanda heated up after the Tutsi massacre of thousands of Hutu in neighboring Burundi. Kayibanda's opponents accused him of not acting decisively against the Tutsi, and the following year a military coup* toppled his government. Major General Juvénal Habyarimana took over as president and appointed members of his

* **assimilate** to adopt the beliefs or customs of a society

* **hierarchical** referring to a society or institution divided into groups with higher and lower levels

* **League of Nations** organization founded to promote international peace and security; it functioned from 1920 to 1946

* **cash crop** crop grown primarily for sale rather than for local consumption

* **coup** sudden, often violent, overthrow of a ruler or government

217

Rwanda

Poetic (In)Justice?

An epic poem written in Kinyarwanda, the language of both the Hutu and the Tutsi, is sometimes used to justify Rwanda's historical social order. In the poem, a divine ruler named Kigwa devises a test to determine which of his three sons will succeed him as king. He gives each boy a bowl of milk to guard overnight. One son, Gatwa, drinks the milk. Yahutu spills the milk while he sleeps. Only Gatutsi guards the milk as he is told. According to legend, this is the reason the Tutsi became nobles, the Hutu became their servants, and the Twa became outcasts.

family and trusted advisers to the most important political positions. Under a new constitution adopted in 1973, only a Hutu could become president.

Military rule in Rwanda ended officially in 1975, but Habyarimana and his political party, the MRND, set up a single-party system. In the 1980s conditions in the nation worsened. The price of coffee beans, Rwanda's major export, fell dramatically on the world market. Meanwhile, Rwandans became increasingly discontented with single-party rule. In 1990 Tutsi refugees based in Uganda staged an armed invasion of Rwanda.

Growing Violence. Tutsi refugees in Uganda had formed the Rwandese Alliance of National Unity (RANU). Ugandan rebel leader Yoweri MUSEVENI recruited RANU members for a force that he used to overthrow the Ugandan army in 1986. In return, Museveni gave the RANU members weapons and military equipment to use in their own invasion of Rwanda. In October 1990, some 6,000 of these Tutsi troops, part of a group called the Rwandan Patriotic Front (FPR), streamed into Rwanda and advanced to within 40 miles of Kigali, the capital city.

France, Belgium, and Zaire (present-day Congo, Kinshasa) all came to the aid of Rwandan president Habyarimana. Zaire's president MOBUTU SESE SEKO sent his presidential guard to fight the FPR, while French and Belgian paratroopers arrived in Kigali, supposedly to protect Europeans there. The FPR was stopped, but Habyarimana was forced to end his one-party rule and allow the Tutsi to share power in a democracy. However, many Hutu wanted the Tutsi excluded from the government. Violence and killings continued and then accelerated in 1993, when Tutsi army officers assassinated the Hutu president of Burundi, Melchior Ndadaye. The assassination led to a wave of ethnic violence in Burundi and forced hundreds of thousands of panic-stricken Hutu to seek refuge in Rwanda.

Civil War and Its Aftermath. In 1994 the violence between Tutsi and Hutu erupted in genocide* and civil war in Rwanda. In April 1994, a plane carrying Habyarimana and the new president of Burundi, Cyprien Ntaryamira, was shot down as it approached Kigali airport. Although Hutu rivals of Habyarimana may have been responsible, Hutu leaders blamed the incident on Tutsi rebels. A horrific bloodbath followed, with Hutu death squads killing Tutsi as well as Hutu political rivals. Over the next five months, hundreds of thousands of Tutsi men, women, and children were mercilessly slain. According to one estimate, at the peak of the violence five people per minute were murdered.

In response to the atrocities, Tutsi FPR forces launched an offensive that crushed the Rwandan military. In July they seized control of the government. Two million Hutu, fearing attacks from the FPR, fled into Zaire. The new Rwandan government consisted of a coalition of Hutu and Tutsi members, with a Hutu president and prime minister. However, the real power lay with the Tutsi commander of the FPR, Paul Kagame, and his regime* became one of the most brutal in Africa. Tutsi also controlled the nation's various districts and towns.

* **genocide** deliberate and systematic killing of a particular ethnic, religious, or national group

* **regime** current political system or rule

See color plate 12, vol. 1.

Although the fighting ended in July, violence against the Hutu continued in Rwanda. Local Tutsi leaders had little control over the actions of the military or the FPR. As a result, Hutu were often arrested for no reason and their property given to returning Tutsi refugees. Meanwhile, millions of Hutu refugees remained in exile, fearing that they would not be safe in Rwanda. In Zaire, Hutu leaders began organizing refugees and providing them with military training. When the Zairian government failed to protect the Tutsi from attacks by the Hutu forces, the FPR threw its support to various rebel leaders.

Several months after the end of the fighting in Rwanda, the United Nations established the International Criminal Tribunal for Rwanda. Made up of three groups of judges, the tribunal was created to hear cases involving genocide and other violations of international law.

The Hutu killed hundreds of thousands of Tutsi people during Rwanda's violent civil war in 1994. After the war, millions of Hutus fled the country, fearing revenge. Although many Hutu refugees have returned to Rwanda, others are afraid to come home.

Rwanda

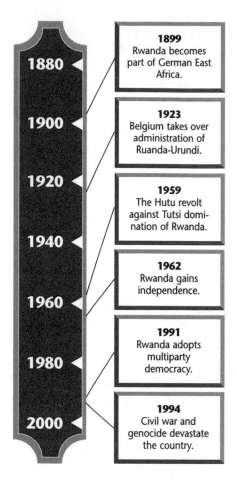

1880

1899
Rwanda becomes part of German East Africa.

1900

1923
Belgium takes over administration of Ruanda-Urundi.

1920

1959
The Hutu revolt against Tutsi domination of Rwanda.

1940

1962
Rwanda gains independence.

1960

1991
Rwanda adopts multiparty democracy.

1980

1994
Civil war and genocide devastate the country.

2000

* **infrastructure** basic framework of a society and its economy, which includes roads, bridges, port facilities, airports, and other public works

Attempts to Unify Rwanda. Since 1994 Rwanda has been ruled by a National Unity Government composed of the FPR, the Hutu-controlled Republican Democratic Movement (MDR), and a coalition of other small political parties. In elections held in 1999, Rwandans chose the Hutu leader Pasteur Bizimungu as president and FPR's Paul Kagame as vice president.

Despite a promising start, the government soon broke apart, and President Bizimungu resigned under pressure in March 2000. The parliament then elected Kagame as president, the first Tutsi to hold that office. This election merely confirmed the fact that Kagame had been the true source of power in Rwanda since the civil war.

Although Kagame called on all refugees to return home, continued violence against the Hutu in Rwanda has led many Hutu refugees to stay in exile. Reunifying and rebuilding Rwanda will be an enormous task. The economy and judicial system are both in shambles, and the continued presence of Rwandan troops in Congo is a source of friction between the two countries. Massive foreign aid is needed to rebuild Rwanda physically. In addition, healing the wounds of civil war and ethnic hatred will take time.

ECONOMY

Rwanda's economy is heavily dependent on agriculture, with coffee and tea the most important crops. Coffee alone accounts for more than half of the country's export revenue. During the years of ethnic violence, export earnings declined by more than half, coffee revenues fell by over 70 percent, and production of tea decreased by nearly two-thirds.

The war left food production in ruins. Before the war, the Hutu formed the bulk of the farming population, but the majority of them either fled the country or were killed during the conflict. As a result, Rwanda's agricultural output was cut in half, and many fields still remain unplanted. European nations are sponsoring a massive rehabilitation program of investment in agriculture and infrastructure*. However, there is some concern that Rwanda's Tutsi-dominated government will allocate little of that money to the Hutu.

PEOPLES AND CULTURES

Before the civil war, the Hutu made up about 80 percent of Rwanda's population, the Tutsi accounted for about 19 percent, and the Twa made up the remaining 1 percent. Since the war, however, millions of Hutu have left the country and hundreds of thousands of Tutsi refugees have returned. As a result, the current population may be as much as one-quarter Tutsi.

The Hutu and Tutsi were once distinguished by physical appearance. The Tutsi were generally tall and slim, while the Hutu were shorter and stockier. However, intermarriage has made it difficult to determine ethnic identity by physical appearance.

Various social and cultural differences appear within the Hutu and Tutsi. For example, northern Hutu are considered a distinct group and are referred to as Kiga by southern Hutu. During the colonial era, some

Republic of Rwanda

POPULATION:
7,229,129 (2000 estimated population)

AREA:
10,169 sq. mi. (26,338 sq. km)

LANGUAGES:
French, Kinyarwanda, English (all official); Kiswahili

NATIONAL CURRENCY:
Rwanda franc

PRINCIPAL RELIGIONS:
Roman Catholic 65%, Traditional 25%, Protestant 9%, Muslim 1%

CITIES:
Kigali (capital), 234,500 (1993 est.); Butare, Gikongoro, Gisenyi, Bitarama, Nyanza, Ruamagana

ANNUAL RAINFALL:
70 in. (1,770 mm) in the west, 30 in. (760 mm) in the northeast and east

ECONOMY:
GDP per capita: $720 (1999 est.)

PRINCIPAL PRODUCTS AND EXPORTS:
Agricultural: coffee, tea, pyrethrum (insecticide), bananas, sorghum, beans, potatoes, livestock
Manufacturing: agricultural products processing, light consumer goods, cigarettes, cement
Mining: tungsten, tin, cassiterite

GOVERNMENT:
Independence from Belgium, 1962. Republic with the president elected by popular vote; special election for president by deputies of the National Assembly and governmental ministers held April 2000. Governing bodies: Assemblée Nationale de Transition (legislative body); Council of Ministers and prime minister, appointed by the president.

HEADS OF STATE SINCE INDEPENDENCE:
1962–1973 President Grégoire Kayibanda
1973–1994 President Major General Juvénal Habyarimana
1994 President Théodore Sindikugbabo
1994–2000 President Pasteur Bizimungu
2000– President Major General Paul Kagame

ARMED FORCES:
47,000

EDUCATION:
Compulsory for ages 7–14; literacy rate 60%

Kiga were incorporated into the Tutsi monarchy. Among the Tutsi are a distinct group of northern cattle herders called Hima. The Hima rarely marry outside their group, and their nomadic lifestyle has always separated them from other Tutsi. (*See also* **Class Structure and Caste, Colonialism in Africa, Genocide and Violence, Tribalism, Warfare.**)

Index

Page numbers of articles in these volumes appear in boldface type.

Index

Index

Index

Index

Index

Index

234

Index

Index

Index

Index

Index

Index

Index

Index

Index